FEMININE ECONOMIES

To Keith, Michael and Lily

JUDITH STILL

feminine economies

THINKING AGAINST THE MARKET
IN THE ENLIGHTENMENT
AND THE LATE TWENTIETH CENTURY

MANCHESTER UNIVERSITY PRESS
MANCHESTER AND NEW YORK

distributed exclusively in the USA by St. Martin's Press

Published by Manchester University Press
Oxford Road, Manchester M13 9NR, UK
and Room 400, 175 Fifth Avenue, New York, NY 10010, USA

Distributed exclusively in the USA by
St. Martin's Press, Inc., 175 Fifth Avenue, New York,
NY 10010, USA

Distributed exclusively in Canada by
UBC Press, University of British Columbia, 6344 Memorial Road,
Vancouver, BC, Canada V6T 1Z2

British Library Cataloguing-in-Publication Data
A catalogue record for this book is available from the British Library

Library of Congress Cataloging-in-Publication Data applied for

ISBN 0 7190 4555 X *hardback*

First published 1997
01 00 99 98 97   10 9 8 7 6 5 4 3 2 1

Typeset in Dante
by Graphicraft Typesetters Limited, Hong Kong
Printed in Great Britain
by Bookcraft (Bath) Ltd, Midsomer Norton

Contents

Afterword   181

Acknowledgements

Earlier versions of sections of chapters have already appeared as follows: 'A Feminine Economy: Some Preliminary Thoughts' in *The Body and the Text: Hélène Cixous, Reading and Teaching*, ed. H. Wilcox, K. McWatters, A. Thompson and L. R. Williams, Brighton, Harvester, 1990, pp. 49–60; 'Dreams of the End of Markets: The Model of Women's Work in Plato, More and Rousseau', *Paragraph*, 15 (1992), 248–60; 'Rousseau's *La Nouvelle Héloïse*: Passion, Reserve, and the Gift', *The Modern Language Review*, 91 (1996), 40–52; 'Questioning Commerce: The Case of Rousseau's *Du contrat social*', *British Journal for Eighteenth-Century Studies*, 19 (1996), 33–46; 'The Gift: Hélène Cixous and Jacques Derrida' in *LIT*'s Cixous anthology, ed. Lee A. Jacobus and Regina Barreca, New York, Gordon & Breach, in press; '*Homo economicus* in the Enlightenment', *Journal of the Institute of Romance Studies*, 5, 1997; and '*Homo economicus* in the Twentieth Century: *écriture masculine* and women's work', in 'Who Speaks? The Voice in the Human Sciences', special issue of *History of the Human Sciences*, ed. Sean Hand and Irving Velody, summer 1997. I should like to thank the editors and publishers for permission to reprint.

I should also like to express my gratitude to the British Academy, which funded a semester's study leave in 1996, enabling me to complete this project, and to the University of Nottingham which provided two earlier periods of study leave.

This book has taken a long time to write, and there are many friends, colleagues and postgraduates who have contributed to it in different ways – all of whom I should like to thank. The Postgraduate School of Critical Theory (including, amongst others, Richard King, Bernard McGuirk, Dave Murray and Douglas Tallack) and the Department of French at the University of Nottingham have proved very stimulating environments in which to think through ideas. Special thanks go to Martin Calder for help with the index and the proofs, and to Joanne Collie, Keith Fairless, Elizabeth Fallaize, Diana Knight, Cath Sharrock, Sabina Sharkey, Madge Still and Michael Worton.

1

Introduction to the market and the gift

In this book I shall be investigating certain textual representations of gift economies, contrasting these with the dominant market paradigm. I shall ask what is the value of a utopic horizon of gift exchange and analyse in what ways the representation of the (sexual or racial) other as economically the same *or* as economically different can have a repressive force. Two points will be selected as particularly significant for analysis: the eighteenth century (in particular the work of Rousseau), an anxious moment of transition from the fixity of feudalism to the capitalist and colonialist market economy; and the late twentieth century (in particular the work of Cixous, Derrida and Irigaray), a moment which, it has been claimed, is somehow post-capitalist and post-colonialist. However, I shall also pause to examine some key precursor texts to these two moments. The representation of the other as economically the same is a device which is associated with the Enlightenment restructuring of relations between self and other. It is indeed to be found in eighteenth-century texts,[1] albeit alongside both overtly repressive (hierarchical and static) representations and, more interestingly, hypotheses of dynamic and reciprocal relations between different people(s). The debate over the virtues of sameness and difference continues today in a variety of guises, from equal opportunities to identity politics.

In the late twentieth century fascination with the gift may not seem self-evident. Readers are less surprised that cultures very distant from us in time or space, such as classical Rome (where Seneca wrote a lengthy treatise on beneficence) or the 'archaic' cultures studied by the anthropologist Marcel Mauss, are exercised by questions such as 'what constitutes a gift?', 'what is the best way of giving?' However, today such questions may seem marginal, since so much has been given over to market or State – even central and fundamental gestures such as giving shelter, food and drink,

---

1 I shall discuss later the reading of Diderot's *Supplement to Bougainville's 'Voyage'* as a work which claims that market principles are universal.

at one extreme are marketed hospitality (hotels and restaurants, cafés and pubs) and, at the other extreme, State safety nets ('Income Support' at subsistence level).[2] But vestiges, remnants of gift exchange remain – there is some excess which overspills the ever-encroaching market and the care of the dwindling Welfare State.[3] And poststructuralist thinkers, such as Jacques Derrida and the so-called French feminists, have been much exercised by this excess (or, from another perspective, this falling short): the question of the gift. This recent debate around the gift has frequently privileged questions of sexual difference or, more particularly, of the feminine. Earlier debates were, at least explicitly, more exercised by ethnographic or historical difference. Feminine 'identity' or non-identity, seemingly a question of *being*, is thus in some texts rephrased economically, subordinated to the question of *having* or of modes of propriation. While this invocation of 'a feminine operation' has been partly fuelled by feminist concerns, and has certainly drawn the attention of feminists, it is also partly fuelled by a more general questioning of ontology. In this first chapter, after some introductory remarks, I shall present the market and the gift as general theoretical models. I shall then examine two concrete fields of investigation in which this opposition has played a crucial role: the study of archaic societies and the study of women's work.

Alongside the opposition of gift and market, it is useful to consider the questions of work (paid or unpaid), exploit and indolence. The logic of the market is that everyone works for wages, and that leisure (broadly encompassing indolence and the time in which to perform exploits) becomes a good to be purchased. The reality of market economies is, of course, that not everyone works, and time not spent working for money is valued in very different ways. The logic of the gift in its most radical form may be antithetical to work, and representations of archaic economies tend to emphasise either indolence or exploit. However, utopias in the style of Thomas More tend to valorise an economy in which everyone works (without wages) in order to contribute to a product held in common. This problematic is highly relevant to the question of sexual difference, since in contemporary Western societies it remains the case that much of women's

---

2 Mauss, writing in 1925, optimistically suggests that State provision could be a return to group morality (*The Gift*, trans. I. Cunnison, London, Routledge and Kegan Paul, 1966, pp. 65–6).

3 Outside 'normal' giving of presents, hospitality and other small services between family and friends, there are the more troubled domains between relatives (such as care of the elderly and infirm), as well as the questions of charity, Aid, and the donation of organs, blood and reproductive elements, which has spawned a considerable literature. See Jacques T. Godbout and Alain Caillé', *L'Esprit du don*, Beauceville, Boréal, 1992, for a general account of contemporary gift 'exchange'. I should like to thank Cathy Wright for drawing this work to my attention.

work is unpaid, that is to say, that it is productive work performed *on behalf of someone else*, without remuneration.[4]

'Market' thinking is to be found in two powerful economic traditions, that of neoclassical economics and that of Marxism; these may both be set against another (sometimes styled utopian) horizon of thinking – that of the gift. It may seem surprising to run neoclassical economics and Marxism together, since there are such obvious differences between them, and neoclassical economics refuses to engage with the question of power, which is fundamental to a class-based analysis. However, it can be argued that both share a certain rationalism and universalism, and certain assumptions about the human subject. Jean Baudrillard, whose works have their utopian qualities, comments in this respect:

> [The system] will never be defeated if you follow its own logic of energy, calculation, reason and revolution, of history and power, or of some finality or counter-finality – on that plane the greatest violence has no purchase, and will only turn back on itself. (*Symbolic Exchange and Death*, p. 36, translation modified)[5]

For Baudrillard, while Marx is enlightening about classical capitalism, contemporary Marxists fail in their analysis of the present social order because they do not see how it thrives on *symbolic* violence; they regard the symbolic as a mere mask or support for material violence.

In France a series of different voices from the late 1960s onwards have argued that it is necessary to address the question of the symbolic order (an expression which has an array of different, albeit related, meanings for different theorists). But if the contemporary symbolic is understood as dominating the way we think, any questioning of it, any reaching out to another symbolic, necessarily involves a kind of leap, a disjunction in logic which is hard to *think*, and which always runs the risk of being incomprehensible in general or risible in detail.[6] A key question is that of the degree to which

---

4 See Christine Delphy and Diana Leonard, *Familiar Exploitation*, Cambridge, Polity Press, 1992, for a detailed explanation of this definition and an analysis of the consequences for women of their position in hierarchical and exploitative family relations. Productive work performed for your own benefit, for example cooking yourself a meal, of course brings its own remuneration.

5 Trans. I. H. Grant, London, Sage, 1993.

6 Poststructuralist thinkers have their widest appeal when they are in negative or critical mode (as analysts of a wide and important range of texts). In positive or utopian mode they fall into two traps which, I would argue, are to some extent gendered. Abstract generalisation, which becomes incomprehensible (even mystical), still has a 'hard' masculine edge, which makes its dangers palatable to some; whereas apparently 'silly' detail, such as Luce Irigaray's advice to women that they should display positive images of motherhood on their walls, drifts towards the feminine in a pre-poststructuralist sense.

the structure of the human subject is considered immutable. Since Lacan's reading of Freud, this has involved consideration of the structure of language. If it is assumed that the human subject, and thus human relations, are necessarily economic, it follows that accounts of the gift as uneconomic will be deemed myths or alibis serving a particular purpose (and thus economic).[7] If, on the other hand, the wager is made that uneconomic acts or relations are possible, that the subject can give without return, then strategies have to be found for writing the dream of change. Hélène Cixous, Barthes, Jacques Derrida and Julia Kristeva (amongst others) have all at various times celebrated avant-garde literary strategies as breaking down the symbolic, at least provisionally.[8] This move to the literary (as a kind of utopia of language) is less surprising than it might seem in view of the post-Lacanian focus on the linguistic structure of the subject. This encourages a certain poetic play, for instance on the 'happy coincidence' that in French the term for expenditure (*dépense*), often used in accounts of uneconomic 'spending', also suggests the undoing of thought.[9] The work of Luce Irigaray since her doctoral thesis has not involved analysis of 'literary' texts in this way, but she too reads philosophy and psychoanalysis in what might be deemed a literary fashion, with close attention to the play of tropes. She proposes the breaking down of the symbolic, and the death of God, as a path to a new symbolic and a new divine. She has used the term *parousia* to refer to a utopia which is not only a destiny but also a here and now, 'the willed construction of a bridge in the present between the past and the future'.[10]

Utopias have to represent economic relations – in the neutral sense of economic – but usually present these as 'uneconomic' or otherly economic, borrowing from gift economy thinking. Economic relations need to be considered in two dimensions, which may be represented as horizontal and vertical axes: the horizontal axis is that of different kinds of economic structures which may coexist at one moment in time, for example: slavery; false beneficence; *market exchange*; beneficence; *gift*. Points about these structures include the following two cautions. First, market exchange does not necessarily involve currency (currency simply reduces the transaction cost) and therefore an exchange of goods which may be *called* gift exchange because no money changes hands can be part of a market structure. Of course, the

7 I should add that, for the purposes of this book, representations of divine (or natural) generosity will be understood as human projections.

8 This is a controversial question to which I shall return – not least because the experiments in form which have caught the attention of these theorists are usually male-authored and frequently appear misogynistic in content.

9 Morag Shiach points to this (serious) play on words in Bataille and Cixous; see *Hélène Cixous*, London and New York, Routledge, 1991, for example pp. 22, 82.

10 *An Ethics of Sexual Difference*, trans. C. Burke and G. C. Gill, London, Athlone Press, 1993, p. 147.

need to assert that a certain kind of transaction has functioned as gift rather than as market exchange may of itself be interesting. Second, these structures may seem to be located strictly in the sphere of consumption (circulation); however, the relation between production and consumption (and even a consideration of the mode of production itself) is usually an important aspect of discussions of gift economies.

The vertical axis is that which links intrapsychic or intracorporal structures, intersubjective or interpersonal relations, and the socio-economic base. The hypothesis that such an axis suggests is that there might be a degree of relationship, even homology, between the different levels – even if historically we have observed the coexistence of different structures at particular moments. For example, a free market may shape, if not determine, behaviour outside the strictly commercial sphere. One classic example is marriage; many present-day economists would argue that the marriage market is not fundamentally different from any other market, and this is not dependent on the legislative contractual dimension, since other forms of pair-bonding are also vulnerable to such an analysis. This has, of course, long been a theme in literature.

Throughout this book there will be a degree of play between *economy* as the management of wealth and *economy* as a certain kind of structure observable in any text, written or otherwise. French poststructuralist writing insistently uses the term *économie*, which is inevitably translated as 'economy', although the English term is somewhat more specific and concrete than its French equivalent. For example, in Irigaray's essay on Plato's myth of the cave, she uses the term *economy* repeatedly.[11] These are just a few examples: 'the economy of that representation' (p. 253); 'the economy of both before and after the fact' (p. 256); 'the phrase *hoion eikos* immediately translates, betrays, and conceals the question of a mimicry of sound and language within the economy of exchanges, notably verbal exchanges' (pp. 257–8); 'the economy of relationships between white and black, as well as between white and white, black and black' (p. 258); 'the economy of this optical jiggery-pokery' (p. 263); 'the sexual economy' (p. 267); 'an economy of values' (p. 272). There is a similar range of references to *economy* in Derrida's writing. Christopher Johnson spends some time on what he calls 'the model of the economy' in *System and Writing in the Philosophy of Jacques Derrida*.[12] He argues that Derrida's uses of the term can be broadly categorised into two: the economy of life or restricted economy is characterised by its finitude, circularity and closure, whereas the elliptical economy of *différance* or general economy can re-embrace violence, death, *anéconomie*,

---

11 'Plato's *Hystera*' in *Speculum*, trans. G. C. Gill, Ithaca, NY, Cornell University Press, 1985.

12 Cambridge, Cambridge University Press, 1993. There is a section headed 'The Economy', pp. 57–64, but there are also relevant sections of analysis in other chapters.

excess, madness, hyperbole, infinity or *démesure*. Johnson relates economising in the second sense of economy to a holding in reserve which is close
to the deferral of *différance*. This division could thus be related to Cixous's
masculine (closed) and feminine (open) economies. What is required is a
balance between recognising that not every use of the term economy should
be weighted towards the mercantile, and that the French term is more
abstract than the English, while taking the economic metaphors seriously.
In order to take them seriously it is necessary to think through what a
market economy means.

The market

How do we define the market? I shall be focusing in particular on the logic
of the market, that is to say, capitalism – although, of course, markets can
exist under different modes of production. A favourite undergraduate economics textbook is *An Introduction to Positive Economics* by Richard G. Lipsey.[13]
In chapter 5, 'A General View of the Price System', Lipsey outlines the
classic assumptions about market economies: division of labour is more
efficient than universal self-sufficiency; specialisation must be accompanied
by trade; efficient division of labour requires the organisation of workers
into large units of production, and so they must sell their labour to firms
and receive wages in return; the allocation of resources is the outcome of
millions of independent decisions made by consumers and producers, all
acting through the medium of markets (the price system) – what Adam
Smith called 'the invisible hand'. In chapter 6, 'Basic concepts of price theory',
Lipsey explains the two major behavioural assumptions behind (neo)class-
ical economics: households (assumed to be the basic decision-taking atom
of consumption behaviour) seek to maximise utility; firms seek to maximise
profit. The maximisation of utility could be loosely subsumed under the
maximisation of profit, if profit were then understood in non-material, as
well as material, terms. I shall go on to consider these assumptions in a little
more detail.

Division of labour is one of the features of the market which was
most fervently discussed in the eighteenth century – and viewed with un-
mitigated enthusiasm by many modernisers. It can be argued that even a
pre-capitalist market requires some specialisation in order for exchange to
be regularly useful. Indeed, as Adam Smith puts it:

> This division of labour, from which so many advantages are derived, is not
> originally the effect of any human wisdom, which foresees and intends that
> general opulence to which it gives occasion. It is the necessary, though very
> slow and gradual consequence of a certain propensity in human nature which

13 London, Weidenfeld and Nicolson, 1983 (1st edn, 1963).

has in view no such extensive utility; the propensity to truck, barter, and exchange one thing for another. (*The Wealth of Nations*, Book I, chapter 2)[14]

When Smith remarks on the many advantages derived from division of labour, he is referring to his conviction that life in contemporary Europe, in spite of its inequalities, was better than life in more primitive societies.

If efficient production requires specialisation, efficient distribution requires the price system. This assumes scarcity – not in an absolute sense, for Smith and many others will argue that it is the market which produces the highest standard of living – but in a relative sense. This scarcity allows a price to be fixed where supply equals demand. Marshall Sahlins points out that descriptions of pre-agricultural economies often present the people's lives as miserable and impoverished – because of what they eat, how they dress or the number of possessions they have – measured on some absolute scale against Western capitalism.[15] However, in relative terms, abundance or affluence is the situation where supply exceeds demand. Market economies breed demand, and thus it can be argued that as well as economic scarcity being a precondition of price-setting, (a sense of) impoverishment is an inevitable consequence of the expansion of the market.

The economic assumption about the subject is that he (I use the masculine advisedly) is dedicated to the rational maximisation of utility, subject to constraints. Freud is usually credited with dethroning the rational conscious subject by his revelation of the role of the unconscious persistently gesturing in the gaps and slips which dot even the most controlled of discourses or behaviours. However, it can be argued that Freud himself, in some ways a man of his time, deploys an economic model in his representation of the drives. Freudian psychoanalysis would suggest that, although in terms of content the unconscious is to be opposed to rationality (e.g. the coexistence of mutually exclusive terms), structurally it functions in an economic mode: energy is a scarce commodity which can be spent or saved. Jean Laplanche and Jean-Baptiste Pontalis claim that 'Economic considerations are brought forward by Freud throughout his work; in his view there can be no complete description of a mental process so long as the economy of cathexes [*investissements*] has not been assessed.'[16] Freud emphasises the need to keep levels of excitation low (although this emphasis takes on different nuances at different stages in his work); in 'Inhibitions, Symptoms and Anxiety', he describes the accumulation of amounts of stimulation in the psyche as an economic disturbance requiring a transformation of libido into anxiety – later he describes this anxiety as a kind of warning signal

14 Ed. R. H. Campbell and A. S. Skinner, Oxford, Clarendon Press, 1976, p. 25.
15 See *Stone Age Economics*, Chicago and New York, Aldine Atherton Inc., 1972, Chapter 1, 'The Original Affluent Society'.
16 *The Language of Psycho-analysis*, with an introduction by D. Lagache, trans. D. Nicholson-Smith, London, Hogarth Press, 1973, p. 127.

from the ego.[17] We learn in *The Psychopathology of Everyday Life* that jokes aim at economising psychical expenditure, and in *Jokes and their Relation to the Unconscious* that seeing the funny side to a tragedy economises pity (p. 125).[18] While Freud's texts are less simple than I am suggesting, the term 'masculine economy' (used by Cixous in opposition to 'feminine economy') is a deliberate and explicit reference to the Freudian theory of (masculine) libidinal development, and to the key role of castration anxiety in that development, amongst other things. As Derrida remarks in *Given Time*: 'Wherever there is castration and problematic of castration [. . .] there is rationality of the border and there is no gift or even a possible problematic of the gift.'[19]

Market economics assumes that value is fixed, that it can be measured and stored.[20] An exchange of one good for another assumes the rational quantification of value (the recognition of equivalence). This also drives language as the exchange of meanings, and truth has often been likened to the gold standard.[21] Language is thus a kind of restricted economy, one of market values, the circulation of objects with certain value (that is to say, meaning). As Derrida comments on Hegel: 'the *circularity* of absolute knowledge could dominate, could comprehend only this circulation, only the *circuit of reproductive consumption*'.[22] It cannot comprehend absolute production and destruction of value, energy which is excessive as such, which must be lost without an aim. Restricted value should instead increase over time according to a model which, since the ancient Greeks, has linked interest on capital to biological reproduction (albeit that fantasmatical parthenogenesis whereby fathers produce sons).[23]

17 *On Psychopathology*, Harmondsworth, Pelican Freud Library, X, 1979, pp. 229–333.

18 *The Psychopathology of Everyday Life*, Harmondsworth, Pelican Freud Library, V, 1975; *Jokes and their Relation to the Unconscious*, Harmondsworth, Pelican Freud Library, VI, 1976. In the latter, Freud describes three kinds of economy in jokes, the comic and humour, respectively economy in expenditure on inhibition, ideation and feeling. He argues that jokes are all based on condensation, a tendency to compression or saving: 'It all seems to be a question of economy. In Hamlet's words: "Thrift, thrift, Horatio!"' (p. 77). The greater the economy, the more the pleasure. The energy saved is discharged by laughing.

19 *Given Time*, trans. P. Kamuf, Chicago and London, The University of Chicago Press, p. 91.

20 Value may be said to be agreed by convention or negotiation, but it may also be said to be imposed by authority. Derrida observes: 'The king or god [. . .] is thus the other name for the origin of value' ('Plato's Pharmacy', in *Dissemination*, trans. B. Johnson, Chicago, The University of Chicago Press, 1981, p. 76).

21 See Jean-Joseph Goux, *Les Monnayeurs du langage*, Paris, Galilée, 1984, for an analysis of this. Derrida presents a brief critique of this work in a footnote to *Given Time*, p. 110.

22 'From Restricted to General Economy. A Hegelianism without Reserve', in *Writing and Difference*, trans. A. Bass, London, Routledge, 1978, p. 271.

23 In 'Plato's Pharmacy', Derrida analyses the Greek term *pater* in *Phaedrus* and the *Republic*. It means variously 'father', 'good', 'head' and 'capital' (e.g. pp. 81–2). He

Barter could be about the satisfaction of needs; ultimately the market understood today (capitalism) is about the desire for profit. This involves a linear understanding of temporality, which permits foresight and thus investment. There has been some debate over the question of temporality and the gift, notably in Derrida's *Given Time*, not only with respect to Heidegger, but also, less abstractly, in relation to Mauss. Certain theorists of the gift economy (for instance, Pierre Bourdieu, writing on pre-colonial Algeria)[24] have insisted on the importance of a temporal lag in gift exchange. Those who claim that the economic is universal answer that such temporal lags are no more than forms of investment. I would underline the role of calculation in economic investment: mathematical formulae will explain how a present investment yields a future return – this makes investment (and insurance, with a risk factor added) rational. Microeconomics terms this 'inter-temporal choice'. The argument runs, in its simplest form, that the interest rate (r) is the rate at which you can trade today for tomorrow: Z_0 today is worth $Z_0 (1 + r)$ tomorrow. It is the combination of a temporal lag with absolute and willed uncertainty (the refusal to calculate a probability) about any return which would divide the gift from economic investment. More radical understandings of temporality are also possible, such as circular time or infinite time, although it can be argued that these are primitivist myths.

Dale Spender claims that sexism, which is one of the principles encoded in our language, comes into the whole process of organising and describing the universe and building theories about it.[25] These theories shape what is observed – a problem for allegedly neutral science, which does not acknowledge its own inevitable partiality, and hence compounds its errors. Objectivity is thus a mask for positions which are currently dominant – part of the masculine imaginary, as Irigaray puts it. This is true of almost all science; economics in particular is perceived as problematic by Irigaray, because it has 'emphasised the phenomenon of scarcity and the question of survival rather than that of life and abundance' (*Parler n'est jamais neutre*, p. 314). We could add the exclusive stress of economic science on the individual (unit) who maximises rationally, and the tendency of neoclassical economics to exogenise the social and ideological domain. Irigaray points

points out that it is a hidden source, both blinding and illuminating, like Plato's sun. This is a theme which returns, for example, in Bataille, and is discussed by Kristeva in *Tales of Love*, trans. L. S. Roudiez, New York, Columbia University Press, 1987. On the reproduction model of revenue, see also Marc Shell, *The Economy of Literature*, Baltimore, Johns Hopkins University Press, 1978.

24 For example, *Algérie 60*, Paris, Minuit, 1977.

25 *Man Made Language*, London, Routledge and Kegan Paul, 1980. See also Luce Irigaray, *Parler n'est jamais neutre*, Paris, Minuit, 1985, e.g. 'Le sujet de la science est-il sexué?', pp. 311 ff., in which she discusses the construction of universal models as a way of appropriating the world, dressing it in your own guise, and also the technical as a way of cutting the scientist off from the object of *his* study.

out that all science is mistaken in its exclusion of these domains – as if the scientist did not have a body or a class position. However, it seems even more strange to ignore the social when your subject is a major part of human behaviour than when it is the natural world.

A key question about the market is whether it is a contingent and historical phenomenon or whether it is a universal structure which simply takes different shapes at different times. One possible story runs as follows: gradually the market as a structure has become more and more dominant, spreading into more areas of the globe and of people's lives. Once the market was a place, containable, now it has spilled out all over the place. This imperialism of market exchange has, however, also affected our *reading* of the past, and so we question whether there was a time or place when exchange was not the dominant principle. In *The Postmodern Condition*, Jean-François Lyotard expresses the argument which is the mainstay of many accounts of postmodernity.[26] This is the thesis that the market has permeated ever more areas of social existence, in particular those concerned with knowledge. This can be related both to Fredric Jameson's adaptation of Ernest Mandel's stages of capital, and to Baudrillard's hypothesis of the new predominance of consumption (over production) – although both of these thinkers have a number of differences from Lyotard. Thus in *The Postmodern Condition* Lyotard adopts the faction of a temporal break (modernity has become postmodernity). However, this is something which the essay appended to the English translation brings into question, at least with regard to the aesthetic realm (thus Montaigne's essays are termed postmodern; the postmodern is that scepticism which has always trailed belief).[27] While postmodernism as aesthetic form and postmodernity as social development need not be taken as identical, the different temporality of the former hints at the advisability of nuancing the latter's easy historicism.

The dominant *narrative* of modernity and of market economics is that of universality and homogeneity – a powerful, potentially liberal narrative, yet one which has been a force for enormous harm. In *Parler n'est jamais neutre*, Irigaray writes: 'In fact, the would-be universal is equivalent to a men's idiolect, to a masculine imaginary, to a sexed world – without neutrality' (p. 311).[28] From a different perspective, Bourdieu remarks in *Algérie 60*:

---

26 *The Postmodern Condition*, trans. G. Bennington and B. Massumi, foreword by F. Jameson, Manchester, Manchester University Press, 1984. Although this short work is not one of Lyotard's most cherished or most thought through, it is, I would argue, deservedly one of his best known. This is in part because of the quality of some other writing on postmodernity.

27 'What is Postmodernism?', trans. R. Durand, in *The Postmodern Condition*, pp. 71–82.

28 Here, of course, Irigaray is echoing a feminist observation which dates back at least as far as Simone de Beauvoir's 'Introduction' to *The Second Sex*, trans. and ed. H. M. Parshley, London, Jonathan Cape, 1953. However, Irigaray goes further in arguing that there is a hidden isomorphism (p. 312) between the male sexual imaginary and

It is the universalisation of a specific class of preferences which is at the root of that justificatory and moralising discourse which transforms what are the objective constraints of *one* economy into universal precepts concerning morality, foresight, denial or saving yesterday, credit, expenditure and pleasure today. Unbeknownst to itself the science of economics, which is still 'the most moral of the human sciences', frequently participates in that discourse. (p. 8)

The assertion of equality and identity seems immediately preferable to the assertion/speech act that there shall be inequality which we associate with premodern times and the fixed hierarchy of the Church and the feudal State. However, the assumption of equality where it does not exist is a potent way of pre-empting reform, never mind revolution. The discourse of economics (the discipline) and economic discourse in general have deployed the assumption that all economic agents are equal and acting of their own free will in a way which has shored up and intensified real inequalities. The radical counter-narratives of modernity such as Marxism, feminism and anti-colonialism have insisted on class, sex or race *opposition* in order to challenge the hegemonic assumption of universality – but have frequently suppressed difference in their ranks and adopted universalisms of their own.[29]

Over recent decades there has been an increasing reference to the postmodern (or post-industrial, post-capitalist, post-Fordist and so on) from both Left and Right. Postmodernity replaces the unitary monoliths of the Modern with a fragmented, temporary, flexible society and economy.[30] I wish to argue that this need mean no fundamental change at all for dominant economic discourse, which has always prized exactly these qualities, endows all agents with them and thus does not let them detract from the assumption of homogeneity. I shall be taking the example of women's work to argue this case.

For difference not to be reabsorbed into homogeneity (we're all different, and therefore all the same) requires combining or alternating *difference* with the lessons of opposition, plurality and mobility with a degree

the scientific project as we know it. The scientist is a partial (or schizoid) man supposedly cut off from his social and sexual self, cut off and confronting nature, rather than part of it.

29 Thus, for example, Marxism stands accused of being sex- and race-blind, feminism of acting in a colonising way towards third-world women, anti-colonialists such as Frantz Fanon of homophobia.

30 David Harvey makes this case in *The Condition of Postmodernity*, Oxford, Blackwell, 1989. See, for example, chapter 9, 'From Fordism to Flexible Accumulation', which argues that after crises provoked by institutional and State rigidity there has been a shift to a new flexible regime of accumulation. For some of the economic and social theory lying behind this notion of changing regimes of accumulation and the various modes of regulation see, for example, M. Aglietta, *A Theory of Capitalist Regulation*, trans. D. Fernbach, London, Verso, 1979.

of fixity. In *The Postmodern Condition* Lyotard combines observation of the expansion of the economic criterion of performativity/profitability (into the domain of education, for instance) with some more ambiguous, if not optimistic conclusions. For instance, he points to the ambiguity of temporary contracts; temporary contracts are ambiguous in that they might be seen as positive in certain social ways (the availability of divorce, for example), and yet they are favoured by the market system because they are cheap and allow a flexible response to changing economic conditions, in so far as people can be laid off (or hired) without incurring costs. He discusses the potential role of information technology in so far as information – knowledge – becomes a public good, because it is difficult to exclude people from acquiring it. Public goods are a problem for economic discourse, since they cannot easily be priced; the price mechanism relies on scarcity, hence excludability. He also analyses scientists' use of small narratives and the increased importance of the unexpected move in a non-zero-sum game of perfect information.[31] The tentative optimism of certain of his hypothetical conclusions may be related to some of the hypotheses thrown out by Irigaray. For example, his 'unexpected move' (which allows innovation) could be profitably juxtaposed with the questions she raises about a feminine language:

> This raises the question whether language uses (could use) potential meaning which has not yet been made reality, while remaining within the same general discursive economy, or whether what women think and could say necessitates a transformation of the linguistic horizon. That would explain the resistances to their entry into the communication networks and all the more so into the theoretical or scientific forums which determine the values and laws governing exchanges. (*Parler n'est jamais neutre*, p. 318)

Lyotard also warns of the danger of terror being used to exclude people from data and block creative paralogical moves. His plea is for 'a politics that would respect both the desire for justice and the desire for the unknown' (p. 67). Thus while this work of Lyotard's is sometimes seen as describing the homogeneity of market expansion (albeit in a fragmented and plural form), in fact he considers it crucial to allow for the radically heterogeneous. This brings us on to one of the forms of thinking the heterogeneous: the gift.

---

31 Lyotard's references to games of perfect information are not without irony, since economists regularly practice the fiction that there is perfect information in building their models – for example, the most standard model, of competitive equilibrium, relies on the assumption of perfect information. Only if consumers know the prices set by the competitors to their supplier can it be assumed that *ceteris paribus* all prices will equalise at zero (or 'normal') profit. Nowadays, economists sometimes use 'rational expectations' as a preferable formula to 'perfect information', since the latter might suggest literal omniscience, whereas the former suggests the use of 'reasonable' assumptions.

The gift

The gift is understood with varying degrees of radicality by different thinkers. Obviously, the more strictly the gift is understood (as *outside* the economic), the harder it is to imagine a giving subject. How radical a structure is to be ascribed to the gift involves a consideration of temporality, spatiality (direct and indirect reciprocity), calculation (rationality), and obligation (legal, social, moral, magical . . .). The question of equality is one of the most thorny: it can be argued that, as we move from slavery to the gift, so equality (or potential for equality) increases. This ethical understanding of the gift would be my own. However, that is to ignore the problem that much of what I would term 'false beneficence' is often understood as gift: for example, aristocratic magnanimity (most common in a feudal or slave mode of production, but possible in other modes), potlatch, Bataillean expenditure and sacrifice, Baudrillard's symbolic violence.

Derrida clearly states the paradox of the gift as impossible, as trapped in a double bind of gift and obligation (*Given Time*, p. 27) – which hits us in a familiar form in the impossibility of perfect altruism or of a disinterested (unmotivated) gratuitous act. There is no gift without bond, but no gift that does not have to untie itself from obligation. The gift must and must not be recognised by both benefactor and beneficiary, must and must not be forgotten. Any recognition, self-recognition or gratitude could become a motivation for the gift, or become a binding contract, demanding repayment, even interest. But, on the other hand, how can one desire to forget the good of the gift? Because circulation is economic, because it is an Odyssean return to the home or hearth (where women find their *non* place), must one say that gifts should not circulate?[32]

Mauss's *The Gift* demystifies gift-giving in archaic societies in so far as it insistently reveals apparently disinterested and generous prestations to be a mere social facade, covering self-interested and obligatory behaviour. However, it also insists upon a series of differences between market transactions and gifts. Mauss argues that gift exchange often exists alongside market exchange in archaic societies, and that those participating are acutely conscious of the differences between the two. However, for Mauss, one of the differences between archaic societies and our own is the ability (or the desire) to distinguish between 'pure gifts' and obligatory prestations, a distinction not clear in archaic societies, according to Mauss. Baudrillard expands upon this question in a footnote to *Symbolic Exchange and Death*:

32 Derrida deals with the paradoxes of the gift over and over again. Another statement runs: 'There is no gift without the intention of giving. The gift can only have a meaning that is intentional – in the two senses of the word that refers to intention as well as to intentionality. However, everything stemming from the intentional meaning also threatens the gift with self-keeping, with being kept in its very expenditure' (*Given Time*, p. 123).

The gift, under the sign of gift-exchange, has been made into the distinguishing characteristic of primitive 'economies', and thus into the alternative principle to that of the law of value and political economy. No worse mystification is possible. The gift is *our* myth, the idealist myth corresponding to our materialist myth – we bury primitive peoples under both of these in one fell swoop. The primitive symbolic process knows nothing of free gifts, it knows only challenge [*le défi*] and the reversibility of exchanges. When the latter has been destroyed, precisely by the one-sided opportunity to give (which presumes the possibility of storing value and of transferring it in one direction only), then the properly symbolic relation is dead, and power makes an appearance: from then on it will do nothing other than develop via the economic apparatus of the contract. It is our (operational) fiction, our metaphysics that it is possible to accumulate on its head (capital) a stock of value, to make it grow and multiply: this is the deceptive lure of accumulation and capital. But it is equally our fiction to think that you can relinquish it absolutely (in the gift). Primitive peoples know that this possibility does not exist, that the fixing of value on one term, the very possibility of isolating one segment in the exchange-process, one side of the exchange, is unthinkable, *that everything has a counterpart*, not in the contractual sense, but in the sense that the process of exchange is unavoidably reversible. Primitive peoples base all their relations on this incessant cross-fire of ambivalence and death in exchange. Whereas we base our order on the possibility of separating out two distinct poles of exchange and making them autonomous, which implies either equivalent exchange (the contract) or inequivalent exchange with no counterpart (the gift). But both, as we shall see, obey the same dislocation of the process and the same principle of the autonomisation of value. (*Symbolic Exchange and Death*, pp. 48–9, translation modified)

For Baudrillard, the gift which is not returned (or reversed) is power, and it is characteristic of capitalist rather than primitive societies. Indeed, in order to confront power in our own societies it is necessary to make a return gift to the powers that be.

For Mauss, one key distinction between gift exchange and economic exchange lies in the kind of analysis required; while economists tend to exogenise sociological material as much as possible, Mauss claims that in order to understand gift exchange you must study the 'total social fact'. Giving is at once economic behaviour and legal, moral, social, religious and aesthetic behaviour. The economic aspect is neither predominant nor isolatable. Another difference lies in the character of what is exchanged, which is, according to Mauss, not inert, but endowed with spirit, such as the Maori *hau*. Gift exchange can thus effect a kind of bonding, on a series of different levels, between people, groups and things. This bond results from the gift exchange, but also requires it: there is an initial obligation to give, just as there is an obligation to receive and to repay (with interest).

The market, by contrast, is characterised by 'freedom'.[33] No one is obliged to sell or buy, although everyone has to pay . . . The market is impersonal and casual, whereas there is a link between giving and sacrifice (giving to the gods). The sentiments aroused by the gift are a mixture of intimacy and fear, both with respect to the object given and to the partner in the transaction: 'In giving [gifts], a man gives himself, and he does so because he owes himself – himself and his possessions – to others' (*The Gift*, p. 45).

Although Mauss does not make a strong distinction between them, it has seemed to some readers that there are important differences between the circle of gifts called the *kula*, a seemingly more peaceable model of the gift, and the highly agonistic model of the *potlatch* in which honour is bound up with 'expenditure' or even 'destruction' of goods. It is the potlatch which has achieved the greatest currency as a model in later writings. Bataille takes it up as emblematic of the principle of loss which he sees as more fundamental to life than the bourgeois economic principle of conservation and growth. He writes, for example: 'It is the constitution of a positive property of loss – from which spring nobility, honour, and rank in a hierarchy – that gives [potlatch] its significant value. The gift must be considered as a loss and thus as a partial destruction, since the desire to destroy is in part transferred onto the recipient.'[34]

A gift economy usually requires abundance, supply exceeding demand in some respect. This may be achieved by an expansion of supply, and writing on the *économie féminine* emphasises the superabundance of love, for example. Classical utopian writing often highlights the power of education and social example to restrict demand – pointing out that inflated demand in market societies is usually the fruit of *amour-propre* (vainglory) or the desire to have more than your fellows. This brings us to the question of ethics. One crucial element in economic discourse is its insistence that its only criterion is efficiency, and that ethics is not properly its concern. Gift economy thinking may be said to have a strong ethical undertone even when, as in Mauss's work, it places itself within the realm of (social) science. Ethics sets up a certain relation to the other. This may be related to disinterestedness in that it involves a forgetting (of the self).

Bourdieu points to some possibilities of interposing a *different* structure via the questions of temporal and spatial deferral, of fragmentation and of non-quantification. The temporal and spatial deferral means that it is

33 Here I am echoing Marx's argument that capitalism 'frees' the worker from ownership of the means of production.

34 'The Notion of Expenditure', in *Visions of Excess*, trans A. Stoekl with C. R. Lovitt and D. M. Leslie, Jr., Minneapolis, The University of Minnesota Press, 1985, p. 122. Bataille's anal–sadistic view of the potlatch is quite distinct from, say, Irigaray's view of the gift.

unclear when, where and by whom a gift would be returned; the fragmentation suggests more radically that any gift is out of the question, that is to
say, that there are only gifts and no return gifts. Non-quantification could
mean no more than that exchange is approximate, rather than the precise
transactions which are enabled by currency; however, it could also imply
a more radical refusal to calculate.

One further point is that of reading. There is a tendency for commentators to engage with Mauss's work in a passionate way. Sahlins hails
it as a gift. Lévi-Strauss writes of his extreme emotion in reading it. Derrida
too takes up this theme, and even raises the issue of Gurvitch's comments
on Lévi-Strauss's reading of Mauss in terms of gift and counter-gift or poison
and counter-poison (*Given Time*, pp. 69, 73). In the introduction to the
English translation of *The Gift*, Evans-Pritchard suggests that Mauss's generosity to his former collaborators (many of whom were killed in the First
World War) entailed a loss to posterity of Mauss's own potential work: 'if
one belongs to others and not to oneself, which is one of the themes, perhaps the basic theme, of the present book, one expresses one's attachment
by subordinating one's own ambitions to the common interest' (pp. v–vi).
That emotions are aroused by reading, that projections are made, that
investments are at stake, and that all these inflect would-be dispassionate
analysis of texts will be assumed throughout this book. A passionate
engagement with a text is, of course, not necessarily a generous one. In
general, I shall attempt to err on the side of the generous reading, while
allowing hard-headed analysis its due.

The archaic gift and its legacy

In this section I want briefly to consider the debate over the representation
of the racial other, the primitive, as partaking in a gift economy which
is somehow uneconomic.[35] Marcel Mauss's *The Gift* has become the *locus
classicus* for such a representation, and a number of later thinkers have used
his short work as a springboard for their own thinking, whether they use
it to prove that everything is reducible to the economic or the opposite.
The questions raised may be summed up as follows: does the gift exist? Is
the assertion of the gift ethnocentric? Does the archaic gift involve the
sacrifice of the woman? One of the striking features of this debate on
the gift is that women tend to be absent or objectified – instead of being
donors or even recipients they are the objects of the exchange.[36] Lévi-Strauss

35 In *The Other Heading*, trans. P.-A. Brault and M. B. Naas, Bloomington and Indianapolis,
Indiana University Press, 1992, Derrida comments on Valéry's representation of Europe
or the European Spirit as supremely economic.
36 This is less striking in Mauss's seminal work, although there are a number of passing
references to the exchange of women.

influentially declares that society is based upon the exchange of women (by men), and would otherwise fall into anarchy.[37] Lévi-Strauss, however, falls into the camp of those who tend to reduce gift exchange to the economic. It is important to note that this debate over the 'primitive' gift does not necessarily present the gift as an ethical act of altruism in the liberal human-ist tradition, but simply as anti-economic. Indeed, far from being altruistic, the archaic gift is frequently agonistic. Outside the self-evidently competit-ive model of the potlatch, the two models most commonly evoked by twentieth-century commentators on the archaic gift are those of the sun and of the artist.[38]

DOES THE GIFT EXIST?

There is a range of different thinkers with quite different approaches who argue for an uneconomic principle in archaic societies. For Thorstein Veblen both the origin of property and its accumulation is not to do with subsist-ence consumption, but with emulation.[39] Although Veblen concedes the presence of an impulse to 'workmanship' in the human subject, for him the dominant motor of human relations has been invidious comparison (some-thing akin to Rousseau's *amour-propre*). Thus what is most prized in society is predatory exploit and pecuniary waste.

Bourdieu's work on pre-colonial Algeria, which is in a very different spirit, raises a number of relevant points, for example, the question of the observing eye which may erroneously perceive the familiar structure of obligation or self-interest in all that it surveys. He insists on the importance of the temporal separation of gift and repayment and on the absence of precise calculation:

> Is generous exchange anything other than the spreading out into a succession of different moments in time of a transaction which the rational contract squeezes into an instant? It is precisely thanks to that intervening interval of time that the gift can seem to the observer like an obligatory step in a continuous series of gifts and return gifts, while it is actually experienced as a disinterested and thoughtful act. Is it not the case that the worst offence you can commit is returning a gift immediately or reciprocating with an identical offering? As long as the return gift is deferred each act of giving can be understood as an absolute beginning and not as the obligatory continua-tion of an exchange process. (*Algérie 60*, p. 35)

37 See, for example, *The Elementary Structures of Kinship*, trans. J. Harle Bell and J. R. von Sturmer, ed. R. Needham, London, Eyre & Spottiswood, 1969.

38 See Derrida, 'Economimesis', trans. R. Klein, *Diacritics*, 11 (1981), 3–25. Derrida analyses Kant's hierarchical distinction between true art which must not enter the economic circle of commercial exchange, which must not be paid, and handicraft or mercenary art. The artist must imitate divine (natural or solar) superabundance.

39 *The Theory of the Leisure Class*, New York, Penguin Books USA, [1899] 1953.

However, Bourdieu's writings on the Algerian situation in particular also ring certain alarm bells for feminists. He presents feudal domesticity in a somewhat idealised fashion (for instance, pp. 111–12). Feminists have long argued that men's exploitation of women's unpaid domestic labour should not be confused with the notion of feminine generosity. Another practical point is the consideration that men's generosity may be enabled by the exploitation of women.

Lévi-Strauss's argument, on the other hand, is that all exchange is economic: Mauss's examples of the gift are in fact gift exchange and can easily be collapsed back into economic forms.[40] If not simply economic change without the mediation of currency, then they are forms of investment. Derrida analyses Lévi-Strauss's reading of Mauss in *Given Time*.[41] He cites Lévi-Strauss's interpretation of Mauss's observation that Papuan and Melanesian have one single term to designate antithetical operations such as buying and selling: 'That is ample proof that the operations in question are far from "opposite"; that they are just two modes of a selfsame reality. We do not need *hau* to make the synthesis, because the antithesis does not exist' (p. 75). Derrida then comments:

> By eliminating or moving into a secondary role what he calls 'affective' notions [such as *hau*], whose intervention would remain 'residual' (and everything that is at stake seems to consist here in this residue, that is, in a remainder that no one knows what to do with), Lévi-Strauss has no trouble privileging the logic of exchange and relation in order to eliminate the question of the thing. And let us recall here the principle guiding us in this reflection on the gift: to reduce the latter to exchange is quite simply to annul the very possibility of the gift. (p. 76)

Gilles Deleuze and Félix Guattari also reject Lévi-Strauss's reading of Mauss.[42] They insist that 'There is a question that Marcel Mauss at least left open: is debt primary in relation to exchange, or is it merely a mode of exchange, a means in the service of exchange? But Lévi-Strauss seems to have closed the question again with a categorical reply: debt is no more than a superstructure, a conscious form whereby the unconscious social reality of exchange is converted into cash' (p. 185). Deleuze and Guattari argue that 'The primitive machine is not ignorant of exchange, commerce,

---

40 'Introduction à l'œuvre de Marcel Mauss', in Mauss, *Sociologie et Anthropologie*, Paris, Presses Universitaires de France, 1950, pp. ix–lii.

41 Derrida also reads Lévi-Strauss's economism in 'Structure, Sign and Play' in *Writing and Difference*, and in *Of Grammatology*, trans. G. Spivak, Baltimore, The Johns Hopkins University Press, [1967] 1976.

42 *Anti-Oedipus Capitalism and Schizophrenia*, trans. R. Hurley, M. Seem and H. R. Lane, London, Athlone Press, [1972] 1984. For Deleuze and Guattari, the key thing about primitive economies is that they are conducted in terms of codes, for example, surplus value of code is the primitive form of surplus value (p. 150).

and industry; it exorcises them, localizes them, cordons them off, encastes them, and maintains the merchant and blacksmith in a subordinate position, so that the flows of exchange and the flows of production do not manage to break the codes in favour of their abstract or fictional qualities' (p. 153). Furthermore, 'Desire knows nothing of exchange, *it knows only theft and gift*'; they claim that if one sees exchange in the unconscious of the gift, 'one does nothing more than hypostatize the principles of an exchangist psychology to account for institutions that on the other hand are recognized to be nonexchangist' (p. 186). They also point to Lévi-Strauss's debate with Leach over the Kachin marriage system – a system which is seen to be in disequilibrium. Leach argues, and Deleuze and Guattari agree, that it is an open and heterogeneous system (and the disequilibrium is functional and fundamental). Lévi-Strauss insists that the disequilibrium is contingent and pathological; Deleuze and Guattari comment: 'the exchangist conception finds it necessary to postulate a closed system, statistically closed, and to shore up the structure with a psychological conviction ("confidence that the cycle will reclose")' (p. 187).

However, Lyotard dispatches gift economy thinking with some swift but important deconstructive moves in *Libidinal Economy* – suggesting that the location of a libidinal 'other' to capitalism is no more than an alibi for capitalism – which is itself permeated with desire, as indeed is Marx's and Marxist thinking about capitalism.[43] Lyotard's own utopic wager in this text concerns the 'bande libidinale' (the libidinal strip or band), a surface imagined rotating in such a way and at such a speed that it disables the bar of disjunction which separates this from non-this (pp. 15–16). He argues convincingly that, with the bar of disjunction in operation, any critique, for instance of capitalism, is liable to fall into the same 'pious' thinking as that which it attacks. This kind of argument with respect to the sustaining of binary oppositions is familiar from a range of French poststructuralist texts. Cixous, indeed, aligns hierarchical binaries with a masculine libidinal economy. The problem is always, and the devil's advocate will always point it out, that, caught within language as we are, thinking insistently falls back into division – even if this division is only the split between willingly supporting binary oppositions and attempting another way of thinking. However, while this may appear to support the necessity of the bar of disjunction, in fact it also muddies distinction – since 'other' thinking cannot escape its opposite. While Lyotard's point that any economy is libidinal seems to me to be incontrovertible (although it was received with hostility), I should like to focus on the significant difference between the mental staking (wager) of a gift economy and those economic ideologies (manifested in homosociality,

---

43 Paris, Minuit, 1974, trans. I. Hamilton Grant, London, Athlone Press, 1993. See particularly the section entitled 'The Desire Named Marx', pp. 95–154.

for example) which repress and suppress desire. While it may well be the case that no pure feminine economy could ever be available to us, the evocation of such a utopic term may enable a displacement in thinking. Barthes has pointed out how utopias, spaces of desire, have generally been taboo in serious revolutionary discourse, and how that has limited the scope of that discourse.[44]

ETHNOCENTRISM

Lyotard's questioning of the division between rational capitalism and societies of symbolic exchange, societies of the gift, includes the argument that such a division is founded on nostalgic, even racist, primitivism. He not only reads economic rationality back into earlier forms, but also works at producing the libidinal in both capitalism and the critique of capitalism (Marxism). He argues that theories (or myths) of Before Capitalism are utopic fantasies which serve to keep capitalism 'pure' – pure rationality, pure calculation and so on, whether you love it or whether you hate it (more likely both). In relation to Baudrillard's *The Mirror of Production*, he argues:

> When Baudrillard says: *'There is no mode of production nor indeed production* in primitive societies, there is no *dialectic* in primitive societies, there is *no unconscious* in primitive societies', we reply: there's no such thing as a primitive society.
>
> First of all, from a methodological point of view (yes, I'm afraid so . . .), that gift and counter-gift society plays the role in Baudrillard's thinking of a (lost, of course) reference, of an (unlocatable) alibi for his critique of capital. Baudrillard doesn't want to hear talk of nature or naturalness. How is it that he doesn't see that the whole problematic of the gift, of symbolic exchange as he gets it from Mauss, with or without Bataille's, Caillois's or Lacan's additions and rewritings, belongs in its entirety to Western imperialism and racism – that it's still ethnology's noble savage, somewhat libidinalised, which is passed down to him along with that concept. (*Libidinal Economy*, p. 106, translation modified)

Derrida had already pointed out the ever-present danger of (reverse) ethnocentrism. In 'Structure, Sign, and Play', he argues that ethnology could only be born as a science at the moment of the decentring of European culture and of metaphysics. The critique of ethnocentrism is, he claims, the condition of ethnology, *and yet*, 'the ethnologist accepts into his discourse the premises of ethnocentrism at the very moment when he denounces them' (p. 282). As he describes it in the section of *Of Grammatology* which again turns to Lévi-Strauss: 'an ethnocentrism *thinking itself* as anti-ethnocentrism,

---

44 See Diana Knight, 'Roland Barthes in Harmony: The Writing of Utopia', *Paragraph*, 11 (1988), 127–42. In a rather different vein, Barbara Taylor, in a study of nineteenth-century Utopian socialism (*Eve and the New Jerusalem: Socialism and Feminism in the Nineteenth Century*, London, Virago, 1983), suggests that it is far more radical in its approach to women and to sexual relations than scientific socialism was.

an ethnocentrism in the consciousness of a liberating progressivism'
(p. 120). He suggests, with ample illustration from Lévi-Strauss, that this
is the legacy of Rousseau. It is a certain privileging of nature over culture
(of speech over writing) and a certain ahistoricism where change has to be
modelled as catastrophe. In fact, Lyotard says, no economy is completely
propre:

> All political economies are libidinal
> Here's the first thing that makes us say: there's no such thing as a primitive
> society, that is, there's no external reference, not even an immanent one,
> where the division between what is part of capital (or political economy) and
> what is part of subversion (or libidinal economy) can always be cleanly and
> properly made; where desire is clearly readable, where its *own proper economy*
> [*économie propre*] is not muddied. (p. 108, translation modified)

WOMEN

Derrida comments with respect to a homosocial scene from Baudelaire:
'You will very quickly suspect that if woman seems to be absent from this
narrative, her exclusion could well be organizing the scene and marking its
tempo like a clock' (*Given Time*, p. 103). The narrative of the archaic gift
informs the aristocratic gift or unproductive expenditure in Baudelaire and
indeed in a whole range of texts up to the present day. The archaic gift is
related to sacrifice – and it sometimes appears that the perfect sacrifice or
gift is a woman. There is a fascination with prostitution, classically linked
to the sacred as well as spectacularly represented as degrading. The 'lost
woman' (*femme perdue*) is a way for men to 'lose', to spend excessively
(both financially and physiologically).[45] In order to detect a *feminine* quality
in these extravagant texts – which are often highly misogynistic in their
representation of women – at least a powerful deconstructive reading (or
an exceedingly generous reading) is required. I shall be dealing with the
exemplary case of Bataille in Chapter Seven. Another instance (which Lyotard
refers to repeatedly in *Libidinal Economy*) is the work of Pierre Klossowski,
author of *La Monnaie vivante*, an attack on industrialisation in the name of
the libidinal.[46]

In *Roberte ce soir*, Klossowski formulates the notorious 'Laws of
Hospitality' in which the husband (Octave) offers his wife (Roberte) to his
friends, or better yet to strangers, in order that he and his guests should
have an essential rather than merely an accidental relationship.[47] Octave, a

45 Bataille, for example, refers to the lost woman in 'The Notion of Expenditure', p. 128.
46 Paris, Losfeld, 1970.
47 *Roberte ce soir* and *The Revocation of the Edict of Nantes*, trans. Austryn Wainhouse,
 London, Calder and Boyars, 1971. *Roberte ce soir* was first published in 1953, within
 a few years of Bataille writing *Blue of Noon* and *Madame Edwarda*, and the publication
 of *Histoire d'O*. All these works pose the question of women's acute pleasure in
 humiliation – in a decade which is one of those which stand out in the century as a
 peak of natalism and a low point of women's participation in the labour market.

Professor of Scholastics led astray by language, 'suffered from his conjugal happiness as though from an illness, firm in the belief that he would be cured of it once he had made it contagious' (p. 9). As the narrator, Octave's nephew, points out, this is a 'hospitality which was practised at my aunt's expense'. Although Octave is abandoning his role as master (possessive and proprietorial), his role as host (generous) is equally abusive of his wife. However, Klossowski presents the situation as inherently paradoxical because of the contradictory position of the hostess:

> For either the essence of the hostess is constituted by her fidelity to the host, and in this case she eludes him the more he wishes to know her in the opposite state of betrayal, for she would be unable to betray him in order to be faithful to him; or else the essence of the hostess is really constituted by infidelity and then the host would cease to have any part in the essence of the hostess who would be susceptible of belonging, accidentally, as mistress of the house, to some one or other of the guests. (p. 13)

This self-undermining could be related to Derrida's analysis of Nietzsche (whom Klossowski translates and comments on) in *Spurs Nietzsche's Styles*.[48] Derrida points out that Nietzsche's woman *se donne pour* even as she *se donne*. As she gives herself, she acts out giving herself or gives herself for a reason. What is presented as a philosophical paradox in Klossowski (who follows his master Sade in combining philosophy with pornography)[49] could, of course, equally be understood as a social double-bind – the impossible position of women historically. Klossowski makes a further classical link: 'such making common property of a cherished living person is not without analogy to the hallowed gaze of an artist' (p. 123).

Thorstein Veblen's entertaining account of (pre)history helps in understanding the process by which the thesis of original expenditure or primitive *dépense* may be allied with a debasement of women. Since my concern is with *representations* of economies rather than the actuality of economies, I shall not question Veblen's scholarly accuracy or originality. He argues that the first division of labour is between men and women:[50] 'the women are, by prescriptive custom, held to those employments out of which the industrial occupations proper develop at the next advance. The men are

48 trans. B. Harlow, Chicago and London, The University of Chicago Press, 1979.
49 Much of Klossowski's own fiction and painting is pornographic; within the text Octave is the voice in favour of pornography and Roberte is the would-be (secular) censor – objecting to the idea that men are only potent when they imagine women as the victims of torture. For Octave, Roberte's attitude is a denial of the spirit. She is punished by (her pleasure in) being ravished by a succession of spirits.
50 Rousseau also puts forward such a hypothesis in his *Essay on the Origin of Languages*. At a number of points Veblen's conclusions about prehistory recall Rousseau, although there are also differences (for example, Rousseau argues that the first form of property is land). Rousseau notoriously produces history as story in which factual details are less important than inner accuracy.

exempt from these vulgar employments and are reserved for war, hunting, sports, and devout observances' (p. 23). Women's work is exercised upon the inert ('brute matter'), whereas men's exploits result from conquering the animate. Women, we might add, synecdochally take on the passive characteristics of the matter upon which they work. Man, on the other hand, as active agent, finds scope for emulation in the killing of formidable competitors and in the acquisition of booty (pp. 30–1). Women, in the shape of female slaves taken as booty, are, furthermore, he tells us, the first form of property. Over time they become, like servants, the means for vicarious consumption. Thus wives of wealthy men in many periods of history have not worked for money because their labour is entirely their husbands' – whether that labour is productive or is to be demonstrably unproductive. Thus, from one perspective, women (objects) represent men's uneconomic, unproductive expenditure – from a feminist viewpoint this may be highly economic, social exploitation.

Lévi-Strauss sees the exchange of women (objects) as economic, but naturalises the economic rather than analysing it as exploitation. Irigaray suggests, in her analysis of Lévi-Strauss and Marx, that the anthropologist's (Lévi-Strauss's) excuse that *women* must be exchanged because they are a scarce commodity is risible. Irigaray points out that women are exchanged because 'women's bodies – through their use, consumption, and circulation – provide for the condition making social life and culture possible, although they remain an unknown "infrastructure" of the elaboration of that social life and culture'.[51] In other words, it is a question of the reproduction of the means of production – in the widest possible sense. Irigaray comments further:

> Mothers are essential to [social] (re)production (particularly inasmuch as they are [re]productive of children and of the labour force: through maternity, child-rearing, and domestic maintenance in general). Their reponsibility is to maintain the social order without intervening so as to change it. Their products are legal tender in that order, moreover, only if they are marked with the name of the father, only if they are recognised within his law: that is, only insofar as they are appropriated by him. Society is the place where man engenders himself, where man produces himself as man, where man is born into 'human', 'super-natural' existence. ('Women on the Market', p. 185)

In her various writings, Irigaray, like a number of other feminists, brings together women's use and exchange value in a material sense (such as the production of children or domestic labour) and in a psychological sense: women's work in supporting men, listening sympathetically, giving positive feedback, and enhancing their self-image both privately and publicly.

---

51 'Women on the Market', *This Sex Which Is Not One*, trans. Catherine Porter, New York, Cornell University Press, [1977] 1985, p. 171.

Women's value in patriarchal terms continuously inflects their role as paid workers in the market economy, although that role is a crucial one, according to the very principles of capitalism. Thus the ebb and flow of capital's demands interact with those of the patriarchal system and with the demands of women struggling to assert themselves as subjects. Both archaic gift economy analysis and the economic analysis of women within the domestic sphere make women into objects or commodities. This reification relates to the lack of freedom of the family as economic institution relative to the market. There is a relation of obligation in the domestic mode of production which makes it closer to a slave or feudal mode of production than a capitalist one – it is generally easier to leave a job than to get divorced or leave your dependent family.[52] Most feminist analyses recognise that the recent emphasis on the woman as (masculine) economic subject (paid worker) masks the continuing reality of women's role as objects, and that, in the Enlightenment tradition, it is crucial to reveal women's double exploitation. However, beyond this common and crucial critique, feminists are divided. Some would seek equality in the labour market and at home (whether by reform or revolution!) on the masculine Enlightenment model. Others would wish to achieve equality *and* to modify this model, using, for instance, notions of a feminine economy.

Women's work

On the whole, this book will be less concerned with empirical evidence than with representations; the focus is on thinking for and against the market, rather than market or anti-market practices. However, any such separation is itself an artificial thought-experiment, since thinking and practice are importantly interdependent. In this section I wish to pause in order to examine briefly contemporary women's participation in the labour market – and would-be 'factual' representations of their participation. This exceptional excursion into the empirical will serve a range of purposes. On the one hand, those thinkers who make reference to a feminine economy are sometimes accused of ignoring the realities of women's lives and, by their ignorant theorisings, reinforcing certain stereotypes which are precisely an integral part of that hegemonic ideology which bolsters up economic and social inequality between the sexes. The connection established (at least on a lexical level) between women and production which is not for exchange on the market can be seen as fostering the tradition of female self-sacrifice

52 Delphy and Leonard analyse a number of the pressures on a wife to work for her husband; they point out that when a wife cannot fulfil her 'domestic obligations' because of the demands of her paid employment it is usually the case that she must pay for child-care or domestic work out of her wages and that she must 'manage' the arrangements in question.

which has long characterised motherhood – but also daughterhood, sisterhood, and a range of aspects of married life. Put crudely, women give more than they get; women 'work' without getting paid. Thus gift economies should not be tied to the feminine in any positive sense, because there is a real connection between women and 'gifts', but we should be struggling to break that connection, since those so-called gifts are really the fruits of exploitation. On the other hand, it can be argued that, even if women used to occupy a space outside the market, this is becoming increasingly rare. Now the large majority of women work for pay just as men do, and their unpaid labour is, like men's, an additional extra which they choose to give. Thus, it is claimed, gift economies should not be tied to the feminine, because there is no real connection between women and generosity today – if there ever was.

I shall focus on the question of work (in the widest possible sense), since it seems to me that it is one of the most important aspects of gift-giving; although it is frequently ignored, as thinkers focus on the exchange of commodities without considering how these commodities were acquired by the giver. On the one hand, some of the most valuable gifts are gifts of labour (such as education, the teacher's labour), and many gifts of objects are directly or indirectly the gifts of the fruits of the giver's labour. On the other hand, it is the distinction between working for wages and working without wages which has become one of the key elements of sexual differentiation in our society.[53] I shall argue that sexual equality as identity is still not a feature of labour relations inside or outside the market economy, that women continue to give more than they get in an importantly different way from men. However, I shall also argue that, while it is crucial to distinguish between a gift freely given and a service extracted in a an exploitative relationship (even if the coercion is ideological rather than physical), certain aspects of the giving historically associated with women should still be positively valorised. First I shall turn to the troubled question of the assumption of equality as an assumption of universality.

In order to analyse the labour market (or any other market), economists have to make certain decisions about the population in question. A key decision from my perspective is whether men and women should be treated as the same or different – and, if different, then how and why. The answers also have great implications for tackling econometric models and for policy evaluation. When neoclassical economists (and I include Keynesians within that broad term) refer to labour markets they assume homogeneity of labour, and this permits the aggregation of individuals, each maximising rationally subject to constraints. They also assume that scarce resources are in general allocated by the market. These are, of course,

53 See Delphy and Leonard, *Familiar Exploitation.*

simplifying assumptions, but are considered to be justified – simplicity not only makes models more elegant, but also more powerful. Universality is a typical assumption of the economic approach,[54] which hypothesises roughly stable preferences over time, place, sex and so on. For those readers less familiar with this way of thinking, I should explain that this need not mean that people have always preferred butter to margarine ('clearly an absurdity'), but does suggest that people have always and everywhere preferred more to less or have acted (on average) 'rationally' to achieve their goals ('common sense'). Taken to an extreme, this implies that discrimination does not exist, since it is not optimal for profit-maximising employers to discriminate. In a competitive equilibrium each person's wage should on average equal the marginal product of her or his labour, and in general the marginal product of the least efficient female worker in any firm should be equal to that of the least efficient male. The same argument applies to racial discrimination: it is not profitable or efficient to discriminate, and so discrimination does not exist.

Economic discourse covers both economic models and econometric practice. In econometric studies of the labour market, the assumption of homogeneity is something which should be tested. Econometricians use misspecification tests to find out whether their population is homoskedastic (in other words, whether it has a constant mean and variance). If that assumption does not hold, then it means that the sample is not normally distributed; it makes it more difficult to know the distribution of the sample and creates a series of problems. Irigaray criticises scientific language for its very emphasis on quantification (rather than quality). She analyses in the following way:

> the *connectors* are:
>   – negation: P or not P;
>   – conjunction: P plus Q;
>   – disjunction: either P or Q;
>   – implication: P entails Q;
>   – equivalence: P equals Q;
>
> Thus there is no sign:
>   – for *difference* other than a quantitative difference;
>   – for *reciprocity* (other than in one and the same property or whole);
>   – for *exchange*;
>   – for *permeability*;
>   – for *fluidity*.
>
>   (*Parler n'est jamais neutre*, p. 313)

---

54 See Gary Becker, *The Economic Approach to Human Behaviour*, Chicago, University of Chicago Press, 1976.

Scientific syntax is dominated by identity (through property and quantity), non-contradiction (which reduces ambiguity) and binary oppositions. If there are two distinct populations within the sample, called m and f for the sake of the argument, then the econometrician may well want to split the sample in order to get two well-specified regressions.

The analyst may discover, for instance, that, whereas the sub-sample f's labour supply is quite elastic with respect to changes in the real wage-rate over time, the sub-sample m's labour supply is quite inelastic with respect to these changes. Put crudely, if wages go up, more of population f choose to work, whereas population m work whatever the wage rate. This could be because income and substitution effects cancel each other out (the economist's diagnosis) or because social pressures dictate that a certain level of work is acceptable for population m, no more and no less. If this is the case, does m equal males and f equal females? Many economists would argue that in 'the developed world' m, who could also be called Group One (implying 'primary workers', and hence muddying the waters still further) should certainly *include* all males, since men's labour supply has been relatively constant over a long period of time.[55] This is the model of (men's) work experience as homogeneous, indeed monolithic.[56] I would hypothesise that the largest group of economists treat labour supply as homogeneous, while the second largest group make a simple split: m equals males, f equals females. That split has been particularly common over the last few decades, for instance in cross-section studies of earnings functions.[57] Some econometricians argue, however, that the sample should not be split on the grounds of sex alone, but on a combination of sex and marital status. One example would be to make m into Group One of males and unmarried

55 This is the labour supply of men of working age (itself a definition which is variable). The stability of men's labour supply, say, since the Second World War, is even more striking if we disregard unemployment by looking at the figures for men in the labour force (that is, we assume men's unemployment to be involuntary) rather than men in paid work; i.e. we are looking at the labour men want to supply. Labour force figures for women have to be attained by questionnaire, as female unemployment statistics have been notoriously unreliable, since benefit laws have often discouraged married or cohabiting women from signing on as unemployed. Thus the labour women want to suppply is underestimated in certain measures. This has a number of ideological bonuses – making the global unemployment rate appear lower; reinforcing certain cultural stereoypes concerning women. In that vein some curious research has been done with work exit questionnaires – used to prove that many women say that they would not work or would work less if money were not a problem. Strangely, in reports on this research there is no mention of the possibility of asking male workers the same questions . . .

56 It is possible to begin to undo that apparent unity, for example, by looking at the participation rates of the over-55s or at the 16–19 age group. Men's participation may not be as solid and unquestionable as sometimes assumed, although equally it may not be as 'flexible' as some would wish.

57 $W_i = \beta X_i + u_i \ (i = m, f)$

females, *f* into Group Two of married females. This works quite well with UK time series data of hours of labour supplied since the Second World War, a period and a place which has seen a gradual drawing of married women into the labour market, from which they were conspicuous by their absence in the inter-war period.[58]

Christine Greenhalgh argues that there are four distinct groups in her regressions of earnings on to a vector of personal characteristics: married males, single males, single females and married females.[59] Setting aside the so-called 'explained differential', for example that due to differences in 'human capital variables,[60] there is a difference of the order of 10 per cent between each category. This 'equality' of differential may be misleading, as over time the gap between single men and women has narrowed whereas the gap between single and married women has widened – in other words, within the category of women, marital status seems to have taken on some of the disadvantage previously associated with sex alone in terms of earning capacity, over a period in which married women have increased as a group, both within the general category of women and within the category of working women. Setting aside the explained differential and attributing the residual to discrimination is common practice, but it means that differential access to the acquisition of qualifications and so on is not taken into account. Unsurprisingly, there is some controversy over what can be incorporated into the explained differential, for example whether or not an industry variable should be included within this.[61]

One might suggest, however, that an even more significant split would be that Group One equals males and females without children (below a certain age), Group Two equals females with dependent children. A factor often cited as contributing to women's increased participation in the labour market is demographic change (in particular, smaller and later families) – a factor which brings in the question of causal antecedence. The single element which has the greatest effect on whether or not a British woman works is the presence of one or more children below a certain age.[62] In France it is the number rather than the presence of children below a certain age which

---

58 One complication, however, is that married women have been increasing in propor-
    tion within the population of all females during this same period. Consideration of
    time-series data which goes back to the First World War and beyond prevents too
    easy an assumption that women's entry into the labour market has simply risen
    gradually over time.

59 See 'Male–Female Wage Differentials in Great Britain: Is Marriage an Equal Oppor-
    tunity?', *The Economic Journal*, 90 (1980), 751–75.

60 Of course, the difference in human capital variables has been crucial, as women have
    acquired less education, training and years of continuous 'relevant' work experience
    than men, for a variety of reasons which are pertinent to the whole debate.

61 This is controversial, because it is indeed the case that the crowding of women into
    certain industries is related to the low pay in those industries (both as cause and
    effect), and hence to the low average wage of women as a whole.

62 In 1981 only 7 per cent of UK women with a child under 5 worked full-time.

is important: three or more children make it significantly less likely that a French woman will participate in the labour market. Mothers of young children usually cannot work in Britain unless their wages at least cover the cost of child-care; in France the State provides high-quality child-care. Surveys of countries as diverse as Canada and Brazil return the same answer that the quality and availability of child-care and the relationship between wages and the cost of child-care is the major determinant of women's labour supply.

The interest in determining homogeneous groups – other than in order to get good regressions – is obviously in order to pinpoint where the difference lies. Analysis of data has not yet provided us with a simple answer to the problem of how to split the population to get a good fit – the empirical, unsurprisingly, does not provide us with our theory. Of course, theories as well as other factors have some influence on what data is available and what kinds of avenues have already been explored.

A large body of current thinking emphasises the convergence of male and female patterns of employment by quoting global statistics, for example: in Britain in 1951 women's economic activity rate was 42.1 per cent,[63] while in spring 1995 71 per cent of British women of working age (16–59) were economically active,[64] compared to 85 per cent of British men of working age (16–64).[65] Another way of putting this is to say that in 1995 44 per cent of all people in employment were women – very nearly half. These kinds of global figures seem to force the view that employment experience is becoming broadly similar for the sexes. In my view this is highly misleading, and I want to ask both what is the reality when the figures are disaggregated, and what is at stake in pressing this false homogenisation upon us. In Harvey's analysis of the transformation of labour markets in postmodernity, he writes:

> Not only do the new labour market structures make it much easier to exploit the labour power of women on a part-time basis, and so to substitute lower-paid female labour for that of more highly paid and less easily laid-off core male workers, but the revival of sub-contracting and domestic and family labour systems permits a resurgence of patriarchal practices and homeworking.
> (*The Condition of Postmodernity*, p. 153)

He takes issue with the notion of convergence between core and peripheral workers (including immigrants and certain ethnic groups as well as women)

---

63 See H. Joshi and H. Owen, 'How Long Is a Piece of Elastic? The Measurement of Female Activity Rates in British Censuses, 1951–1981', *Cambridge Journal of Economics*, 11 (1987), 55–74.

64 In other words they were either in work or registered unemployed. The figure for working-age women in employment is 66 per cent.

65 These figures (prepared by the Government Statistical Service) are taken from Frances Sly, 'Women in the Labour Market: Results from the Spring 1995 Labour Force Survey', *Labour Market Trends*, 104 (March 1996), pp. 91–113. All further figures will also be taken from Labour Force Surveys (LFS), unless otherwise indicated. LFS figures are grossed up from interviews with about 60,000 households.

except in so far as the core has become smaller, and so some white males have been thrown into what may be variously termed the secondary, peripheral or reserve sector. I too would argue that the reality is a series of differences,[66] and that these differences should be treated seriously both in order to achieve more equality as idéntity where that is appropriate, and to foster different, non-market values where possible.

The crucial difference is the mode of employment: full-time or part-time. Only 37 per cent of women of working age work full-time (34 per cent are not working; 27 per cent work part-time; 2 per cent did not answer the question). The proportion of women in part-time work tends to be higher in Britain than in other European countries, but it is generally true that part-time work is much more common for women than for men. The idea of part-time work itself needs to be analysed, as different surveys have different definitions. In general it covers a wide range of hours – between 1 and 30 hours a week – and thus covers a range of different work experiences. In the past decade it has become more common for men to take part-time jobs – evidence of the gradual casualisation of the workforce in general, and cited as evidence of the gradual convergence of men's and women's work experience. However, men tend to work part-time at particular stages in their life-cycle, for example when they are students. Women often work part-time in their mature years, when men are at the peak of their earning capacity.

The segregation of the workforce remains a crucial factor in depressing women's wages, and making a difference between women's work experience and that of men.[67] Economists describe this situation of 'crowding' (women working largely in 'women's occupations') as 'labour market segmentation'. It can be hard to pass from a secondary segment to a primary one, and thus segregation is perpetuated. What they find difficult to explain is the causality: why are women predominantly to be found in certain kinds of work?

Shirley Dex, Heather Joshi and Susan Macran argue that in the 1990s two populations of women, indeed two populations of mothers, have emerged.[68] The first is well educated, has children later in life, benefits from maternity leave, and returns to full-time work with the same employer shortly after

---

66 For example, 66 per cent of women of working age are in employment, compared to 76 per cent of men. However, since 'working age' is deemed to end at the 60th birthday for women, but not until the 65th birthday for men, this difference already skews the figure, depressing the male participation rate.

67 The majority of women work only with other women, and the majority of men work only with other men. See J. Martin and C. Roberts, *Women and Employment: A Lifetime Perspective*, London: HMSO, 1984. Part-time jobs are more likely to be predominantly female than full-time jobs.

68 'A Widening Gulf among Britain's Mothers', *Oxford Review of Economic Policy*, 12 (1996), Special Issue 'Inequality', pp. 65–75. It is interesting to note that this kind of investigation is not common in economics journals, and that the population of academics carrying out such research is quite small. (Fourteen of the twenty-six publications cited in the bibliography to this article include Dex or Joshi as one of the authors.)

bearing a child. This (minority)[69] population is beginning to approach equality with men. The less highly-educated majority follows the opposite pattern: it has children early, is less likely to be eligible for maternity leave, unlikely to return quickly to full-time work and unlikely to remain with the same employer. Motherhood used to be a leveller for women in terms of their own careers, although not in terms of their spending power, which was dependent on their husbands. Now social class impinges not only on disposable income and assets, but also on independence.

A further key factor is, of course, domestic labour. As I have suggested already, it is erroneous to see the household chiefly as a consuming unit; there is a large amount of productive work performed within households, although most of this is not recognised by measures of national production such as GNP, because it is not production for exchange on the market. This is in no way intrinsic to the tasks performed, but is due to the relations of production in question. At some income levels women can afford to pay others (usually other women, usually unqualified, usually very low-paid) to perform a range of domestic tasks on their behalf (at which point, if declared to the State, the tasks are deemed productive) – although a degree of unpaid administration and management results from buying in these services. Even highly-paid, highly-skilled wives continue to contribute more unpaid work to the maintenance of the household than their husbands – for example, running social relations with family and friends. At lower income levels the dual shift is even heavier, since no money can be spared to buy in services other than the minimum of child-care. Delphy and Leonard point out that the invention of ever more 'labour-saving' devices has hardly reduced the amount of time spent on housework by women. Instead, labour-saving devices either replace buying in services (the washing machine replaces the servant who did the washing) or enable a higher standard of living (more frequent changes of clothes). Delphy and Leonard are concerned to emphasise the *obligatory* nature of women's unpaid labour for others within the family system – and their emphasis is still a very necessary corrective to the frequent misrepresentations which are part of the narrative of free choice. Nevertheless, without going quite as far as Annie Leclerc's *Parole de Femme*[70] in a celebration of women's particular biological

---

69 In 1991 only 21 per cent of British women had qualifications above A level; this rises to 33 per cent if we broaden the category to A levels or above (Dex, Joshi and Macran, 'A Widening Gulf Among Britain's Mothers', p. 66). This still represents a very significant increase over the post-Second World War period, and a considerable narrowing of the gap between men and women.

70 Paris, Grasset, 1974. Extracts have been translated in a number of collections of French feminist writing, such as Toril Moi (ed.), *French Feminist Thought*, Oxford, Blackwell, 1987 – one of the more sympathetic presentations is in Elizabeth Fallaize, *French Women's Writing*, London and Basingstoke, Macmillan, 1993. This work is the main target of Delphy's 'Proto-Feminism and Anti-Feminism' in *French Feminist Thought*, pp. 80–109.

and domestic pleasures, I would still suggest that there is something to be redeemed and recuperated from the notion of unpaid work as a gift – *where there is no obligation to be exploited.*

Women's work, a range of disparate experiences now and in the past, is described and analysed by economists and historians in a way which purports to be objective science. In fact it is narrativised: the story told will either be that of women biologically predisposed to choose mothering and domestic labour (deemed unproductive by government statistics) or that of women as just the same as men, meaning men as they are taken to be here and now (working full-time for the whole of their working lives, maximising their utility). I would argue that neither is true. Most women's work experience is not the same as men's, and that difference affects even those women whose experience is closest to the masculine pattern. At the same time, when women have the opportunity of paid work, then certain rational calculations will usually enter into play as they do for men: the amount by which the income and wealth to which they have access without paid work falls below their perceived needs; the difference between the wage they can command and the costs they incur by working (such as child-care or travel); the satisfaction derived from paid work as against the physical and mental toll.

Women's inferior position in the labour market, and their general economic inferiority, renders them less capable of acting as great public benefactors than men. Women's acts of generosity therefore tend to take place in the domestic sphere – or to consist in the gift of their labour (charity work). Both these categories of gifts are ambiguous, because of the dominant relations of production between men and women in our society.[71] In early utopian texts, it is often suggested that a precondition of the just society is that all should work, and this has specifically included women, but not on the masculine model of full-time work for wages (which, in a full market model, would equal the marginal product of labour). Rather all should work for the collectivity, and should receive reward according to their needs (or their socially contained desires). Recent work on the *économie féminine* has borrowed a vocabulary of female biology and women's traditional nurturing tasks to hint at the possibility of new social relations for both men and women.

Narratives

I have touched on the subject of scientific discourse and its relation to the theory of economics and to the masculine imaginary. Against scientific

---

71 Veblen provides an interesting analysis of charity work and vicarious consumption in *The Theory of the Leisure Class.*

discourse (supposedly) there is the figural and the narrative (supposedly, because in fact scientists do use the narrative function). The narrative form is hospitable to a variety of language games – as Lyotard would put it. He remarks that traditional knowledge arises through apprenticeship; the one-time listener becomes a speaker in his turn (*The Postmodern Condition*, p. 21). Lyotard points out that narrative knowledge is tolerant towards scientific discourse as a variant in the family of narrative cultures, but that the opposite is not true:

> The scientist questions the validity of narrative statements and concludes that they are never subject to argumentation or proof. He classifies them as belonging to a different mentality: savage, primitive, underdeveloped, backward, alienated, composed of opinions, customs, authority, prejudice, ignorance, ideology. Narratives are fables, myths, legends, fit only for women and children. At best, attempts are made to throw some rays of light into this obscurantism, to civilize, educate, develop. (*The Postmodern Condition*, p. 27)

For Lyotard this is part of the history of cultural imperialism. The question of narrative thus brings us to the link between the sexual other and the racial other. However, while 'women and children' and the 'savage' or 'primitive' are lumped together here by the scientist, thanks to their irrationality, neither group as a social reality would necessarily see its interests lying in maintaining that alliance rather than in establishing its own superiority. And in celebrations of the primitive economy, of desire over economic reason, women are often, or so it would seem, the sacrificial object.

The gift of reading

The critical question that emerges from my brief survey of these debates is that of reading. The evidence that exists, or the texts that present the evidence, can either be read economically, according to Hegelian strategies of mastery and exclusion, or they can be read and rewritten with a degree of generosity. Texts are the result of readings and rewritings of other texts, and that intertextuality can be modelled according to a range of forms of exchange, just as the intertextuality which is my encounter with the text can follow different paths.[72] Cixous has presented a model of reading in her theory, or rather practice, of *écriture féminine*, which, I would argue, is no more, and no less, about writing than about reading. Both practices relate to the practitioners' model of intersubjective relations. Writing and reading, for Cixous, need not be locked in violent, if cerebral, combat in which one's survival means the other's death.[73] Instead there can be a sensuous

---

72 See my article 'From Eliot's "raw bone" to Gyges' Ring: Two Studies in Intertextuality', *Paragraph*, 1 (1983), 44–59.

73 For the explicitly political dimension of Cixous's work, for example the colonial and postcolonial analysis, see Shiach, *Hélène Cixous*.

amorous wrestling of reader (to be writer) with text. I use the metaphor of wrestling, since a degree of struggle is inevitable even in reading the most 'fluid' of texts (Clarice Lispector's, according to Cixous), never mind those with a tendency to dry (you) up. Cixous's metaphors of birth (indeed, of giving birth to one's own 'mother'), or mastication, never imply simple passivity, even as they reject that activity which seeks the annihilation of what is not the (*propre*) selfsame. Margaret Whitford has likewise argued for a maternal – feminine reading of Irigaray, and for an understanding of Irigaray as herself engaged in a creative and loving dialogue with other texts, instead of a suspicious reading.[74] Barthes's, Derrida's and Kristeva's readings of Bataille are examples of a way to find the feminine in what may at first seem unpromising material. These will be explored further in later chapters.

74 See 'Luce Irigaray: The Problem of Feminist Theory', *Paragraph*, 8 (1986), 102–5.

2

Key pre-texts on the gift economy: Plato, More and Montaigne

This chapter attempts a brief analysis of three key pre-texts to Enlightenment (and later) gift economy thinking. The three texts I have chosen are Plato's *Republic*,[1] More's *Utopia*[2] and Montaigne's *Essays*,[3] in particular Book I, Chapter 31, 'On the Cannibals'. Of course, others could have been selected, but these authors have haunted later debates in important ways. This selection entails a focus on explicitly constructed social virtue (the line that runs through these works by Plato, More, Rousseau, Diderot and Scott) rather than chronological primitivism or theses of natural goodness.[4] Montaigne's 'On the Cannibals' may seem to be the token example of a text taken to be an account of archaic expenditure or natural goodness, but I shall argue that this too has a crucial strand of constructed social virtue. Plato remains an absolutely privileged, if tortured, point of reference, particularly for the poststructuralist and feminist philosophers I shall be discussing in more detail in Chapter Eight. His major work of political philosophy explores both the conditions of possibility of the just state, and

1 *The Republic of Plato*, ed. F. M. Cornford, Oxford, Oxford University Press, 1941.
2 *Utopia*, trans. Ralph Robinson, introduction by Richard Marius, London, Dent, [1516] 1985.
3 *The Essays*, trans. and ed. M. A. Screech, Harmondsworth, Penguin, 1991. The *Essays* were first published in 1580, but substantially revised in subsequent editions – Montaigne was still adding to his text when he died in 1592.
4 An important complementary strand of influence would be the representations of the Golden Age (such as those of Hesiod, Virgil, Horace, Ovid or Tacitus). In fact it is difficult to make watertight distinctions between different kinds of what I call representations of gift economies. Dominic Baker-Smith in 'The Escape from the Cave: Thomas More and the Vision of Utopia', *Dutch Quarterly Review of Anglo-American Letters*, 15 (1985), 148–61, critiques J. C. Davis's division of what he would broadly term utopian writing into five categories: utopia, millennium, arcadia, cockaygne and perfect moral commonwealth (p. 149). Baker-Smith argues that in practice most texts cross these boundaries; for example, while millennial texts might be thought to owe their specificity to their insistence on divine intervention, in fact they tend to operate figuratively, so that, say, a pastoral element (milk and honey) represents unrestricted divine intervention. Equally, utopias tend to have 'historical' foundations such as the work of King Utopus, and these could be related figuratively to divine intervention.

the fundamental ontological and epistemological questions about human nature. On a heuristic level, the *Republic* appears surprisingly sexually egalitarian, but Plato nevertheless stands accused of privileging 'the same', that is to say, the masculine. *Utopia* names a genre.[5] Utopian writing is not simply political theory, and could be said to use fiction and the figural as it does because of the inadequacy of available political concepts. It is a genre which is to be intimately linked to economies of abundance, and which raises the question of the imaginary other. 'On the Cannibals' at once evokes an ideal primitive gift economy and makes explicit the importance of colonialism in defining the terms of the encounter with the primitive 'other'.

Plato

It is very difficult to overstate the influence of Plato in general, and of *The Republic* in particular. In 'Plato's Pharmacy', Derrida remarks that ' "Platonism" [. . .] sets up the whole of Western metaphysics in its conceptuality' (*Dissemination*, p. 76), claiming that it is therefore all the more significant that Platonism is a striking example of a schema which assigns the origin and power of the word to the paternal position. All the other writers whom I shall be analysing have to measure themselves in some way against Plato, as founding father, whether this agon is made explicit or not. In *The Post Card*,[6] Derrida suggests that Plato wants us all to be his sons – and even wants Socrates to be his son. This passage from father to son is a kind of reproduction of the same – what Irigaray would call an anal logic and an anal economy.[7] I shall briefly discuss *The Republic* as a text in itself,

5 For a seminal analysis of utopic form, see Louis Marin, *Utopics*, trans. R. A. Vollrath, London and Basingstoke, Macmillan, 1984. For Marin utopic texts are historically restricted to the formative period of Western capitalism, although he gives contemporary examples which he views as ideologically regressive. He argues that 'Utopia is [. . .] the neutral moment of a difference, the space outside of place; it is a gap impossible to inscribe on a geographic map or to assign to history [. . .] This figurative representation [. . .] will cancel out the "objective" difference displayed by historical reality, as picture and fiction in the text. It will do so by extending the limits of Western civilisation, if not to the unlimited universe, at least to a space whose spherical nature excludes the notion of limits' (pp. 57–8). Marin's analysis attempts to reconstitute the masked history from the textual traces which remain. His insistence on the *neutral* quality of utopia sits uneasily with contemporary feminist work on utopias.

6 trans. A. Bass, Chicago and London, The University of Chicago Press, 1987.

7 Derrida uses the motif of the *a tergo* in his analysis. Johnson comments: 'In Plato's closed shop (as in Hegel's circular economy), reproduction is ideally the return of the same, son is like father, the paternal seed always arrives at its destination. As Derrida remarks in "Envois", Plato, through the written deposit of his dialogues and letters, through Socrates to whom he dictates, wants to send himself his own child [*The Post Card*, p. 101]. This is the mono-sexual (circular, restricted, ideal) economy of auto-insemination [. . .] The problem is that reproduction, the emission or transmission of seed, requires an exit from the homely economy of the same' (*System and Writing*, p. 175).

and then move on to some of the intertextual relationships which it has generated.

Plato was writing in the fourth century BC, a very different economic context from that of any of the other writers I shall be considering – in other words, a slave economy rather than a stage of capitalism. His just state taken as a whole is less radical in economic terms than More's Utopia or Rousseau's republic in *The Social Contract*: a market economy still operates for the lower classes (the artisans) as a means of distributing their products, and these are produced with maximum 'efficiency', thanks to the division of labour. However, it is not the just state taken as a whole which has caught the attention of readers. Frequently readers of *The Republic* have focused on the far more radical society within the state, that is the society of the Guardians (the two upper classes), and on the parable of the cave. Readers have, of course, approached Plato through burning problems of their own – most recently logocentrism and the politics of sexual difference. At the same time Plato is of particular interest where he hypothesises social existence without market exchange; from the time of Thomas More, the time of 'New Economics' (nascent capitalism), it has seemed urgent to interrogate the combination of the market mechanism and excessive political power.

Plato is taxed by the intersection of moral and political philosophy: the question of which form of socio-political organisation would enable individuals to realise their potential for virtue. He is worried by economic inequality because it threatens to bring about civil strife, and so is a major political problem. It is also a moral problem, since it fosters excessive desire for material goods and negative emotions towards those at the opposite end of the wealth spectrum. He says of riches and poverty: 'The one produces luxury and idleness, the other low standards of conduct and workmanship; and both have a subversive tendency' (*The Republic*, p. 109). To prevent extremes of wealth and poverty there must be restrictions on accumulation and hence restriction of private property; this both implies and is implied by restrictions on trade, particularly the trade in labour.

This line of argument bears on the question of sexual difference not only because the abolition or near abolition of the labour market removes one key difference between the sexes, but also, indirectly, because it is often believed that discouraging private ownership means calling family life and the private sphere into question. Plato/Socrates makes more radical suggestions in this respect (with regard to the community of the Guardians) than most of his successors – and even in the late twentieth century his ideas can still seem sufficiently threatening that they must be dismissed as a joke. Plato was a major moral influence on More and Rousseau; they are worried by the same kinds of questions as those he raises in the *Republic*, and yet they are unwilling to advocate such a radical reduction of sexual difference and indeed the abolition of the family.[8] Of course, it is hard to distinguish anxiety generated by other sources from that generated by the peculiar psychic relationship between master text and ephebe text, a relationship which is itself often phrased in terms of the hierarchy of sexual difference – the later and influenced text being emasculated or feminised.

Plato's Guardians may not possess any private property beyond the barest necessities. They may not possess any dwelling or storehouse which is not open for all to enter at will (p. 106).[9] Furthermore Socrates claims that the maxim he cites, 'friends have all things in common', applies also to women and children. When challenged, he expands on the metaphor he first used for the Guardians, that of sheep-dogs, with some rhetorical questions:

> Which do we think right for watch-dogs: should the females guard the flock and hunt with the males and take a share in all they do, or should they be kept within doors as fit for no more than bearing and feeding their puppies, while all the hard work of looking after the flock is left to the males? . . . Can you employ any creature for the same work as another, if you do not give them both the same upbringing and education? (p. 145)

Having thus suggested that women should be given equal opportunity with men, and that those women whose merits mark them as ranking as Guardians should receive the same education as the male Guardians, and eventually perform the same tasks, Socrates then proposes that the family be replaced by a social structure in which spouses and children are held in common. To that end, and also to prevent the formation of private families (and private loyalties), children should be reared in communal nurseries. 'Marriages' would be skilfully organised on eugenic principles. Amorous passion and sexual modesty would be replaced by a rationalisation of sexual conduct and a rational vision of the human body in which men and women can exercise naked together in order to be fit for war (p. 115).[10]

8 I shall argue in Chapter Four that Rousseau's *La Nouvelle Héloïse*, to some extent, and Sarah Scott's *Millenium Hall*, to an even greater extent, produce fictional near-ideal communities which replace the family unit based on biological and legal bonds. While both novels contain explicit statements in favour of the family, both show how it can produce unhappiness and describe moral, social bonds which appear preferable.

9 This transparency or lack of privacy is typical of many later texts in this tradition – including Diderot's *Supplement to Bougainville's 'Voyage'*.

10 It has been suggested that Plato's (or Socrates') position on women shifts from the more egalitarian line of the *Symposium* or the *Republic*, which reflects the medical theories of Hippocrates, to a line which anticipates Aristotle's more hierarchical theories in the *Timaeus* and the *Laws*. See Anne Dickason, 'Anatomy and Destiny in Plato's Views of Women', in *Women and Philosophy: Towards a Theory of Liberation*, ed. C. Gould and M. Wartofsky, New York, Capricorn Books, 1976, pp. 45–53. It is, of course, Aristotle's strange version of biology which is preferred by the medieval Church.

Plato as intertext

The longer title of More's *Utopia* is *De Optimo Reipublicae Statu* (usually translated as *The Best State of a Commonwealth*). In other words, it could be said to place itself immediately in the tradition or category of works *De Republica*.[11] These are works of political philosophy which also deploy dialogue, fiction, allegory and irony. When Socrates discusses the holding of all things in common he says that he indulges a fancy 'like one who entertains himself with idle daydreams on a solitary walk' (*The Republic*, p. 153) – language which reminds the modern reader (of the translation) of Rousseau's *Rêveries of the Solitary Walker*, and a notion which was echoed in More's invention of Hythloday, the speaker of nonsense. Each of these thinkers is aware that his invention will be disparaged as 'utopian' (even *avant la lettre*), but also that the question of realism could have personal consequences for him – as each lived under conditions of real political tyranny to a greater or lesser extent. More deals wittily with the question of verisimilitude by his very coinage 'Utopia', with its ironic eymological double (at least aurally) of *u* (no-place) or *eu* (pleasant-place), and this is echoed in a series of place-names within Utopia. The name 'Hythloday' and various place-names are often given as an example to support the case that *Utopia* is no more than playful nonsense, modelled less on Plato than on Lucian. (Importantly, the name Morus also means 'folly' . . . perhaps More could not help that, but equally he was bound to be aware of it.) But readers of Plato (such as Allan Bloom) as well as More (such as C. S. Lewis) have been much exercised by the question of irony. Where an otherwise respected thinker puts forward a position with which one strongly disagrees, it is no doubt a temptation to assert that the great man must have been joking. The same claim has been made of the letters from other important humanists such as Erasmus or Peter Giles which praise More's *Utopia* and are sometimes published alongside it.[12] Both Plato and More do have playful moments and are accomplished ironists when they choose, and therefore the possibility that outrageous suggestions such as educating women alongside men or abolishing private property are far from serious could remain in suspense. Without entering into the complexities of the

11 Baker-Smith points this out, and cites Cicero as well as Plato as an obvious intertext ('The Escape from the Cave', p. 151). Cicero's *De Republica* is known only in fragments; More would have had available to him Macrobius' commentary called the *Somnium Scipionis*.

12 See Warren J. Wooden, 'A Reconsideration of the Parerga of Thomas More's *Utopia*' in *Quincentennial Essays on Saint Thomas More*, ed. M. J. Moore, Boone, NC, Albion, 1978, pp. 151–60. More had enormous respect for Erasmus's *In Praise of Folly*, and wrote defending it against criticism; *Utopia* should no doubt be seen in this context. See Germain Marc 'Hadour, 'Thomas More in Emulation and Defense of Erasmus', in *Erasmus of Rotterdam: The Man and the Scholar*, ed. J. Sperna Weiland and W. Th. M. Frijhoff, Leiden, Brill, 1988, pp. 203–14.

debate (and my conclusion would be that it seems improbable that any elements of non-seriousness are of the order of those humanists simply laughing among themselves at such ludicrous suggestions), I would claim that the historical importance of the works has lain above all in the possibility of their radical propositions having serious significance. By More's device of an imagined observer he can also play on the contention that Utopia is a reality, compared to Plato's imaginary state: 'If so be that I should speak those things that Plato *feigneth* in his weal-public, or that the Utopians *do* in theirs . . .' (*Utopia*, p. 48, my italics). The dialogic scenario allows for questions of material detail to be posed.

More makes a number of direct comparisons between Utopia and Plato's *Republic*. His spokesman, Raphael Hythloday, is compared to 'the ancient and sage philosopher Plato' (p. 15), and is said to be better versed in Greek than Latin because the writings of that civilisation are more to his purpose. The comparisons are made on the grounds that both in Utopia and in the Republic 'all things be common' (p. 48). Hythloday tells More that when he considers the problems of different nations:

> Where possessions be private, where money beareth all the stroke, it is hard and almost impossible that there the weal-public may justly be governed and prosperously flourish [. . .] I hold well with Plato, and do nothing marvel that he would make no laws for them that refused those laws whereby all men should have and enjoy equal parts of wealth and commodities. (p. 50)

He also raises, in the first book of *Utopia*, the thorny question of the relationship between philosophers and kings, with reference to Plato's comments (pp. 34, 49) – both Plato and More experienced this as a personal dilemma, as well as a theoretical one. Peter Giles concludes of *Utopia* (in one of its parergonal texts) that it is 'as far excelling Plato's *Commonwealth*, all people should be willing to know' (p. 136).[13]

Some commentators have claimed that *Utopia* points to the superiority of Christianity over paganism, that More's concerns are strictly spiritual and quintessentially medieval. R. W. Chambers suggests that *Utopia* is written to show Christians what can be achieved with the four cardinal virtues alone (wisdom, fortitude, temperance and justice), so that they can imagine what far greater good could come when the three Christian virtues (faith, hope and charity) are added.[14] *Utopia* could shock Catholics into recognising that some Christians are worse than some heathens, who are guided by reason alone. Against the Catholic and spiritual and the politically conservative readings of More,[15] there is the seminal reading of Karl

13 Erasmus's marginalia also highlight links to *The Republic*.
14 *Thomas More*, London, Jonathan Cape, 1935.
15 See Gerard Wegemer, 'The Rhetoric of Opposition in Thomas More's *Utopia*: Giving Form to Competing Philosophies', *Philosophy and Rhetoric*, 23 (1990), 288–307.

Kautsky.[16] Kautsky claims that More is the true father of Utopian Socialism and that *Utopia* is the product of the social evils and incipient economic tendencies of the day, *rather than* an imitation of Plato. Much energy has been expended on the question whether More is concerned with a moral or an economic issue in *Utopia*. I would insist that for him (as for Plato, many of More's contemporaries and up to the Age of Rousseau), the two could not be separated.

Montaigne's *Essays* are famously studded with names of classical authors (as well as attributed and non-attributed quotations and misquotations). Plato is a particular favourite, alongside Aristotle, Herodotus, Plutarch, Virgil, Cicero and Seneca, to name but a few.[17] Montaigne's essay 'On the Cannibals' contains a series of references to Plato, beginning with the story of Atlantis (from the *Timaeus*) which introduces some comments on continental drift.[18] Diderot too begins the *Supplement* with observations on the tearing apart and bringing together of land masses, the disappearance and discovery of places and peoples. Both authors are creating an atmosphere of natural change and instability, and gently questioning any given state of human knowledge.[19] Both play with the problems of observation and speculation, and the kinds of knowledge which may result from these activities. Later Montaigne states, with respect to the native Brazilians he calls cannibals:

> It irritates me that neither Lycurgus nor Plato had any knowledge of them, for it seems to me that what experience has taught us about those peoples surpasses not only all the descriptions with which poetry has beautifully painted the Age of Gold and all its ingenious fictons about Man's blessed early state, but also the very conceptions and yearnings of philosophy. They could not even imagine a state of nature so simple and so pure as the one we have learned about from experience; they could not even believe that societies of men could be maintained with so little artifice, so little in the way of human solder. ('On the Cannibals', pp. 232–3)

Here the belated writer, living in a degenerate society amongst degenerate thinkers, less potent than those of classical antiquity, can nevertheless outdo the greatest lawgiver and the greatest thinker about social justice of classical

---

16 *Thomas More and his Utopia*, trans. H. J. Stenning, London, Lawrence and Wishart, 1979. Sir Ernest Barker, in *The Political Thought of Plato and Aristotle*, London, Methuen, 1959, also asserts that whereas Plato's motives for communism are moral, More's are economic.

17 See the Introduction by Judith Still and Michael Worton to *Intertextuality: Theories and Practices*, ed. M. Worton and J. Still, Manchester, Manchester University Press, 1990, especially pp. 8–12.

18 More's Utopia is located in the general area where Atlantis was believed to have existed.

19 Utopia is, however, a man-made island – it was a peninsula until King Utopus dug a channel cutting it off from the mainland.

times. Paradoxically, this is through his knowledge of peoples contemporary with himself and yet 'earlier' than his forefathers.

Rousseau, an even later comer, asserts – when the Genevans burn his books – that the *Social Contract* is a mirror of the real Genevan constitution: 'They [his enemies] were satisfied with relegating the *Social Contract* to the land of daydreams along with Plato's *Republic, Utopia* and the *Sevarites*'.[20] Rousseau has a complicated and ambiguous relationship with Plato in general and the *Republic* in particular. For example, Glaucon, Socrates' key interlocutor in the *Republic*, who evokes the mythical and dystopic figure of Gyges, appears more than once in Rousseau's most personal and introspective writing.[21] Rousseau claims to find Socrates' 'idle dream' totally aberrant:

> In the *Republic*, Plato suggests women do the same exercises as men; I'm not surprised! Having got rid of the family in his state, he didn't know what to do with the women and so was obliged to turn them into men. That great genius had worked out his plans in every detail and provided for every contingency; he even answered an objection which perhaps nobody would ever have thought to make, but he did not succeed in meeting the objection which everyone does make. I am talking about the alleged sharing [*communauté*] of women for which people have so often reproached him, thereby proving that they have never read him: I refer to that political promiscuity which everywhere confuses the two sexes, assigning the same work, the same occupations to both, which cannot fail to engender the most intolerable abuses; I refer to that subversion of the sweetest natural emotions, sacrificed to a social [*artificiel*] emotion which can only exist by their aid; as if the bonds of conventions would hold firm without some natural ground; as if the love which you hold for your nearest and dearest were not the principle behind the love you owe to the state; as if your heart does not learn devotion to the homeland via the home; as if it weren't the good son, the good husband, the good father who make the good citizen. (*Émile*,[22] p. 326, translation modified)

Rousseau makes two points: the first is that Plato's dissolution of sexual difference will lead to *abus intolérables,* and the second is that familial love

20 *Lettres écrites de la montagne,* in *Œuvres complètes,* ed. B. Gagnebin and M. Raymond, Paris, Bibliothèque de la Pléiade, 1959–95, III, p. 810. The third denied influence refers to Denis Veiras d'Alais, *Histoire des Sévarambes,* Paris, 5 vols, 1677–79, a novel which is little read today but which was influential in the eighteenth century. Rousseau ordered a copy in 1764, and probably had access to one when he was writing the notes for the *Discourse on Inequality.* See G. Chinard, *L'Amérique au 18ᵉ siècle,* Paris, Droz, 1934, p. 349. Emanuel von der Mühl, in *Denis Veiras et son Histoire des Sévarambes 1677–79,* Paris, Droz, 1938, places Veiras firmly in the line which runs from Plato through More to Rousseau.

21 See my *Justice and Difference in the Works of Rousseau,* Cambridge, Cambridge University Press, 1993 particularly chapter 5, or 'From Eliot's "raw bone" to Gyges' Ring: Two Studies in Intertextuality'.

22 trans. B. Foxley, London, Dent, 1974.

is a prerequisite for patriotism. The first point is familiar from other of Rousseau's writings (such as the *Letter to d'Alembert*), and it is typical that Rousseau should prescribe absolute sexual difference and indeed segregation (while describing and enacting something more fluid, as we shall see in Chapter Five). The second point, that concerning the family, is more of a pressure point, even on the level of overt prescription. It is a question on which Rousseau performs a series of reversals. In many of his works Rousseau portrays, or even advocates, the replacement of the familial blood-tie by a conventional bond, based on the natural emotion of *pity*, which, in his *Discourse on Inequality*, is the *only* natural emotion not to be directed at the self but at the other. In both the *Discourse on Political Economy* and *The Government of Poland* he suggests that the way for children to be raised as patriots is via State education rather than education in the bosom of the family. Rousseau does not subscribe to Filmer's patriarchal theory of society, which claims that the relation of (absolute) ruler to his people is a natural development of, and thus founded upon, the relation of the father to his household.[23] He argues in the *Discourse on Political Economy* that the conventional or contractual relationship of citizen to Republic should supplant the relationship of child to father, for example, concerning education:

> If the public authorities, by replacing fathers and taking on this important function [educating their children], acquire their rights in carrying out their duties, fathers have the less grounds for complaint in that, in this respect, all that happens, properly speaking, is that they are described differently, and that in the name of citizens they hold the same authority, in common, over their children as they had separately in the name of fathers. (p. 23, translation modified)

On the other hand, in the *Confessions*, Rousseau ascribes his youthful sin of abandoning all his and Thérèse Levasseur's children to his (mis) identification with Plato's *Republic*.[24] On many occasions this father who never knew his own children writes lyrically of the potential pleasures of family life, although he is also ready to describe the suffering which can be brought about by paternal tyranny, such as that of Julie's father in *La Nouvelle Héloïse*.[25]

I shall take just one late twentieth-century example of engaging with or rewriting Plato – of course, there are many. Irigaray analyses Plato's myth of the cave (*Republic*, VII) in *Speculum* (pp. 241–364). She reads the cave perversely or against the grain as a sexed metaphor, which tells of

23 See his *Discourse on Political Economy and The Social Contract*, trans. C. Betts, Oxford and New York, Oxford University Press, 1994, e.g. pp. 3–6.

24 *The Confessions*, trans. J. M. Cohen, Harmondsworth, Penguin, [1781] 1953, p. 333.

25 Readers of Rousseau often choose to focus on whichever element in his highly complex *œuvre* fits their argument – to take one example, James Miller, 'The Household', in *Rousseau, Dreamer of Democracy*, New Haven, Yale University Press, 1984, pp. 28–32, presents Rousseau's work as an androcentric panegyric of fatherhood.

men's painful attempt to obliterate maternal–feminine materiality. The cave itself has undoubted womb-like qualities (Socrates is famously described as a midwife), while the men (of indeterminate sex?) imprisoned within are phallic in the detail of their description. When a prisoner is released to the Truth, then the economy of the same to which he was always already subjected becomes a question of more (reason, truth, light, masculinity) or less (sensuality, fantasm, darkness, maternal-femininity). Plato fantasises a primal scene in which the father engenders alone – which is, of course, impossible. Irigaray's focus on Plato's will to the reproduction of the same is similar to that of Derrida in 'Plato's Pharmacy', which was first published in 1968, but she takes Derrida's insight concerning Plato's will to paternal parthenogenesis much further.[26] If we relate her analysis to Plato's depiction of the Guardians, then we would be forced to say that, on a philosophical level, the female Guardians are made into (masculine) subjects – as Rousseau claimed. Whitford comments in this respect: 'Plato's ideal republic, despite appearances, is not at all egalitarian; his city is homosexual, his women are all "men" – they accede to all the civic functions in so far as they resemble men and renounce their specificity.'[27] In so far as Plato's women are women, they are the sensible, the material or *becoming* – all this must be left behind as much as possible in favour of ideal truth or *being*. Thus, for Plato, the feminine is the enemy of truth, and as Whitford points out, Nietzsche's writings on women draw the consequences.[28] For Irigaray, Plato's flight from castration, or from mortality, in the *Republic* thus places him, and his *polis*, largely within a masculine economy.

Irigaray also writes on Plato in 'Sorcerer Love: A Reading of Plato's Symposium, Diotima's Speech'.[29] This is a much more optimistic analysis, albeit tempered by the knowledge of the Platonic tradition, the 'sons' of Plato. Diotima is not physically present at the banquet (another dematerialisation), but her words of wisdom concerning love are reported enthusiastically by Socrates. She presents Eros as an intermediary, neither one nor the other, never fulfilled, always becoming, both mortal and divine. He is the child of Plenty *and* of Poverty.[30] Love thus participates in a kind of feminine

26 Derrida often appears to be an intertext for Irigaray, although this is not always explicit. She does write on his work explicitly in 'Le v(i)ol de la lettre', where she suggests that Derrida too has a certain tendency to dematerialise. See *Parler n'est jamais neutre*, pp. 149–68. This question of Derrida's dematerialisation of the female body is interestingly pursued in relation to Virgil and Plato, as well as Gloria Naylor's *Linden Hills*, in Margaret Homans, 'The Woman in the Cave: Recent Feminist Fictions and the Classical Underworld', *Contemporary Literature*, 29 (1988), 369–402.

27 *Luce Irigaray*, London and New York, Routledge, 1991, p. 106.

28 See Irigaray, *Marine Lover*, trans. Gillian C. Gill, New York, Columbia University Press, 1991.

29 trans. E. H. Kuykendall, *Hypatia*, 3 (1989), 32–44. Also in *An Ethics of Sexual Difference*.

30 Tina Chanter draws links between Irigaray's analysis here and that of Levinas, as well as pointing out the influence of Nietzsche and Heidegger. See her *Ethics of Eros*, New York and London, Routledge, 1995.

economy, 'energy pouring forth', rather than being hoarded. However, Irigaray sounds a final note of caution: Diotima, as reported by Socrates, runs the risk of being reduced to the metaphysics which Plato is setting up, that is to say, to the privileging of the immortal over the carnal.

More

As well as seeing More as a participant in an intertextual debate (which I believe he was), it is crucial to see him in his own socio-historical context – and he explicitly frames the description of the imaginary island of Utopia with fictionalised scenes from that political, material reality. In the first book of *Utopia*, Hythloday presents the case against enclosures, which left many husbandmen disposessed of the means of production (land) and un-employed. He also points out:

> And although the number of sheep increase never so fast, yet the price falleth not one mite, because there be so few sellers; for they be almost all come into a few rich men's hands, whom no need forceth to sell before they lust, and they lust not before they may sell as dear as they lust. (p. 27)

This could be (and has been) interpreted as an early pro-merchant (and so prototypically bourgeois) position, that is to say, an argument for the free-ing of the market. However, I would suggest that More is less optimistic about the workings of the market than such an interpretation would imply, and that this is why in Utopia, a society is which there is no unemployment and no poverty, transactions are so strictly regulated. The context of Hythloday's claim is his impassioned plea to Cardinal Morton that it is both unjust and ineffective to hang people for theft. It would be better to have less cruel punishments for theft, and to improve the social conditions which drive people to steal.

In *Utopia* More describes an economy of abundance rather than an economy of scarcity. He claims that this is the case because *everybody* works (and the majority *produce*), whereas 'how great a part of the people in other countries liveth idle. First, almost all women, which be the half of the whole number' (p. 66), then the priests, then the wealthy and those engaged in unproductive labour on their account (servants for example) – none are 'set to profitable occupations'. In Utopia everyone is expert in husbandry and also in one of the few necessary crafts. They are watched to make sure that they work, but they are also persuaded that work is virtuous – and no one is made to work as hard as the labourers of More's own time. The goods they produce are distributed as follows:

> The works of every family be brought into certain houses, and every kind of thing is laid up several in barns or storehouses. From hence the father of every family and every householder fetcheth whatsoever he and his have need of, and carrieth it away with him without money, without exchange, without

any gage, pawn or pledge. For why should anything be denied unto him, seeing that there is abundance of all things, and that it is not to be feared lest any man will ask more than he needeth? For why should it be thought that any man would ask more than enough which is sure never to lack? (p. 71)

There is no internal market, 'the whole island is as it were one family or household' (p. 76); trade is reserved for relations with peoples from the outside world, to whom they sell surplus products and from whom they buy mercenaries. Hospitality unsurprisingly (following the classical tradition) replaces the need for taverns, but, in addition, the sick are cared for by the whole community in hospitals, and most of the population eat communally rather than in their families. Houses are the property of the community, and so they are never locked: 'Whoso will may go in, for there is nothing within the houses that is private or any man's own. And every tenth year they change their houses by lot' (pp. 60–1).

Utopia is far less egalitarian than the Republic in terms of sexual difference – there is a clear family hierarchy (p. 70) which is more reminiscent of Plato's Laws (917a). However, there are certain remnants: women, as well as men, practise war exercises, women can be priests, women are shown their wooers naked (as well as the reverse) (p. 99). That last, as well as being even-handed, reminds the reader of Plato's rationalisation of sexual conduct – More's Utopians point out how carefully potential buyers inspect horses before parting with their money and wonder at the folly of acquiring a spouse after a less careful inspection. Diderot's Tahiti is one step further in the rationalisation of sexual conduct – for breeding (and happiness). Transparency – mutual visibility – replaces privacy as a goal in most utopias. It is generally an ideal for Rousseau, as Jean Starobinski has famously demonstrated; there are moments of emotional transparency in La Nouvelle Héloïse, as there is political transparency in The Social Contract. However, sexual transparency – which does not pay its due to eros – seems to imply sterility for Rousseau. Diderot's Tahiti takes visibility to its limit, including the conduct of sexual relations. Bougainville refers to Tahiti as Utopia, and the first report published from his voyage focuses on Tahiti and refers to Utopia particularly with respect to the public conduct of sexual relations. In both these dream locations and in The Republic, the practical rather than erotic approach to procreation is said to have no adverse effect on fertility – quite the reverse. Rousseau is perhaps the most modern of these writers, in that his texts are crossed with traces of anxiety whenever he imagines a definitive lifting of the veil.

Montaigne

Montaigne's account of the native Brazilians (in particular, the Tupinamba tribe), like most of the texts I am considering, is a slippery and much disputed text. It can be read largely as a critique of his own society, and the negative, privative (as Todorov puts it) quality of his description of the Brazilians can be used as evidence for this. Even as critique, it is open to debates over the degree to which it is ironic or simply an exercise in putting forward certain points of view.[31]

It is of particular interest in the context of gift economies for two reasons. The first is the degree of common ownership in the society Montaigne describes, the second lies in Montaigne's description of cannibalism as symbolic exchange. I shall discuss the representation of the New World as a place where private property and trade are called into question, and then move on to the question of symbolic exchange. The discoveries in the Americas produced a range of representations of peoples without commerce, for instance, the various indigenous tribes of North America, the ancient Peruvians, and, later, the Jesuits in Paraguay. Montaigne writes:

> I would tell Plato that those people have no trade of any kind, no acquaintance with writing, no knowledge of numbers, no terms for governor or of political superior, no practice of subordination or of riches or poverty, no contracts, no inheritances, no divided estates, no occupation but leisure, no concern for kinship – except such as is common to them all – no clothing, no agriculture, no metals, no use of wine or corn. Among them you hear no words for treachery, lying, cheating, avarice, envy, backbiting or forgiveness. How remote from such perfection would Plato find that Republic which he thought up – 'viri a diis recentes' [men fresh from the gods].
> Hos natura modos primum dedit.
> [These are the ways which Nature first ordained.]
>
> ('On the Cannibals', p. 233)

Towards the end of the essay, Montaigne asks some native Brazilians for their response to France, and they express their horror at the material inequality they have observed, and their surprise that the poor do not rise up in bloody revolt. After the self's account of the other, the other is thus asked to respond to the self – even if, as Montaigne laments (although it is perhaps inevitable) it is a dialogue mediated by an inadequate translator.

The first quotation in the extract cited above is from Seneca's *Letters* (XC); the second from Virgil's *Georgics* (II, 20). Even as Montaigne wishes that the ancients had come into contact with the native Americans, he uses

31 Frank Lestringant, 'Le Cannibalisme des "Cannibales" I: Montaigne et la tradition', *Bulletin de la société des amis de Montaigne*, 9–10 (1982), 27–40, gives a helpful discussion of some of the various interpretations of this essay. He points out that some of the claims that 'Montaigne must have been joking' ignore the fact that the details he gives are also reported in other (earlier as well as later) accounts of the Brazilian Indians. Thus the role of women in warming the men's drink or the reference to hammocks need not be read as self-evidently 'comic asides' (pp. 28–9).

the words of the classics to sum them up. In 'Des coches' ('On Coaches')[32] (III, 6, written about 1586–87), he wishes that it had been the ancients who had colonised the New World rather than the men of his own day – for that would have been a mutually beneficial encounter, each giving something to the other.[33] Instead, his own contemporaries have only *taken*: their commercial desire for plunder means that they have not only taken precious metals, spices and stones, but also that they have dimished the very being of those they have robbed:

> We [. . .] took advantage of their ignorance and lack of experience to pervert them more easily towards treachery, debauchery and cupidity, toward every kind of cruelty and inhumanity, by the example and model of our own manners. Whoever else has ever rated trade and commerce [*de la mercadence et de la trafique*] at such a price? So many cities razed to the ground, so many nations wiped out, so many millions of individuals put to the sword, and the most beautiful and the richest part of the world shattered, on behalf of the pearls-and-pepper business! Tradesmen's victories! [*mechaniques victoires*] At least ambition and political strife never led men against men to such acts of horrifying enmity and to such pitiable disasters. (p. 1031)

Montaigne is not only contrasting war to peace – but two modes of commerce (in the sense of intercourse or relationship). The first is commercial in our sense, using other people as means to an end (profit), and this involves warfare of every kind, from literal bloody slaughter and destruction to what we might call ideological warfare or moral degradation. The second is noble (rather than *mechanique*) 'brotherly fellowship', a kind of exchange between (at least potential) equals. This may still involve warfare – the relations between 'cannibals' which Montaigne describes include considerable violence, and the Greeks and Romans he admires are also warriors.[34] However, it is 'disinterested' warfare (p. 114), warfare where the only possible defeat lies

---

32 Translated by Cohen as 'On Vehicles'. See Montaigne, *Essays*, translated by J. M. Cohen, Harmondsworth, Penguin, 1958.

33 'Oh why did it not fall to Alexander and those ancient Greeks and Romans to make of it a most noble conquest; why did such a huge transfer of so many empires, and such revolutions in the circumstances of so many peoples, not fall into hands which would have gently polished those peoples, clearing away any wild weeds while encouraging and strengthening the good crops that Nature had brought forth among them, not only bringing to them the world's arts of farming the land and adorning their cities (in so far as they were lacking to them) but also bringing to the natives of those countries the virtues of the Romans and the Greeks? What a renewal that would have been, what a restoration of the fabric of this world, if the first examples of our behaviour which were set before that new world had summoned those peoples to be amazed by our virtue and to imitate it, and had created between them and us a brotherly fellowship and understanding' (p. 1031).

34 Montaigne is an important and interesting intertext for Bataille. Marcel Raymond, in 'Montaigne devant les sauvages d'Amérique', *Etre et dire* (1970), 13–37, suggests that 'Montaigne explains, if he does not justify, cannibalism, whose true motive, which is

in admitting, verbalising, or 'taking in' defeat. Thus Peruvians or Mexicans will sometimes fast to death when they are captured, rather than accept food from their captors, Montaigne tells us. In other words, Montaigne is contrasting the peoples of the New World and the ancient world with the *homo economicus* of his own time.

Montaigne is variously described as a liberal cultural relativist, as a closet universalist, and as a writer who (unwittingly or deliberately) presents contradictory and indeed mutually incompatible positions – such as relativism alongside absolute standards. In his Cannibals essay, he is said to be contradictory in that he argues both that the practices of the native Brazilians are only defined as barbarous and savage because they are different (cultural relativism), and that the Brazilians are not barbarous because they produce Anacreontic poetry (applying Greek standards as absolute and universal).[35] Todorov argues that Montaigne's undeclared universalism is dangerous and susceptible to annexation. From a postcolonial perspective it is, of course, possible to argue that invoking *reason* (as a universal) is a colonising gesture – however, we should at least note two points in Montaigne's defence: one is that he has an expansive notion of reason which will comprehend the symbolic exchange of cannibalism, and the other is the impossibility of stepping outside rationality and judgement.[36] While of course any writer is to some extent a product of his or her time, and its implicit prejudices, and equally any writer's declarations can be appropriated to the worst political

of the order of the sacred, he could not appreciate' (p. 33). Montaigne is brushing up against *the sacred*, even if he does not know what it is he is describing. In the 'Apology', Montaigne claims that if he were not a Christian, he would worship the sun.

35 Edwin M. Duval 'Lessons of the New World: Design and Meaning in Montaigne's "Des Cannibales" (I, 31) and "Des coches" (III, 6)', *Yale French Studies (Montaigne: Essays in Reading)*, 64 (1983), 95–112, argues that Montaigne deliberately presents conflicting judgements. For example, he extracts five perspectives from Montaigne's remarks on the Cannibals: (1) they are *barbares* in the sense of *different*; (2) they are *sauvages* in the sense of *natural*; (3) they are *barbares* in their cannibalism, but less barbarous than warring Europeans; (4) they are not *sauvages* because they are so valiant in war; (5) they are not *barbares* because their poetry is so artistic. For Duval both this essay and 'On Coaches' are performances of what Montaigne recommends as pedagogical method in 'On Educating Children': these essays are apprenticeships in judgement.

In the same volume of *Yale French Studies*, Tzvetan Todorov argues that Montaigne's apparent tolerance of other customs and practices masks the individualism which becomes the universalism of the rising mercantile bourgeoisie. He points to Montaigne's use of economic imagery in his self-figuring ('L'Etre et l'Autre: Montaigne', 113–44).

36 Zhang Longxi, 'The Cannibals, the Ancients and Cultural Critique: Reading Montaigne in Postmodern Perspective', *Human Studies*, 16 (1993), 51–68, remarks in this respect that 'Todorov's relativist who "does not judge others" does not yet exist' (p. 62). Foucault's famous heterotopia (Borges's Chinese encyclopedia) presents us with an exotic non-Western Other, whose conceptual monstrosity threatens to destroy the usual categories of thinking and naming in language.

ends, I would rather construct a more generous reading of the essay (emu-
lating, in a rather belated fashion, Montaigne's own practice with respect to
the native peoples of the 'New World'). It seems to me that Montaigne's
range of positive points with respect to Brazilian cannibals are part of an
imaginary rhetorical debate with those who wish to condemn the cannibals
for a range of contradictory reasons. Thus he can at the same time say that
we tend to condemn those who are different from us, which is an irrational
gesture (and thus flawed by our own standards), and that *if* we do judge
them by our own measure, then they are better than our (that is to say,
Montaigne's) contemporaries, and, indeed, equal to the Greeks. I should
add that even in our postmodern end of the twentieth century there are
plenty of critics who still find Montaigne's attitude to the Brazilian Indians
ludicrously, even offensively, generous. Moishe Black[37] takes the 'common-
sense' view that it is natural and reasonable to see France as superior to
Brazil (p. 25) and to find cannibalism revolting (p. 26). Black reads the essay
as a succession of rhetorical tricks designed to destabilise the 'Middle Reader'
(neither the very simple nor the very clever reader) so that Montaigne can
impose his own views. Maryanne Cline Horowitz claims that the essay is
a subtle plea for positive international law, since it shows that natural law
alone will not stop men from behaving like beasts and eating each other . . .[38]

In 'An Apology for Raymond Sebond', Montaigne again refers to the
key encounter with the Tupinamba:

> I once saw men brought to us from distant lands overseas. We could under-
> stand nothing of their language; their manners and even their features and
> clothing were far different from ours. Which of us did not take them for
> brutes and savages? Which of us did not attribute their silence to dullness
> and brutish ignorance? After all, they knew no French, were unaware of our
> hand-kissings and our low and complex bows, our bearing and our beha-
> viour – such things must, of course, serve as a pattern for the whole human
> race . . . (p. 521)[39]

Montaigne's observation that people tend to react with prejudice, dismissing as inferior those who are different from themselves is often taken to
mean that it is impossible to make judgements, in particular, across cultures. In fact, Montaigne neither proclaims the impossibility of judging, nor
refuses to judge – he simply warns us that even excellent judges, such as
the ancient Greeks, fell victim to their own cultural prejudices (*doxai*) when

---

37 'When Montaigne Conducts You on a Visit to his Cannibals, Take Care not to get
Eaten by the Guide', *Dalhousie French Studies*, 16 (1989), 15–36.

38 'Montaigne's "Des Cannibales" and Natural Sources of Virtue', *History of European
Ideas*, 11 (1989), 427–34.

39 This passage could very usefully be juxtaposed to Bougainville's account of Parisian
reaction to Aotourou, the Tahitian who accompanied him back to France – and soon
longed to return to Tahiti.

faced with foreigners. The oscillation in the essay between deferring hasty condemnation where we see cultural difference, and making a favourable judgement where we can immediately recognise merit, can be read as a deliberate play on sameness and difference, to promote a generous (and as rational as possible) interpretation of the facts available – and to confound the contradictory self-interested 'knowledge' (we would call it ideology) which will support the colonial enterprise.[40]

Montaigne's 'cannibals' exist within a frugal economy of abundance; they have what is necessary, and do not desire what is superfluous. This is common to all the utopias or gift economies which I shall be considering. Within that category they fall into the subsection of natural or 'indolent' abundance, which is also characteristic of Diderot's Tahiti. In other words, it is not suggested that all must work in order for abundance to be achieved. In 'On Coaches', Montaigne's descriptions of the Aztecs and Incas feed into another tradition – the El Dorado tradition of abundance of precious stones and metals.[41] Montaigne's cannibals, like Diderot's Tahitians, do not exist in a complete state of nature, but a relative one.[42] They are socialised in that they are educated in the moral (and aesthetic) values of their society. Their indolence makes them natural relative to Europeans, but their learnt *constance*, or stoicism in the face of pain, and their love poetry makes them socialised relative to a hypothetical animal state. Their indolence is a gift, in that it makes their society a static one, but this in itself makes them vulnerable to the shock of the encounter with Europeans. The dormant state of their capacity to adapt and change (Rousseau's *perfectibility*) has kept them outside history – now they will become historical outsiders.[43] This dormancy of the two-sided quality (to progress and degenerate) is not necessarily to be seen as an innate lack, but more a question of the environmental determinism

40 In 'On Coaches', Montaigne adopts the classical line that beneficence must be tempered by justice – the king who showers money from the public purse without due consideration is not behaving responsibly, and will not earn the gratitude of his subjects. Montaigne's own generosity towards others is likewise to be tempered by a just rationality.

41 Two very different versions of this are to be found in Margaret Cavendish's *New Blazing World* (1666), in *The Description of a New World, Called the Blazing World*, ed. Kate Lilley, London, William Pickering, 1992, and Voltaire's *Candide* (1759), in *Candide and Other Stories*, trans. R. Pearson, London, Dent, 1992. In the former, the jewels are used as signs of distinctions, despite their abundance, and the 'lady' who chances upon this fantastic world refuses to take any of the riches back to her own country. In *Candide*, more typically, the inhabitants do not prize what the Europeans place such a high price upon – and, in a parody of the early phase of the colonial adventure, Candide and his friend carry away as much as they can.

42 It has been compared to Rousseau's stage of life in *cabanes* (huts).

43 Raymond comments in this respect on the different sense of temporality of Montaigne's cannibals: it is fragmentary rather than cumulative, moments simply substitute one for another ('Montaigne devant les sauvages d'Amérique', p. 34).

which becomes so common in the eighteenth century. A favourable climate and abundance of food fosters 'indolence', and geographical isolation creates a closed society.[44]

One final aspect of 'On the Cannibals' which has been linked with the Tupinamba rejection of private property is their polygamy. The link might seem somewhat surprising, as the Tupinamba warrior's acquisition of wives may appear to us as a form of property. However, Montaigne presents this as emblematic of the lack of possessiveness of the Tupinamba. Unlike European women, the Tupinamba women, he tells us, are happy to share their men with other women. They delight in offering choice women to their husbands.

Symbolic exchange

The particular 'gift economy' known as potlatch, which has been famously discussed by Mauss and by Bataille, is associated with the native peoples of North America. In Montaigne's account of the Tupinamba, cannibalism can be interpreted in a similar fashion. The prisoners defiantly offer their bodies to be eaten with a series of verbal insults; the cannibals eat them as the culmination of their return insults and challenges (such as the repeated offer to set them free if they submit). The celebration of the sovereign humanity exemplified in this economically disinterested violence – what can be seen as an aesthetic act – comes to play a particular role in theorisations of gift exchange.[45] The question will be raised whether or not it is a sexually specific role – certainly in Montaigne's essay the polygamous cannibals only eat men.[46]

Frank Lestringant gives a particular and convincing analysis of the cannibalism of Montaigne's Brazilians in terms of an economy of abundance, as opposed to the model of scarcity found in other works on cannibalism.[47] According to Lestringant, investigations of cannibalism divided

---

44 For Rousseau, only a series of catastrophes will awaken the human potential for change.

45 Michel de Certeau, 'Le Lieu de l'autre. Montaigne: "Des cannibales"', Œuvres et Critiques, 8 (1983), 59–72 remarks: 'Montaigne is writing himself into a long tradition (stretching both before and after him) when he transforms these two 'monstrosities' [cannibalism and polygamy] into forms which are 'beautiful' relative to their function in the social body' (p. 61). The question of what is beautiful (as a social question) will return in all the eighteenth-century texts, and the treatment of 'monsters' (monstrous bodies) notably in *Millenium Hall*.

46 Traces of violence are retained in some feminine theorisations of the gift, for example (another Brazilian example) Hélène Cixous's account of Clarice Lispector's 'The Foreign Legion'.

47 The bulk of the argument with respect to Montaigne is in the article already cited, but further interesting detail on the competing traditions in discussions of cannibalism is given in 'Le Cannibalisme des "Cannibales" II: De Montaigne à Malthus', *Bulletin de la Société des Amis de Montaigne*, 11–12 (1982), 19–38.

early into a medical discourse which explained cannibalism by hunger and a *moraliste* discourse which sought the social and moral meaning of the practice. Montaigne opens his essay with a refusal to place the cannibals on the *island* of Atlantis; instead, he locates them on a continent whose vastness he is at pains to emphasise (*un pais infini*). The 'medical' (what becomes the *materialist*) explanation of cannibalism favoured an insular origin,[48] where shortage of food and concern about over-population is more credible. Montaigne emphasises the abundance of food available to his cannibals, and thus contributes to his argument that their cannibalism is part of a symbolic rather than a material economy.[49] It is a luxurious, noble and glorious *dépense* which has nothing to do with *need*. Lestringant concludes: 'Montaigne brings the Brazilians' cannibalism into the domain of discourse; and the prisoner's flesh melts into word: challenge, insult, or song of agony and revenge, which not only gives the true meaning, but also constitutes the ultimate stake, of cannibal exchange' (I, pp. 39–40). It is Montaigne's example of European cannibalism (the siege of Alésia) which participates in the economy of scarcity: 'The Cannibal's gift of self is set against the implacable *usure* – in both senses of the word [usury and use/using up] – of the enclosed, starving and tortured bodies of old Europe' (p. 35). European cannibalism is thus interested, the satisfaction of a need. Lestringant argues that the increasing prevalence of the argument that, far from being a symbolic (and thus supremely human) gesture, cannibalism is an animal need makes it easier to hunt down and kill the animals in question.[50]

Leaving aside the New World, what is Montaigne's own favoured mode of exchange? Todorov claims that Montaigne's use of economic language reveals the individualist, even the nascent petty bourgeois ('L'Etre et l'Autre: Montaigne', pp. 134–5) latent in the *Essays*. He argues that Montaigne does not wish to exchange with others because he wishes only to be wedded to himself, indeed only to feed upon himself (*autophagie*) (p. 131). He cites Montaigne's essay 'Of husbanding your will' (III, 10): 'Mon opinion est qu'il se faut prester à autruy et ne se donner qu'à soy-mesme' ('My opinion is

48 As Lestringant points out, this is the tradition in which Diderot places himself in his discussion of Lancers Island in the *Supplement* and in his additions to (and subtractions from) Raynal's *History of Trade in the Two Indies*. While his account of Tahiti has much in common with Montaigne, in this case he is part of the 'modern' materialist line which Lestringant links to Malthus.

49 Lestringant makes one specific reference to Bataille and his theory of the accursed share (p. 33), but his vocabulary reintroduces Bataille as an intertext on more than one occasion.

50 In another article, Lestringant analyses Columbus's first writings on the caribs/cannibals, in which he suggests that they have dogs' heads. As Lestringant points out, *canis* slips in as one of the sources of the word. Rabelais also introduces cannibals with dogs' heads. See 'Le Nom des "Cannibales" de Christophe Colomb à Michel de Montaigne', *Bulletin de la Société des Amis de Montaigne*, 17–18 (1984), 51–74.

that we must lend ourselves to others and give ourselves only to ourselves'). Exceptional friendship is only with 'celuy qui n'est pas autre: c'est moy' ('the one who is not another man: he is myself') (p. 134). It seems to me that Montaigne's warning against too freely giving oneself to others could be read as a proto-Rousseauian critique of the slavery of false social intercourse. The statement Todorov quotes: 'Personne ne distribue son argent à autruy, chacun y distribue son temps et sa vie' ('No one distributes his money to others, everyone distributes his time and his life on them') (p. 132), could equally be read as a caustic comment on those who consider the narrow demands of justice and reason (rather than generosity) where their purse is concerned, but are lavish beyond justice and reason with their selves.

Montaigne does use economic vocabulary in a range of circumstances; his essay 'De trois commerces' (III, 3) is a good example of the tension between the notion that commerce is a neutral term encompassing quite different relationships and the notion that it implies some similarity of structure. The modern *first* sense of 'buying and selling' is elided in Montaigne's essay – even though it is also a primary meaning of the Latin *commercium*. However, there are at least two economic themes (or tropes) which predominate in the essay: personal profit and reserve. Montaigne, as I have observed, writes himself with reference to a series of classical forefathers, Plato, Plutarch, Seneca and Cicero, to name only some of the most obvious. This writing returns insistently to the question of self-knowledge (which is often metaphorically related to profit) and to a kind of discipline of the self – self-stylisation, as Foucault puts it in referring to the classical period.[51] On Montaigne's medal, struck in 1576, he has 'Que sçais-je?' famously inscribed on one side; on the other side, just as significantly, there are the Greek words which translate into French as 'Je m'abstiens'. This is self-stylisation as an economy of reserve.

The title 'De trois commerces' is translated by Cohen as 'On three kinds of relationships',[52] which works as a reinforcement of any neutralisation; the essay deals with Montaigne's commerce with friends, with women and with books – arguing indeed for important differences between the

51 *The History of Sexuality*, vols II (*The Use of Pleasure*) and III (*The Care of the Self*), translated by Robert Hurley, Harmondsworth, Penguin, 1985, 1986. Foucault emphasises the classical focus on the need to know oneself in order to form oneself as an ethical subject (II, pp. 86–7). He wishes to establish an opposition between classical Greek and Christian modalities (e.g. II, p. 92); I would argue, however, that both Montaigne and Rousseau, despite their adherence to Christianity, borrow as much, if not more, from the classical concern with active freedom and with an aesthetics of existence as from the Scholastic codification of acts. Foucault claims that there was a general tendency towards a restrictive economy in classical Greek thinking (which he distinguishes from Christian prohibition), e.g. pp. 118, 130, 139 – a perceived advisability of expending less (while producing more or better quality).
52 Screech translates the title as 'On three kinds of social intercourse'.

three kinds of commerce, and that it is quintessentially human to be able to adopt different structures or forms of behaviour. Commerce with (male) friends can attain perfection, but commerce with the common herd of men requires an expansiveness which Montaigne finds that he tends to check. Commerce with women has the advantage of exercising the body as well as the mind, and yet has the danger of tending to lead the man into reckless passion – it also withers with age.[53] Montaigne appears, therefore, to conclude by privileging his relationship with books, whose main disadvantage is no more than the fact that they do not exercise the reader physically; books provide the greatest profit for the least expenditure. For a writer so intriguingly wedded to both acknowledged and unacknowledged debts to his precursors to deny that element of desire and anxiety characteristic of amorous passion in his commerce with books (with the great dead) may smack of denial. However, it is in the name of a kind of moderate hoarding of self (not the sterile miserliness of self-contemplation), that Montaigne chooses betweeen the three kinds of 'commerce': an economic moral decision.

Montaigne's choice relates to the argument that Seneca makes in *De Beneficiis*: that generosity and justice should moderate each other. It also relates to his socio-political context, his experiences of the Wars of Religion at home and his knowledge of the horrors of colonial expansion abroad. At home, as he tells us in 'On the Cannibals', men 'ate each other alive', a more barbarous act than anything performed by the Tupinamba. Montaigne has no access to the noble symbolic exchange of the cannibals, and his only access to the ancients is through books. Thus he devours books, and as they become part of him, he feeds upon himself. The Tupinamba are told by their prisoners that in eating them they are eating their own fathers and grandfathers, whom the prisoners ate when they were last victorious.

The battles which have been fought over the correct interpretation of Plato, More and Montaigne often relate to the question of laughter. Some critics have seen the irony in the texts in question as a means by which wise men can wittily communicate with each other, sure in their knowledge that certain aspects of the status quo go without saying. Women should not be educated on an equal footing with men, property should not be held in

---

53 Montaigne incorporates into his discussion a critique of women who parade learning in an imitation of male pedants. He likens this to the artifice of make-up hiding natural beauty. Women should, in his view, devote themselves to two kinds of learning only: poetry and practical knowledge – both of which return us to love and marriage, women's natural domains. I would argue that this relates to a Rousseauian structure (although Rousseau would place his boundaries differently) and to a complicated argument about natural being and the artifice of appearance. Neither thinker (contrary to certain readings of Rousseau, at least) straightforwardly privileges the natural, untutored self – hence their advocacy of education. However, both claim that education should be 'for living', and thus in conformity with nature, up to a point.

common, Christians are better than heathens, the practices of Renaissance France are superior to those surviving from pre-Columbian Brazil and so on. Other critics, and I include myself amongst them, see the irony, the laughter, as less complacent and conservative – more a means of making the reader see the status quo *differently*. Perhaps unsurprisingly, all these texts have a certain drive towards an economy of *the same*, often brought out by reading them in terms of sexual difference. However, I wish to argue that a productive tension between sameness and difference can be distilled both from their common speculations on economy in the narrow sense of the term, and from a common disturbance of the linguistic economy by play.

3

The eighteenth century I:
the rise of the market

A moment of transition

The (European and North American) eighteenth century can be perceived as the location of a shift in the relationship between economic thinking and moral thinking; briefly, that whereas a discursive tradition dating from classical antiquity subordinated the economic to the moral, the eighteenth century witnessed a move to establish the primacy of the economic (a move sometimes defended as promoting virtue). In this chapter, I shall attempt to sketch the 'new' attitude to the market which is struggling for dominance, with respect to a selection of English, French and Scottish writings of the period.

The argument that the positive 'science' of economics developed in the eighteenth century is not very controversial in so far as the case has often been made that alongside – and, in part, because of – certain developments in the economic base itself (including colonial expansion), the Enlightenment produced a series of radical, indeed, revolutionary theses – all of which fed into, say, the French Revolution or the rise of capitalism. The argument can, however, be challenged on a number of grounds – not least the difficulty of locating an epistemological break without immediately discovering a chain of precursors to what succeeds the apparent rupture. In this instance, one could discuss the physiocrats and the mercantilists and then the scholastics – a chain which would eventually take us back to Aristotle. The birth of capitalism, for instance (whether an epistemological or a non-epistemological break!), has been located in so many different centuries, the defining characteristics of capitalism have been detected in so many different eras, as to render the term almost as universal as its most devoted advocates could ever wish it to be.[1] Equally, produced in a

---

1 Neil McKendrick discusses the attempts to locate the birth of a consumer society in a moment earlier than the eighteenth century, attempts which can throw up much interesting material, and provides a convincing rationale for rejecting them. See N. McKendrick, J. Brewer and J. H. Plumb, *The Birth of a Consumer Society*, London, Europa Publications, 1982.

moment of transition, Enlightenment discourse can prove difficult to diagnose, enabling, for instance, a maverick interpretation such as that of Foucault in *The Order of Things*,[2] where he asserts that from about 1750 to about 1800 what is produced is Analysis of Wealth – and that there is an epistemological break between that discursive production and modern political economy.

J. G. A. Pocock argues that the British eighteenth century is indeed characterised by a debate between Country and Court, in which the Country party represents the civic humanist tradition (Machiavelli out of Aristotle again, with a touch of Harrington).[3] This tradition grounds virtue in land and rejects specialisation (particularly a professional army), and also speculation. The Court party, on the other hand, tends to favour commerce and thus, necessarily, credit. But the dangers of the lack of any check on credit were feared even by the otherwise 'progressive' David Hume. As Pocock makes clear, the division is far from clear-cut: in general, virtue and land were not to be simply 'against'. (Rather as today no political party wishes to be 'against' prosperity, growth or freedom, it is a question of defining terms and strategies.) Thus in *The Spectator* Steele will argue that there should be agreement between trade and land as between different parts of the body,[4] a point which echoes Defoe's use of the fable earlier in the year with the statement that 'your land might go a begging but for trade; and for the landed men to rail at trade, is like the members mutinying against the belly'.[5] While both texts score points against land, they acknowledge that it has a role to play.

In the same number of *The Spectator* Sir Roger de Coverley is roundly out-argued by Sir Andrew Freeport when he attempts to suggest that the only possible virtues for a trader are frugality and parsimony, which are virtues far beneath the 'gentleman's charity to the poor, or hospitality among his neighbours' (p. 186). Sir Roger is a 'stereotypical' example of the anti-trade landowner, and often acts as straw man or straight man in the pages of *The Spectator*. In this issue it is noticeable how few lines he gets relative

2 Trans. A. Sheridan, London and New York, Routledge, 1989. While Foucault's work in general has been the subject of massive critical attention, this controversial account of the Analysis of Wealth has been largely ignored. One short article which attempts to suggest why that has been the case is Claude Ménard, 'L'Autre et son double', in L. Giard (ed.), *Michel Foucault*, Grenoble, Jérôme Millon, 1992, pp. 129–40. Ménard criticises Foucault from a number of perspectives, notably, for example, his reliance on incomplete and often inaccurate translations of Smith and Ricardo. I am grateful to Ian Maclean for pointing out this article to me.

3 *The Machiavellian Moment*, Princeton and London, Princeton University Press, 1975. Part Three deals with 'Value and History in the Prerevolutionary Atlantic'.

4 *The Spectator*, ed. D. F. Bond, 5 vols, Oxford, Oxford University Press, 1965, II, p. 185, no. 174, Wednesday 19 September 1711.

5 *Review*, 1 May, 1711, also cited in Bond, II, p. 185.

to Sir Andrew. Sir Andrew succeeds in rejigging 'virtue' so that he can simultaneously claim that the merchant is truly virtuous, and make a series of arguments which deploy the latest economic criteria of efficiency, rather than ethics. Sir Andrew thus responds in progressive style:

> It would be worth while to consider, whether so many artificers at work ten days together by my appointment, or so many peasants made merry on Sir Roger's charge, are the men more obliged: I believe the families of the artificers will thank me, more than the households of the peasants shall Sir Roger. Sir Roger gives to his men, but I place mine above the necessity or obligation of my bounty. (p. 187)

He goes on to comment ironically that 'If it were consistent with the quality of so ancient a baronet as Sir Roger, to keep an account or measure things by the most infallible way, that of numbers, he would prefer our parsimony to his hospitality' (p. 187). This contrasting of quality and quantification has a progressive air in the eighteenth century, when the sweeping away of ancient (feudal) privileges was radically necessary. In my final chapter I shall be considering twentieth-century critiques of this position, such as those which promote a 'feminine economy'. Sir Andrew continues with a discussion of a Dutch proverb which describes a man's failure as 'not keeping true accounts', and places the highest value on the accurate calculation of expense.[6] The discussion had opened with Sir Roger's quotation of a Roman proverb which represents the word of the Carthaginians as the epitome of dishonesty – the Carthaginians, he points out, being a notorious trading nation. Sir Andrew challenges the particulars of this reference to the ancient world, and then sweeps it away with his example of a modern

6 'Numbers are so much the measure of everything that is valuable, that it is not possible to demonstrate the success of any action or the prudence of any undertaking without them. I say this in answer to what Sir Roger is pleased to say, that little that is truly noble can be expected from one who is ever poring on his cash-book or balancing his accounts. When I have my returns from abroad, I can tell to a shilling by the help of numbers the profit or loss by my adventure; but I ought also to be able to show that I had reason for making it, either from my own experience or that of other people, or from a reasonable presumption that my returns will be sufficient to answer my expense and hazard; and this is never to be done without the skill of numbers. For instance, if I am to trade to *Turkey*, I ought beforehand to know the demand of our manufactures there as well as of their silks in *England*, and the customary prices that are given for both in each country. I ought to have a clear knowledge of these matters beforehand, that I may presume upon sufficient returns to answer the charge of the cargo I have fitted out, the freight and assurance out and home, the customs to the Queen, and the interest of my own money, and beside all these expenses a reasonable profit to my self.' (p. 188) Sir Andrew contrasts this economy with the gentleman's choice of hunting, whose 'only returns must be the stag's horns in the great hall, and the fox's nose upon the stable door'. Thanks to such extravagant negligence of business, it is only by intermarrying with merchants that the gentleman can keep his home at all.

trading nation: Holland. Sir Andrew's position should be compared with *The Spectator*, No. 232, Monday, 26 November 1711, in which he expresses his hostility to charity, which keeps potential workers idle. He argues that even if more workers mean that wages should fall (to the benefit of the merchant), those workers will be better off, since prices will inevitably fall as the increased workforce means increased division of labour (as Sir William Petty has shown), and so goods will be produced more cheaply. In No. 549, Saturday, 29 November 1712, Sir Andrew shows in his plans for retirement that a merchant can outdo a Country gentleman even in the practice of (useful) generosity.

In spite of mutual influence (seen in Montesquieu, for instance), there are, of course, crucial historical differences between Britain and France, where the moral high ground is more easily occupied by the *philosophes*, who are, in a less commercially developed context, largely in favour of commerce. Rousseau remains the outstanding exception in both contexts for his scandalous assertion of the contradiction others were trying to live with (as Pocock puts it): the role of commerce in impoverishing as it enriches. At the same time, I would add, he crucially rejects the Country, aristocratic, claim that inheritance and leisure are necessary components of the Republic.

In spite of the real possibility of challenging any location of a significant shift in thought assumptions, I want to maintain the hypothesis that the eighteenth century has that significance even if it is no more than a convenient fiction which serves the purpose of enabling me to theorise here and now. That notion of my having constructed (or in this case, adopted) what may be no more than a convenient fiction (which could be a spatial trope as much as a temporal one) raises the question of my relationship to that past moment. What is taken from the text is what can be received by me, granted my historical and political location, and what I desire to receive; and yet this is not to be deliberate exploitation, nor the violation of complete invention. My relationship to the text of history, or to any specific text, is indeed modelled on forms of gift exchange. I would like to evoke the need for a certain ethics of reading – a responsibility to the text, to the otherness of the text, which involves taking time and at least establishing what Derrida has called a 'garde-fou' of historical scholarship – while recognising the forces which shape the production of a reading: the socio-political intertext, the cultural intertext and, not least, the psychic intertext of the reader.[7] It is a deliberate reference to these intertexts which inspires

7 See *Of Grammatology*: 'To produce this signifying structure obviously cannot consist of reproducing, by the effaced and respectful doubling of commentary, the conscious, voluntary, intentional relationship that the writer institutes in his exchanges with the history to which he belongs thanks to the element of language. This moment of doubling commentary should no doubt have its place in a critical reading. To recognize and respect all its classical exigencies is not easy and requires all the instruments of

me to evoke, for example, a 'feminine economy', when writing about Rousseau. Even as there is a desire for some kind of coming together, there should be a recognition of the difference between us.

Commerce: areas of anxiety

Commerce is still understood in a number of senses in the eighteenth century, as it was in the Renaissance. Furthermore, the eighteenth century is overt in its interrogation of economic values in a diverse range of relationships. I shall briefly evoke three levels of concern even for those writers broadly in favour of the market, before passing to the promotion of trade. The first is the equivocation over the pacific or aggressive character of trade; the second is the relation between the market as a way of organising the distribution of goods and services within and between societies and individual character; the third is temporality.

It is possible for a writer to be in favour of the commercial in all spheres (just as Rousseau is opposed to it in every sphere) on the understanding that the commercial is pacific and dispassionate. As Montesquieu states, in the best-seller *The Spirit of the Laws* (1748), 'Peace is the natural effect of trade' (XX, 2), thanks to the reciprocal dependency of two nations who trade with each other.[8] In the previous chapter he asserts: 'Commerce is a cure for the most destructive prejudices; and it is almost a general rule, that wherever we find agreeable manners [*des mœurs douces*], there commerce flourishes; and that wherever there is commerce, there we meet with agreeable manners' (XX, 1). This is part of an argument about historical progress: society has moved on from the time of rude Spartan or German warriors, and now it is civilised and cultured, thanks to trade. This pacific quality of trade is, indeed, sometimes used against it (or at least evokes a certain anxiety which has to be dissipated in some manner) in the presentation of commercial society as effeminate. At the same time, Montesquieu mentions a tendency to lose certain virtuous practices (such as hospitality) in societies such as that of Holland, where everything is for sale – but this seems a small price to pay for the move out of barbarianism, as he puts it.

When we are considering a putative shift in relations between European powers (from war to trade), then trade may indeed seem a gentler and

traditional criticism. Without this recognition and this respect, critical production would risk developing in any direction at all and authorize itself to say almost anything. But this indispensable guardrail has always only *protected*, it has never *opened*, a reading' (p. 158). Another way of theorising the problem of the relationship between the reader's present and the pastness of the text is what Jauss refers to as the shifting 'horizon of expectations'.

8 *The Spirit of the Laws*, trans. T. Nugent, New York, Hafner Publishing Company, 1949.

preferable mode of intercourse. However, 'colonial' trade introduces a new set of complexities: European powers become competitors in the race to expand overseas – so that France and England make war in Canada, for example. Relations between the metropole and its colonisers overseas may, of course, be highly profitable to both (and, indeed, peaceful). However, the concomitant relations between colonisers and indigenous colonised peoples, or between colonisers and slaves imported from elsewhere, are not necessarily peaceful – and Enlightenment thinkers develop a range of responses to that problematic. Montesquieu, for example, is strikingly clear-sighted about colonial trade (for instance, the deaths of indigenous American peoples in Spanish silver mines (XXI, 22)). These details may to us seem a new barbarism, and to contradict his general assertions about trade, but it is crucial to be clear that eighteenth-century support for trade does not necessarily arise from ignorance about (but rather from acceptance of) some of the consequences. Indeed, the aggressive quality of trade is frequently recognised – particularly in terms of the conquering of markets overseas, but that kind of aggression is not necessarily explicitly presented as contradicting the claim that it is peaceful. Montesquieu seems untroubled by his remark with respect to the peoples of Africa that: 'Every civilised state [tous les peuples policés] is [. . .] in a condition to traffic with them to advantage, by raising their esteem for things of no value, and receiving a very high price in return' (XXI, 2). One strategy for dissipating worry about the savagery of colonial expansion is to project it on to the particular cruelty of a competitor trading nation – notably the Black Legend of the Spanish conquests in the Americas. I shall return briefly to the question of slavery in my discussion of Diderot's Supplement to Bougainville's 'Voyage'. It is interesting to note that the tissue of voices which make up the Abbé Raynal's History of Trade in the Two Indies produces a series of chapters (Book XI, chapters 22, 23, 24) against slavery – ending with the evocation of bloody revolution and the final remark: 'Until that revolution comes along, negroes are groaning under the yoke of burdensome labour, whose description can only make us more and more concerned about their fate.' Yet Book XI, chapter 30 is a calm, 'dispassionate' account of the highly profitable cultivation of sugar-cane ('it would be hard to find a more profitable form of agriculture'), giving encyclopedic details on botany and agriculture. To calculate the size of profits, slaves and their food simply become part of the costs of production – and there is a striking ranking of 'Blacks' alongside 'animals' and other 'necessary things' (the necessary reification produced by slavery), juxtaposed to 'hommes', men being a term which refers to those who profit (homo economicus). The reader is also told that these men who make such high profits have a commensurately high level of consumption – thanks to a very high level of imports from the metropole.

The commercial can be celebrated in terms of world relations of trade (rather than warfare), and yet disparaged in interpersonal relations – there are many examples of refusals of commercial values in social intercourse from those who nevertheless celebrated commerce (free trade) as a source of prosperity and peace.[9] Montesquieu points out that 'in countries where the people move only by the spirit of commerce, they make a traffic of all the humane, all the moral virtues; the most trifling things, those which humanity would demand, are there done, or there given, only for money' (XX, 2). There is a real difficulty in distinguishing between the structures which are operational in different spheres of life. A free market operating in the commercial sphere may shape, if not determine, behaviour in other areas.

As indicated above, commercial society is sometimes presented as effeminate, relative to an earlier period; for instance, specialisation (the division of labour) is said to be leading to the controversial professionalisation of the army. The role of the gentleman as bearer of arms to defend his country, his family and himself is gradually becoming an anachronism. This alleged feminisation is in part accepted (as 'civilisation'), and in part warded off by a range of moves, some involving considerable hostility towards women. With respect to the complexities of the sexual division of labour, it should be noted that while the dictionary definition of 'commerce' begins with 'exchange between men', the definitions of 'economic' or 'economy' begin with an etymological flavour, relating economy to the management or organisation of a household (*oikos*). It can be argued that this sense of economy as household management was primary until the sixteenth century, when capitalist structures began to erode feudal ones with real vigour. One question which could then be posed is to what extent the task of managing the household as economic unit is a gendered one. Another question is then that of the homology (or not) which some thinkers would wish to establish between family structure (the way in which the head of the household relates to – his – household members) and the structure of the State. Furthermore, a by-product of a commercial society is usually held to be a taste for *luxury* – a morally ambivalent term in the eighteenth century, when it is often contrasted with liberty and virtue. (Indeed, its gradual shedding of pejorative connotations over time is doubtless related to the flourishing of the market.) Luxury is again semantically associated with the feminine (and with the Orient). These are frequent concerns in novels and plays of the period, and I shall return to them in my next chapter.

---

9 Rousseau, on the other hand, argues that property encourages warfare, unlike, say, Hobbes, who locates the root of war in man's natural pride, and therefore comes to very different conclusions about the best form of government.

A final concern is that of temporal degeneration – and this is to be seen even in the work of Adam Smith, both on the level of society as a whole (a classic historical pessimism) and on the level of the alienated factory worker (my anachronism pointing to his foresight). Pocock highlights on the one hand, the Republican fear of *corruption*, on the other, the Whig fear that the National Debt might grow to the point of disaster for all but the almost universally vilified stockjobbers.

With respect to the primary domain of *commerce*, buying and selling, Voltaire typically proclaims to Roubaud: 'I am indeed persuaded as you are that the country where trade is most free will always be the richest and most flourishing of countries.'[10] However, once 'commercial' or economic structures have been defined (say, as Voltaire suggests, that prices are established by the force of free competition – a fundamental tenet if we assume a market structure), how do we restrict the commercial sphere? Would women be included amongst the products which men exchange? Do market structures (such as profit maximisation) also predominate in friendship? A second domain of the term *commerce* is indeed that of social relations or friendship; a third is intercourse between the sexes; a fourth the interchange of letters or ideas, the reading of books or communication with God. No dictionary definitions (and I have also consulted the addenda) offer a sense of the economic which matches that of present-day mainstream economists, that is to say, neoclassical economists. Economists have a rather particular understanding of commerce, and it is that particular understanding which, I shall argue, can be (for the sake of the argument?) dated from the eighteenth century. Before I turn to the *locus classicus* for the new understanding of commerce, Adam Smith's *The Wealth of Nations* (1776),[11] I should like to invoke the general temper of the period. This is what allowed Smith's words, far from falling on fallow ground, to be taken up in a particularly pointed fashion. The kind of thinking which will underpin the rise of capitalism privileges questions of efficiency; it posits a real scarcity of whatever goods are in question and claims that individual profit maximisation (calculated by a rationality which should be largely unfettered) will lead efficiently, by the law of the market, to social wealth, a society of *luxe*. That is not to say that eighteenth-century thinkers who tend towards this kind of position ignore moral and social questions altogether – after all, apart from anything else, this is a period of transition. Voltaire, indeed, regularly praises virtue, and attempts to analyse its conditions and elements.

10 *Lettre à Roubaud*, 1 July 1769.
11 It has been argued that there is little that is new in *The Wealth of Nations*, but that it is a systematic pulling together of ideas found in a series of precursor texts. This makes it all the more useful to our purpose. To take the example of the division of labour: the editors point out that analyses can also be found in the writings of Mandeville, Turgot or, indeed, Sir William Petty.

However, he is determined that there should be no confusing poverty with virtue.

In praise of the market

In his *Letters on England*,[12] Voltaire devotes letter X to the benefits brought to England by trade: 'Trade, which made the citizens of England rich, also helped make them free, and that freedom, in its turn, encouraged the expansion of trade' (p. 51, translation modified). In other words, trade and prosperity help to bring about a free society, just as freedom (from antiquated 'prejudices' or hidebound practices) promotes trade. Voltaire's largely idealised representation of England throughout the *Letters on England* is particularly appropriate in this context. England underwent a financial revolution in the first half of the eighteenth century, while it was colonising markets throughout the world, and entering a new era of conspicuous consumption – different from that of the *ancien régime* over the water in that it pointed the way to the future. The South Sea Bubble disaster of 1721 in fact educated a generation into the ways of money markets, and had quite different effects from Law's great experiment in France (1717–20).[13]

While there was ideological opposition to aspects of this transition, such as that of the Tory Scribblerians (Pope, Swift and Gay), there were also many voices praising the new expanded market. Joseph Addison celebrates members of the merchant class in *The Spectator*:

> They knit mankind together in a mutual intercourse of good offices, distribute the gifts of nature, find work for the poor, add wealth to the rich and magnificence to the great. Our *English* merchant converts the tin of his own country into gold, and exchanges his wool for rubies. The *Mahometans* are clothed in our *British* manufacture, and the inhabitants of the frozen zone are warmed with the fleeces of our sheep. (*The Spectator*, ed. Bond, I, p. 296)[14]

This quotation is a sandwich: the first sentence is heart-warming in its description of pure and active benevolence. Men are to be cosily *knitted* together in relations of reciprocity. This homely sociability is encouraged

---

12 First published in 1734. *Letters on England*, trans. L. Tancock, Harmondsworth, Penguin, 1980.

13 See Thomas M. Kavanagh, *Enlightenment and the Shadows of Chance*, Baltimore and London, Johns Hopkins University Press, 1993, in particular chapter 3, 'Law's System and the Gamble Refused'.

14 No. 69, Saturday, 19 May 1711. Also quoted in Colin Nicholson, *Writing and the Rise of Finance*, Cambridge, Cambridge University Press, 1994, p. 26; this highly pertinent study focuses on texts such as *The Rape of the Lock*, *Gulliver's Travels*, *The Beggar's Opera* and *The Dunciad* as a campaign against the civic effects of the new financial institutions (even while their authors may have invested in stocks and shares). The position from which Pope, Swift and Gay attacked the new economic culture is, of course, quite different from Rousseau's.

by the merchant as handmaid to Mother Nature. Imbued with her milk of kindness, merchants humbly give to each his share.[15] *Work* to the needy, and to those who already have riches and nobility – a supplement in kind. The third sentence reflects that busy generosity, specifying that it extends overseas, for the merchant will clothe the naked heathen and warm those who are cold, by association with the wool, the lost sheep. It is the middle sentence which gives the sandwich its *raison d'être, profit*. Almost magically, tin becomes gold and wool becomes rubies. A simple society becomes a society of *luxe*, thanks to the alchemical skills of the merchant. *The Spectator*, while proclaiming political neutrality, is generally received as favouring Whig sensibilities, that is to say, the views of the merchant class. These are epitomised in the character Sir Andrew Freeport, mentioned above, of whom Steele writes 'there is not a point in the compass but blows home a ship in which he is an owner' (no. 2, Friday, 2 March 1711). Number 69 (quoted above) is a typical statement which shows all nations harmoniously negotiating together in London's Royal Exchange, proclaiming general benefit, and yet implying particular profit for England. The celebration of the availability of goods of all nations both to enrich the table and to adorn the lady stands in marked opposition to Rousseau's passionate self-sufficiency and containment. Voltaire's Letter X on commerce also conjures up colonial expansion of trade in his celebration of the power of the merchant, 'who enriches his country, issues orders from his office to Surat or Cairo, and contributes to the well-being of the world' (p. 52). *The Spectator*, no. 69 on the Royal Exchange becomes 'one of the classic expositions of the value of the merchant class to the nation' (Bond, I, p. 296). An epigraph from Virgil's *Georgics* suggests how Nature's laws dictated that different fruits would grow in different places, and that India would produce ebony, while Tmolus would produce saffron. The essay celebrates the superiority of civilised society, in which trade allows us to enjoy 'the fruits of *Portugal* [. . .] corrected by the products of *Barbados*: the infusion of a *China* plant sweetened with the pith of an *Indian* cane' (p. 295).[16] Colonial relations are represented as a meeting of equals, but all is to the profit of London, and the merchant refers with an affectionate proprietorial air to the Spice Islands as 'our hotbeds; the *Persians* [as] our silk-weavers, and the *Chinese* [as] our potters' (p. 296). Then the emotional Addison, weeping with joy at the sight of the men of so many nations gathered in harmony at the Royal Exchange, moves on to another favourite theme, the adornment of woman: 'The single dress

15 *Nomos* signifies both law in general and *nemein*, the law of distribution, of sharing or partition (See Derrida, *Given Time*, p. 6). As soon as there is law, there is partition (or vice versa).

16 The pleasures of the table are a typical area for rhetorical exchange with respect to the value of trade – Rousseau, Sarah Scott and Diderot's Tahitians pleading for self-sufficiency.

of a woman of quality is often the product of an hundred climates. The muff and the fan come together from the different ends of the earth. The scarf is sent from the torrid zone, and the tippet from beneath the pole. The brocade petticoat rises out of the mines of *Peru*, and the diamond necklace out of the bowels of *Indostan*' (p. 293). Woman's body, like the table, is to be decked with rich and exotic goods. Metonymically woman is the commodity, although the emphasis is on the commodities she displays. Anthropologists tell us today that society is marked by the exchange of women, hence the prohibition of incest. *Homo economicus* is a prudent father and husband, and his dependent wife and children display his accumulated wealth.

In his poem 'The Man of the World' ('Le Mondain', 1736), Voltaire mocks the 'primitivists' such as Fénelon or Huet, who praise the simplicity of earlier times:

> Our ancestors lived in innocence
> Knowing neither thine nor mine.
> What could they know? They had nothing,
> They were naked; and one thing is clear
> Someone who has nothing, has nothing to share.[17]

In this poem it is clear that *innocence* means *ignorance*. Knowing (*connaître*) is dependent on having (*avoir*). While Rousseau is usually understood as privileging being (*être*) over having (*avoir*), for Voltaire having takes precedence. 'Ils étaient nus' is polysemic: Adam and Eve are naked and have no clothes to cover them, and equally they have no knowledge, no morality, no possessions. Progress is progress in every sense, unlike Rousseau's paradoxical representation of the human trait of perfectibility, which suggests that every gift of advancement (*alteration*) has its poisonous side. For Voltaire, progress, commerce, wealth are all enabling – it is not surprising that he is so scornful of Rousseau's *Discourse on Inequality*, with what he (mis)perceives as its 'back to nature' tone.[18] But as Rousseau, and later Marx, will argue, *luxe* can equally be read as poverty for the majority of the population. In

---

17 Voltaire, *Mélanges*, ed. J. van den Heuvel, Paris, Bibliothèque de la Pléiade, 1961 (p. 203). All unacknowledged translations are my own.

18 Voltaire's other eulogistic references to trade are too numerous to mention. I shall confine myself here to one further example: the *Manners and Spirit of Nations* (Harmondsworth, Penguin, [1749] 1977), with its praise for Venice, Portugal and Holland. Voltaire's harshness towards slaves in this work puts him at odds with some of his fellow *philosophes*. In the 'Recapitulation' he writes: 'We make household slaves only of the Negroes; we are severly reproached for this kind of traffic [*ce commerce*], but the people who make a trade of selling their children are certainly more blamable than those who purchase them, and this traffic is only a proof of our superiority. He who voluntarily subjects himself to a master is designed by nature for a slave' (p. 531).

a number of different senses, there are only poor people because there are rich ones (Rousseau, *Fragments politiques*, *Œuvres Complètes*, III, p. 521). The *philosophes* in general, disciples of Francis Bacon,[19] believe in progress through the increase in ('scientific') knowledge – the Preface to the *Encyclopédie* stands in direct contrast to Rousseau's notorious polemical attack in his first Discourse, where he reinterprets the Baconian trope of earthly abundance as *luxe*.[20]

The stance of the *Encyclopédie*, and of Diderot, towards trade is very largely and, indeed, polemically positive. The very choice of subjects to be included (or excluded) and the relative length of articles devoted to manufacturing industry as opposed to 'higher' concerns was a gentle form of combat – and received as such. For example, the length of the article on 'Bas' ('stockings') is explicitly polemical, and comes after the article 'Bas' ('low', as opposed to 'high').[21] At the same time, Diderot and his contributors could insert their pleas for *freedom* into articles which might not immediately catch the short-sighted censor's eye.[22] The committed reader would be inclined, and would soon learn how to trace a path through the forests of useful information. Freedom *from* the excessive privileges of others crucially included freedom *to* trade. In the article 'Aiguille' ('Needle'), Diderot inserts a typical polemic against monopolies:

19 Voltaire's Letter XII of his *Letters on England* is in praise of Bacon, as Letter XIII is in praise of Locke. It is interesting to note how Voltaire's admiration for Locke's philosophical stance slides into economic language: Locke is a man who 'in truth does not possess enormous wealth, but whose funds are well secured, and who enjoys the most established of properties without any ostentation' (Voltaire, *Philosophe ignorant*, 1766, ch. XXIX).

20 See also Rousseau's attack on 'Soft and effeminate philosophy' ('Luxury, Commerce and the Arts', *Fragments politiques*, *Œuvres complètes*, III, p. 518). R. Derathé suggests that one of Rousseau's direct targets here may be Hume's *Refinement in the Arts*, which had been translated into French in 1753 (a year after its publication in English) (Rousseau, *Œuvres complètes*, III, p. 1529).

21 Diderot's lyricism in the face of the *manufacture* of stockings should be read in the light of Barthes's essay 'The Plates of the *Encyclopedia*' in *New Critical Essays*, trans. R. Howard, Berkeley and Los Angeles, University of California Press, 1990, pp. 23–39. Barthes emphasises the continual reassuring presence of man, the human relation to the machine, the absence of social ills and the repetition of images of hands. He writes: 'Thus the *Encyclopedia* constantly testifies to a certain epic of substance, but this epic is also in a sense that of the mind: the trajectory of substance is nothing, for the Encyclopedist, but the progress of reason: the image has a logical function *as well*. Diderot says as much explicitly apropos of the machine for making stockings, whose image will reproduce structure: "*We may regard it as a single and unique reasoning of which the work's fabrication is the conclusion; therefore there reigns among its parts so great a dependence that were we to remove even a single one, or to alter the form of those regarded as least important, we should destroy the entire mechanism*"' (pp. 32–3).

22 The censor being less the enlightened Malesherbes than the watchful clerics and others who sought to stop or delay publication of the *Encyclopédie*.

> Granting a company the exclusive right to manufacture a product which a
> number of people could make, is equivalent to wishing that that product,
> instead of improving in quality, will degenerate, and be sold at an ever higher
> price.[23]

Diderot's article 'Art' aggressively mingles the fine with the mechanical arts
and prizes both at least as high as the martial skills of France's traditional
defenders:

> In the judgement of those who today hold healthy ideas about the value of
> things, he who populated France with engravers, painters, sculptors and artists
> of every kind; who snatched from the English the machine for making stock-
> ings, velvet from the Genoans, mirrors from the Venetians, hardly did any-
> thing less for the state, than those who fought its enemies and took their
> strongholds from them.

Diderot's choice of luxury rather than subsistence goods is also polemical.
Note in addition that the value of life, reproduction, *peupla* ('populated') is
opposed to that of death, *battirent* ('fought'). Later in the same article Diderot
introduces the key question of the division of labour:

> The speed of production and the quality of the product depend entirely on
> the number of workers gathered together. When there is a large number in
> one workshop, each task is done by a different man. One worker only does
> and will only ever in his life do one particular thing; another, another thing:
> with the result that each thing is done well and quickly, and that the best
> made product is also the cheapest. Besides, when there is a large number of
> workers, inevitably their taste and their way of making things will improve,
> because it would be surprising if there were not some who were capable of
> thinking, of putting ideas together, and of at last finding the only means
> which will put them above their kind: the means either to save raw material
> or to get more done in the time or to increase output by a new machine or
> by a more convenient way of making things.

Arthur M. Wilson points out that Deleyre's article 'Epingle' ('Pin') illustrates this principle of the division of labour by the *eighteen* stages in the
manufacture of a pin – and asks whether an influence may even have
trickled through to the great Adam Smith.[24]

The article 'Représentants' ('Representatives') argues:

> Today trade is a source of strength and wealth for states. The merchant
> enriches himself and at the same time enriches the state which encourages

23 All translations from the *Encyclopédie* are my own.
24 *Diderot*, New York, Oxford University Press, 1972, pp. 235–6. Smith's famous
   example of the pin factory in the very first chapter of *The Wealth of Nations* also
   describes eighteen stages in the manufacture of the pin. Wilson comments on a range
   of articles from the *Encyclopédie* throughout this work.

his enterprises; he always shares his good fortune and his setbacks; therefore he cannot be reduced to silence without an injustice being done; he
is a useful citizen and capable of giving his opinions in the councils of a nation
whose prosperity and power he increases [. . .] The citizen's voice should
carry a weight in proportion to his possessions in the national assemblies
of government.

Property, rather than birth, makes the citizen, and the citizen should have
a vote [voix] and thus a voice [voix]. The question of who should represent
whom (who should enjoy that power), and whose voice should be heard,
is a question which also has racial implications – hinted at in Diderot's
Supplement to Bougainville's Voyage. This article is unattributed, and so we
could ascribe it provisionally to the Editor, who, in any case, takes ultimate
responsibility for all articles – Diderot. Today, he writes (unlike those bad
old Dark Ages), it is trade which is a source of power and wealth for states
– undoubtedly the author is thinking of the great trading nations of the day,
of which the prime example, for the French Enlightenment, is England.
England, where court and merchant work together, where there is plenty
of venture capital to fund colonial expansion, and where the merchant is
truly honoured. This is a theme rightly associated with Voltaire in his Letters on England or in his Epîtres dédicatoires to Zaïre (dedicated to Falkener).[25]
In dedicating a play to a merchant (whose hospitality he enjoyed during his
stay in England) rather than to an aristocratic patron, Voltaire is celebrating
the high status enjoyed by merchants in England – as he makes clear in the
Dedication. The difference between France and England which he laments is
then demonstrated by the mockery with which the Dedication was received
in Paris, and Falkener is lampooned as an uncultured sailor in a play written
by the Abbé d'Allainville. Characteristically, Voltaire fires back with a second
Epître dédicatoire. In fact, his friend is not only a successful trader, but was
also appointed to the post of ambassador at Constantinople – again emblem-
atising the different attitudes of the two countries.

While Voltaire in France or the collective voice of Mr Spectator in
Britain both reflect and help to create a climate favourable to commerce, it
is The Wealth of Nations which is crucially to shape a number of professional
economists' assumptions about market economies: division of labour is more
efficient than universal self-sufficiency; specialisation must be accompanied
by trade; efficient division of labour requires the organisation of workers
into large units of production, and so they must sell their labour to firms
and receive wages in return; the allocation of resources is the outcome of
millions of independent decisions made by consumers and producers, all
acting through the medium of markets (the price system) – what Adam
Smith called 'the invisible hand'. In his very first chapter Smith stresses the

25 Ed. E. Jacobs, London, Hodder and Stoughton, 1975, pp. 58–66, 69–75.

importance of the division of labour; it is specialisation which enables an increase in the productive powers of labour, and thus an increase in general wealth. He has a voluntaristic view of division of labour, which he presents as a technical, rather than a social, question. In other words, he imagines workers voluntarily innovating in dividing up tasks into ever smaller component parts in which individuals can specialise. (As we have seen, here he is echoing views already expressed in the early volumes of the *Encyclopédie* by Deleyre and Diderot.) But history suggests that the interdependence of technical and social divisions of labour has been crucial. People become defined by the work they do, just as the work they do is valorised by social processes; consequently battles are waged over the designation 'skilled' or 'unskilled' – and sexual difference has frequently been a factor in deciding such designations. For Smith, what tends to limit the extent of specialisation is the size of the market, and so free trade is of paramount importance to him – as much as the elasticity of demand.

A further and related reason why *The Wealth of Nations* is the preferred point of reference for neoclassical economics is the famous 'Invisible Hand' theory that it is perceived advantage rather than benevolence which leads to human co-operation (*The Wealth of Nations*, p. 26). Markets need not be planned, but should be the result of numerous independent decisions made by self-interested individuals. A third reason why Smith is more often cited than other classical economists is that he rejected the labour theory of value for any society other than a 'rude' one. Smith's emphasis on the control of monopolies, his comments on the tendency of masters to combine in order to keep wages low (pp. 83–5) or on the role of fellow-feeling in tempering self-love are perhaps less often cited.

Susan Buck-Morss[26] argues that Smith attempts to call 'upon traditional notions of civic virtue to compensate for the moral inadequacies of the laws of political economy. This is a weakness in his thought, because the civic society he desires is founded on principles inimicable to the economic society he describes.' She claims that it is Hegel who draws out the philosophical consequences of political economy. What Smith and Hegel still share is an understanding of 'political economy as belonging to a more general philosophical discourse, one that entailed critical reflection – a normative dimension – as a necessary part' (p. 461). This is what divides them from neoclassical economists from the late nineteenth century onwards, who 'professionalise' their discipline thanks to their claim to be doing science, which has entailed reducing 'their vision of the polical economy to a point of normative indifference' (p. 462). Herein lies the power of neoclassical economics, but at the cost of self-imposed blindness.

26 'Envisioning Capital: Political Economy on Display', *Critical Inquiry*, 21 (1995), 434–67. I am grateful to Steven Daniels for drawing my attention to this article.

4

The eighteenth century II: gift or investment? Diderot's *Supplement to Bougainville's 'Voyage'*

In this chapter my focus for analysis will be Diderot's *Supplement to Bougainville's 'Voyage'* (first version, 1772).[1] I have chosen this text for detailed consideration because of its hybridity with respect to debates over the market, and because of the way in which it relates the market to the question of relations between the sexes and between potential colonisers and colonised. In certain ways, as I have already suggested, it is an ephebe text to Montaigne's 'On the Cannibals', although it also has its debts to Plato and More. While Rousseau's *Social Contract* gives general principles on which any just society should be based, Diderot's *Supplement to Bougainville's 'Voyage'* is a dialogic description of one particular 'primitive' society which might hypothetically be considered, if not perfectly just, then at least more just than the one in which Rousseau and Diderot lived. Diderot's dialogue can also be read as a utopia, fitting perhaps most comfortably into the tradition whereby utopias are used to critique contemporary ills, rather than to provide a blueprint for the future.[2] It is certainly not easy to judge to what extent Diderot would advocate any aspects of the exotic Tahitian lifestyle, although it seems highly likely that he would join the wise Tahitians (whose speech, we are told, has a peculiarly European resonance) in condemning the hypocrisy of Catholic priests. Diderot is the hardest to pin down of all the celebrated figures of the Enlightenment. He

1 *Supplement to Bougainville's 'Voyage'*, in Diderot, *Rameau's Nephew and Other Works*, trans. J. Barzun and R. H. Bowen, Indianapolis, Bobbs-Merrill Company, 1964, pp. 177–228.

2 See Mary Louis Berneri, *Journey through Utopia* [1950], London, Freedom Press, 1982; this covers utopias from antiquity to the time of writing. Her two main examples of 'Utopias of the Enlightenment' are the *Supplement* and Gabriel de Foigny's *Les Aventures de Jacques Sadeur dans la découverte de la terre Australe* or *A New Discovery of Terra Incognita Australis* (1676). Australia was a favourite location for utopias at one time. (After these two, the most quoted source in that chapter is Sade.) I should like to thank Diana Knight for bringing this work to my attention. Bernard Papin, 'L'Utopie tahitienne du *Supplément au Voyage de Bougainville* ou le "modèle idéal" en politique', *L'Information littéraire* 36 (1984), 102–5, discusses various types of utopia and concludes that Diderot's Tahiti functions like an aesthetic model.

speaks in many tongues, not only in the sense that a text like the *Supplement* conjures up a range of interlocutors whose proximity or distance from 'Diderot' is a matter for conjecture, but also in that his collaborative style of working means that it is often hard to tell what books or what passages in books should be attributed to him. He contributed some key passages to the Abbé Raynal's *History of Trade in the Two Indies*, which is a productive intertext for the *Supplement* – and yet distinguishing the different voices in that work is a difficult task.[3] While Diderot's work is certainly progressive in its critique of the *ancien régime*, there is considerable controversy over two other key aspects of the text: the degree to which his account of sexual relations is anti-patriarchal and the degree to which his writing position can be seen as an anti-colonial one. Benot has argued that it is in his anti-colonial stance that Diderot comes closest to a rejection of the Enlightenment valorisation of material progress which has to be grounded in private property and hence social inequality. However, Diderot has been treated less generously in more recent postcolonial theory.

One of the first questions to be posed of this slippery text is: what is 'Tahiti', or, how does 'Tahiti' function in this dialogue? To what extent is there an attempt to represent an other culture and society; to what extent is Tahiti a device, a thought-experiment, to enable analysis of matters closer to home? Eighteenth-century (and earlier) utopian texts are sometimes set in lands known to exist but still fairly mysterious to the majority of Europeans, rather like some twentieth-century science fiction which uses a location such as Mars or Venus. Diderot's *Supplement to Bougainville's 'Voyage'*, however, presents itself as a discussion of Tahiti in the wake of Bougainville's self-proclaimed factual account, his *Voyage autour du monde*. And the very difference between armchair speculation about a distant location and first-hand experiences of exploration is itself discussed and disturbed in the dialogue. *The Supplement* may still be seen as a discussion of France via its account both of an other place, and of the naively horrified reactions of others to the reader's contemporary reality. Diderot's Tahitians would be somewhere between Montaigne's native Brazilian cannibals (in so far as they represent the voice of nature) and Montesquieu's Persians (the voice of a different sophistication). In this respect the *Supplement* would differ from the 'utopian' works by Rousseau or Scott which will be discussed in the next chapter, which may have a range of oneiric wish-fulfilment qualities, and yet are *in earnest* with their claims that life at Clarens or at Millenium

3 See Yves Benot, *Diderot, de l'athéisme à l'anticolonialisme*, Paris, Maspéro, 1970, for a substantial analysis of the *History of Trade in the Two Indies*, and of Diderot's radical contribution to it. See also Michèle Duchet, *Diderot et l'Histoire des Deux Indes*, Paris, Nizet, 1978, for a detailed breakdown of Diderot's contributions. Duchet places greater emphasis than Benot on the thesis that Diderot, like Voltaire and Montesquieu, praises commerce as peaceful.

Hall is better in every sense than life in Paris or London. However, perhaps we should not be too hasty in assuming that Diderot does not give a voice to Tahitians or to the colonised other in general.[4] Perhaps his hints about the difficulty of translating Tahitians into French (or vice versa), and about the contemplative, if not imaginary, input into the observations arising from the real voyage, bring the reader closer to a (non)encounter with the other.[5]

In order to tackle these complexities with a degree of clarity, I shall schematise my argument as follows. First I shall present the heuristic and generous reading of the text as a positive representation of a gift economy. Then I shall examine some of the more suspicious accounts of *The Supplement* which make a powerful case for integrating it into the property-owning, colonising and patriarchal ideology of the day. While I want to question some of the details of these suspicious accounts, and I want to preserve some of the elements of the generous reading, I shall conclude by focusing on Diderot's universalisation of self-interest and on a disturbing slip in his customary stance against slavery.

A non-market society

The Supplement can easily be presented as a critique of property in general, and in particular a critique of the practice of treating people as property. One of the main targets is a marriage system which reduces women to chattels, another is the colonial ambition of European powers who 'discover' 'new' territories and put up signs saying 'This belongs to us'. The Tahitian patriarch whose apostrophe follows the opening dialogue between A. and B. in *The Supplement* says:

> 'Orou! You who understand the speech of these men, tell every one of us, as you have told me, what they have written on that strip of metal – "This land belongs to us." This land belongs to you! And why? Because you set foot in it? If some day a Tahitian should land on your shores, and if he should engrave on one of your stones or on the bark of one of your trees: "This land belongs to the people of Tahiti", what would you think?' (p. 188)

4 With this rather inelegant phrase I am trying to conjure up at least three categories of people discussed by Diderot: those who had been colonised, those who were about to be colonised and slaves brought to work in the colonies.

5 Dena Goodman, 'The Structure of Political Argument in Diderot's *Supplément au Voyage de Bougainville*', *Diderot Studies*, 21 (1983), 123–37, gives a pertinent analysis of the dialogic and supplementary structure of the text – which she presents as a powerful call for political reform. Georges Van Den Abbeele's much more critical reading nevertheless concludes with a measure of approval for Diderot's 'transvestite ventriloquism': 'In a way, the Diderotian polyphony remains true to the voices it gives us to hear, since it tells us that its imitation of those voices is not just an imitation but an imitation of an imitation, or a supplementary imitation.' ('Utopian Sexuality and its Discontents: Exoticism and Colonialism in the *Supplément au Voyage de Bougainville*', *l'esprit créateur*, 24 (1984), 43–52 (p. 52)).

Here Diderot echoes the opening to the second part of Rousseau's *Discourse on Inequality*, where Rousseau locates the origin of the unjust society in the rich man's speech, 'this belongs to me'. In Rousseau's example the speech must be heard and accepted by those foolish enough to believe that the institution of laws to protect property will benefit everyone, rich and poor. Diderot's example also echoes the even bleaker historical moment at the close of Rousseau's *Essay on the Origin of Languages*, where the imbalance of power has reached the point at which speech is no longer necessary, 'communication' is achieved in silence via the barrel of a gun and placards saying 'give money'. This could well be (amongst other things) an allegory of the colonial situation where there is no need for a common tongue establishing the fiction of equality. The addressee of the French sign in *The Supplement* is another colonial power; the Tahitians are reduced by it to things rather than 'men', they are part of that which belongs (to us). Diderot imagines a Tahitian (a man and not a thing) who can read and respond to the imperious sign; this kind of prosopopoeia is a feature of his various interventions on the subject of colonialism.

Diderot's chief concern in this short text is to tackle the question of the regulation of relations between the sexes, and the political economy of Tahiti is treated incidentally. However, the two matters are closely interlinked, and Diderot's character B., repeating the words of the Tahitian Orou, claims that the first way in which Europeans have gone wrong is by 'the tyranny of men, who have converted the possession of a woman into a right of property' (p. 223). Diderot's Tahitians do not believe that one person can own another. The general principle of the island is that of an economy of abundance. This is true with respect to subsistence needs as well as with respect to women. A venerable old Tahitian explains: 'All things are for all [*Ici tout est à tous*]' (p. 187) – almost everything is held in common,[6] and everyone works (but not very hard – a slightly different emphasis from the other utopias, which may relate to typical eighteenth-century environmental determinism). There is plenty to share, since the Tahitians have not created any 'superfluous wants [*besoins*]' (p. 189) for themselves. This is a typical utopian feature, although achieved without the strong emphasis on education found in other utopias, presumably because the Tahitians are deemed to be so close to nature.

One of the most striking features of the *Supplement* is its regulation of sexual relations. The prevalence of a sexual instinct, but the absence of amorous passion (until the arrival of the French) could seem to bring the Tahitians close to a state of nature (such as that portrayed by Rousseau in

---

6 'The work and the harvesting are done in common. Their sense of the word *property* is very limited; the passion of love, reduced to a simple physical appetite, produces none of our disorders' (p. 217, translation modified). Common ownership is thus linked to the control of amorous passion.

his *Discourse on Inequality*). However, many earlier utopias are marked by their attempt to banish eros, and so to regulate sexual relations *rationally*, and this seems to be the spirit in which Diderot represents Tahiti, although, of course, reason is *in accordance with* nature. Anthropology, in the shape, for instance, of Lévi-Strauss, famously argues that the passage from nature to culture is marked by the prohibition on incest (what he describes as men exchanging women). This is Rousseau's position in the *Essay on the Origin of Languages* (as Derrida has emphasised).[7] However, I would like to argue that Tahiti is presented as a society (albeit one in accordance with Nature) in spite of its failure to prohibit any form of incest – the text insists that there are other laws and prohibitions operative in Tahitian society. Consequently the lack of an incest taboo is highly significant as an anti-patriarchal element. Irigaray comments in her analysis of Lévi-Strauss and Marx:

> As mother, woman remains on the side of (re)productive nature and, because of this, man can never fully transcend his relation to the 'natural'. His social existence, his economic structures and his sexuality are always tied to the work of nature: these structures thus always remain at the level of the earli-est appropriation, that of the constitution of nature as landed property, and of the earliest labour, which is agricultural. But this relationship to productive nature, an insurmountable one, has to be denied so that relations among men may prevail. This means that mothers, reproductive instruments marked with the name of the father and enclosed in his house, must be private pro-perty, excluded from exchange. The *incest taboo* represents this refusal to allow productive nature to enter into exchanges among men. As both natural value and use value, mothers cannot circulate in the form of commodities without threatening the very existence of the social order. ('Women on the Market', *This Sex Which Is Not One*, p. 185)

Tahitians have not attempted to transcend fully their relation to the 'natural' – they have only appropriated land as a society and not as individuals. It could be argued that they accept the impossibility of absolute transcendence, and that they embrace what Irigaray will term a 'sensible transcendental'.

In eighteenth-century Europe children were bought and sold on the marriage market of the middle and upper classes – Diderot himself was imprisoned by *lettre de cachet* because he would not marry the woman chosen by his father. As Irigaray remarks:

> The virgin [. . .] *is pure exchange value*. She is nothing but the possibility, the place, the sign of relations among men. In and of herself, she does not exist: she is a simple envelope veiling what is really at stake in social exchange

7 For a discussion of the treatment of incest in eighteenth-century French philosophical writings, see G. Benrekassa, 'Loi naturelle et loi civile: l'idéologie des Lumières et la prohibition de l'inceste', *Studies on Voltaire and the Eighteenth Century*, 87 (1972), 115–44. It should be noted that Bougainville himself does not raise the question of incest in Tahiti.

[. . .] Once deflowered, woman is relegated to the status of use value, to her entrapment in private property; she is removed from exchange among men. (p. 186)

In Tahiti, the virgin does not have exchange value.

A point of comparison with Diderot's anti-colonial stance in *The Supplement* is his writing on the Hottentots. Benot points out his apostrophe to the Hottentots – asking them either to flee the European oppressor or, better still, to kill him with their poisoned arrows – as evidence of Diderot's passionate anti-colonialism and philosophical support for a war of liberation. He compares this passage (introduced into the chapter on the Cape of Good Hope in the *History of Trade in the Two Indies* in 1781) to Diderot's similarly revolutionary rhetoric with respect to slaves – and this appeal to slaves to rise up and kill their masters is a more immediately practical proposal, soon to be put into practice in Haiti. Post-colonial theory has pointed out that the figure of the good savage could just as well serve the colonising purpose as that of the horrifying cannibal. While the cannibal can legitimately be slain, the good savage could be converted into the good worker. Equally the elegaic tone of many tributes to (and prosopopoeias by) the noble savage is a tone of historical resignation – it goes without saying that his time is past, thanks to the European's superiority (in destructive power). This charge can be, and has been, laid at Diderot's door, for instance with respect to the old man's farewell in the *Supplement*. In his defence it may be said that the implication that it is almost inevitable that the European will defeat the native American, Hottentot, Tahitian is surely not surprising, and that Diderot encourages, where he can, any feasible resistance.[8] From a different perspective, Elizabeth de Fontenay analyses Diderot's writings on Hottentot sexual characteristics – contrasting his account with Buffon's description of an ape-like creature and with the notorious case of the Hottentot Venus.[9]

Sexual capitalism

Many recent critiques of *The Supplement* have focused on the economics of the sexual relations described by Diderot, and have argued that these are organised on capitalist principles. This sexual capitalism, it is argued, sets up a general capitalist economy. Some critics have also argued that Diderot's description of the sexual economy undermines any anti-colonial pretensions previously ascribed to the text.

It may be thought that Diderot's Tahiti, in which partners need not stay together any longer than one lunar month, in which childbirth is

---

8 See Benot on the Black Spartacus (*Diderot, de l'athéisme à l'anticolonialisme*, pp. 212 ff.).
9 *Diderot ou Le Matérialisme enchanté*, Paris, Grasset, 1981. See 'Fuyez, malheureux Hottentots', pp. 103–12.

always a cause for celebration and the concepts of incest or illegitimacy do not exist, is an erotic paradise.[10] However, while sex is far less regulated than in the *Republic*, *Utopia*, *La Nouvelle Héloïse* or *Millenium Hall*, nevertheless it is firmly dedicated to reproduction.[11] Men and women deemed not to have reached sexual maturity, women past child-bearing age, pregnant women or menstruating women are all forbidden to have sexual relations. The purpose of Tahiti's sexual libertarianism is an economic one: to increase the population;[12] and individuals *profit* from procreation. It is the same goal as Rousseau's, but whereas Rousseau believes that sexual licence leads to infertility, Diderot's Tahitians have a more straightforward approach: the more often fertile adults have sex, the more children will be born. Diderot's Tahitians have an economic aim in the sense of desiring an increase in the social wealth which they perceive children to be. Georges Van Den Abbeele suggests that the text is deeply patriarchal in its emphasis on reproduction – he calls it an economy of sexploitation.[13] *Vénus féconde* simply replaces the *Vénus galante* and is just as restrictive – the *il ne faut pas* has simply been replaced by *il faut*. *Contra* Diderot's claim that men, women and children circulate, Van Den Abbeele points out that only women and children circulate – men own the huts in which they live. A child is only wealth in so far as he is a male child, able to be a soldier, farmer or fisherman. Woman is the proletariat: producer of the only wealth; and only men have a voice in the text. We may also ask whether the insistence on reproductive

10 David Spurr seeks to place the *Supplement* in the Orientalist tradition brought to recent critical attention by Edward Said, which represents the Oriental other as full of sexual promise (and threat). See Spurr, *The Rhetoric of Empire*, Durham, NC and London, Duke University Press, 1993; I should like to thank Keith Fairless for bringing this work to my attention. He particularly focuses on the two tropes of *unveiling* (the female body) and *repetition* (of substitutable sexual partners). With respect to unveiling, Spurr quotes Diderot on the Tahitian girl who is 'eager that her mother, authorized by her puberty, will remove her veil and lay bare her breast' (Spurr, p. 174). It seems to me, however, that this is importantly different from the repetitive and staged unveiling which is a typical erotic form. In Diderot's Tahiti, those (girls and boys) who are not sexually mature are covered up. At the moment deemed to be puberty they are uncovered and remain so. Their nakedness is neither shameful nor transgressive, and functions rather differently from that, say, of the Algerian women in the postcards gathered by Malek Alloula, to which Spurr compares them.

11 Janet S. Whatley comments: 'Diderot's Tahiti is not ultimately a relaxed Arcadia, but a strict Utopia, however garlanded, in which the social mechanisms guarantee such efficiency that duty and responsibility are never felt as compulsions' ('*Un retour secret vers la forêt*: The Problem of Privacy and Order in Diderot's Tahiti', *Kentucky Romance Quarterly*, 24 (1977), 199–208), p. 201. She notes Bougainville's evocations of the European pastoral tradition in his descriptions of Tahiti – alongside details which evoke a more troubling and bloody exotic. Diderot removes most of Bougainville's classical references to Venus, nymphs and so on.

12 See, for example pp. 195, 203, 223.

13 A similar point is made by Elizabeth de Fontenay, pp. 121–3; she argues that other texts by Diderot are more egalitarian than the *Supplement*.

sex enforces sexual opposition. It is true that Diderot tells us that Tahitian women and men select sexual partners who look good for breeding, which might suggest exaggerated sexed characteristics (sometimes an element in racist stereotyping).

Wilda Anderson also makes the point that sexual relations in Tahiti are not governed by desire but by economic self-interest.[14] She argues that for Diderot 'nature is continuous with a notion of property (and therefore with "culture"), not antithetical to it' (pp. 138–9), and that his position therefore contradicts Rousseau's in his *Discourse on Inequality*, where 'the notion of property once abstracted drives the wedge between man and nature by forming the epistemological foundation of culture' (p. 139). She argues that leisure, *le repos*, is the only commodity purchasable with the excess cash accruing to children. She further claims that the enrichment process in Diderot's Tahiti is self-accelerating, in that the more children you have, the more desirable you are as a sexual partner *and* the more leisure time you have for sex, and thus the most desirable, rich in children and leisurely individual is the patriarch. (It cannot be a matriarch, because women's child-producing capacity is limited by the menopause.)[15] This does, of course, assume that child-care does not absorb excess leisure time, and that when a woman leaves half of their joint children with their father (when she chooses a new partner), he will immediately find someone else to look after them. But all this is speculation! Anderson argues that Diderot's Tahitians have institutionalised the fixed image of their own naturalness and have abandoned adaptive interaction with the natural changing world (in this instance, the Europeans). She suggests that this is revealed by the patriarch's speech to the departing Europeans, which rejects all that they represent, and which precedes Orou's creed of adaptation. Further, the inflexibility of the Tahitians is synecdochally marked in Aotourou's tongue, which cannot produce European sounds. I am not sure whether Anderson is suggesting that Diderot is blaming the victim, or simply that that is the message we could take from his text. Her argument is powerful, and yet (perhaps inevitably) seems one-sided, in that it takes certain elements to their farthest conclusion and leaves others aside. For example, she says of Orou's claim with respect to his daughters ('elles m'appartiennent [. . .] elles sont à elles' ('they belong to me, they are their own women')) that: 'the first half of his statement speaks the truth, while the second half presents

---

14 *Diderot's Dream*, Baltimore, Johns Hopkins University Press, 1990. See particularly 'Dismantling a Utopian Economics'. I am grateful to Michael Moriarty for recommending this work.

15 While it is true that old women are denied access to sexual pleasure in Diderot's Tahiti, it should be remembered that the one-sixth of the Tahitian national product which is put aside for redistribution is not only given to those who have children, but also to the elderly (p. 162). This 'welfare state' aspect of Tahiti is rarely commented on.

the self-image that his society believes in and that masks its true functioning'
(p. 141).[16] When we compare Orou's paternal power with that of his European counterpart (which Diderot's text invites us to do), it does not appear
to be the case that his post-pubescent daughters belong to him in any sense
other than that they *choose* to do so because of their affection for him. At
any time they are free to leave his hut; they can choose any mature male
sexual partner who equally chooses them. It is true that Diderot does not tell
us that women can own their own homes, but neither does he tell us that
they cannot do so – and his emphasis is on women's freedom of movement.

Simon During suggests that Diderot, in common with other Enlightenment thinkers, projects a patriarchy very similar to that of his own time
on to all 'unpoliced' societies, including Tahiti.[17] This enables a progressive
insistence that civilisation is non-filiative: progress both does and should
mean that a father's wealth and position is not passed on to his sons. While
I agree with his argument that it is important to understand the anti-filiative
strains in much Enlightenment thinking, I am not convinced that Tahiti
is represented as patriarchal. Everything Diderot tells us about Tahiti suggests the contrary: there is no incest taboo, fathers do not possess wives or
children and have almost no rights over them, there is no system of inheritance, there is no greater weight placed on sons than on daughters.

There is, however, an eccentric hospitality scene to which During
refers – which may be set up simply because Diderot cannot resist the anti-
clerical joke potential, or which may, indeed, reveal an eighteenth-century
patriarchal strain creeping into the text in spite of all we are told about the
absence of property in Tahiti. A father presses first his three daughters
(starting with the youngest) upon his clerical guest, and then finally his
wife. As time passes, the almoner succumbs to all three and performs like
a man even as he cries out: 'But my religion, my holy orders' (pp. 194 ff.,
translation modified). Hospitality is a virtue firmly attached to the ancient
world and to 'primitive' peoples by the eighteenth century: commentators
are divided as to the degree or significance of its decline in their own time.

During also comments as follows:

16 We might note that in another episode (much less frequently commented on) it is
   mothers who offer their daughters (p. 151) in a gesture of hospitality.
17 'Rousseau's Patrimony: Primitivism, Romance and Becoming Other', in *Colonial dis-
   course/postcolonial theory*, ed. F. Barker, P. Hulme and M. Iversen, Manchester, Manchester University Press, 1994, pp. 47–71. I am grateful to Keith Fairless for bringing
   this to my attention. During's aim is 'to trace a number of trajectories from the
   enlightened critique of filiation through modes of self-othering to the larger processes
   of European expansion and back' (p. 47). In the process he claims that 'the *philosophes*
   who articulated Enlightenment ideals projected a version of these relatively recent
   historical formations on to the species's so-called immaturity' (p. 52). While it is
   clearer to me that Rousseau (unlike the Diderot of the *Supplement*, analysed pp. 54–
   6) claims that the first societies were broadly 'patriarchal' in the sense of filiative or
   based around kin relations, I do not agree that he projected eighteenth-century patriarchy with all its domestic tyranny on to these hypothetical early societies.

Tahiti-as-nature teaches us that social relations are, in the last instance, based on men's power over women. Men are more sexually aggressive, naturally more proprietorial [. . .] because a woman's sexual response is slower than a man's. Women need to be pressured into sexual activity: every sexual act is a rape *in petto* – where I am using 'rape' in its modern sense as an act of sexual violence [. . .] Diderot argues [. . .] that it is from this primordial difference that socio-political hierarchies develop – in a form which ensures that they can break male power only at the risk of offending their own basis in nature. Diderot's Tahiti, then, offers both a glimpse of familial freedom (a society in which monogamous domesticity does not exist) and a confrontation with equality's limits (just because men always come first). (p. 56)

I find this a puzzling analysis. I believe it to refer to A. and B.'s discussion of *pudeur* (sexual modesty), a virtue which society has particularly attached to women. B. asserts (in conformity with Rousseau in his *Discourse on Inequality*) that the only absolutely natural *pudeur* is common to both men and women, and is a natural caution about being discovered by a predator in a moment of weakness. He tells A. that the almoner remarks that in Tahiti neither men nor women blush at the sight of an erection. A. asks why it is always men who make the first step, and B. responds that this is not the case in Tahiti: 'the gap which divides a man from a woman would be crossed first by the more amorously inclined of the two' (p. 222). However, 'But after women have learned through experience and education what more or less painful consequences can follow a blissful interlude, their hearts tremble at a man's approach. The man's heart is far from trembling; he is urged on by his senses and he obeys' (p. 222). This statement does not seem to me to apply to Tahiti; rather B. is again contrasting Tahiti, where pregnancy is always welcome and sexually transmitted diseases unknown, with Europe or North America, where the results of sexual activity are 'plus ou moins cruelles' for a woman. Earlier B. had told the tale of Miss Polly Baker of Connecticut, who had been fined and whipped because of her illegitimate offspring – while the man who first seduced her sat honourably amongst her judges (pp. 165–6). (This tale is also told in the Abbé Raynal's *History of Trade in the Two Indies*.) Small wonder that such a 'civilisation' means that women are forced to be reserved, and then 'need to be pressured into sexual activity'. In other words, in so far as Diderot refers to rape in this text, it would seem to be a *social* rather than a *natural* phenomenon.

It is interesting to focus on the *supplementary* quality of the text's relation to Bougainville's own account of his voyage, which was published in the previous year and aroused considerable interest.[18] The *Supplement* begins with A. and B. (two Frenchmen, we presume) discussing the weather

---

18 Spurr refers to the text as 'a dangerous supplement [. . .] which reveals the repressed sexual content of the *Voyage*' (p. 173). William W. Stowe's 'Diderot's Supplement: A Model for Reading', *Philological Quarterly*, 62 (1983), 353–65, is an attempt to analyse the supplementary quality of Diderot's writing.

(fog), and passes to a discussion of the explorer, Bougainville, since B. is *occupying himself during the bad weather* by reading Bougainville's account of his voyage. I shall return to the role of the text as a distraction from certain irritating aspects of material reality – figured as fog (perhaps an unconscious link to the English, irritatingly more successful than the French at this juncture). The account of Bougainville the man raises a number of relevant points. Most importantly, Bougainville is said to be 'a true Frenchman' ['un véritable français']; he is exemplary of that nation's love of pleasure ['il aime les femmes'], ballasted by its theoretical and practical exploits. Bougainville is a mathematician (he was given since his youth to that most rational and universal of languages), and he is a practical man. We could add from another Bougainville text, his *American Journals*, that he is a man of his moment, holding the view that 'it is trade which most of all civilizes man'.[19] This practical *commercial* side is elided by Diderot in favour of the philosophical debate over Tahiti, although it returns as economic universalism. Derrida tells us in *The Other Heading*, with respect to universality and exemplarity, that Valéry (his main text in that essay) believes that Frenchmen feel that they are particularly universal (*The Other Heading*, p. 73). The more French, 'a real Frenchman', the more European, the more universal. A. and B. are perhaps also true Frenchmen, engaging in philosophical debate, intellectual inquiry, and finally ending their commerce (I mean, their conversation) with a typically Gallic evocation of women (underlining its own typicality, 'Toujours les femmes!' ['Women again'], Diderot, *Supplement*, p. 228), and a comment on women's tendency to say the opposite of what they think. These 'men of the world' are both well acquainted with a range of travel narratives; they have a globe at hand on which to trace out a route, and they can discuss the relative merits of different accounts of the Patagonians or turn to debate exotically different forms of birth-control – which all in the end are simply means to achieve the 'universal' human need to regulate population where resources are scarce.

Van Den Abbeele claims that:

> Bougainville's circumnavigation traces a line around the world, a line which defines a zone of property belonging to France in the form of colonies. So if, on the one hand, the traveler never leaves the France of his house-boat, on the other hand, every place that house-boat lands becomes metonymically assimilated to and appropriated by France. Bougainville, having economically sublated difference in his voyage, returns home, himself a celebrity and a hero for having made France greater. ('Utopian Sexuality', p. 45)

19 *Adventures in the Wilderness*, trans. E. P. Hamilton, Norman, University of Oklahoma Press, 1964 [French printing in Quebec, 1924] (p. 123). Bougainville does not see native Americans as 'noble savages'; he refers (negatively) on several occasions to their cannibalism (for instance pp. 122, 143, 144, 150).

This is seductive and convincing up to a point – but we must remember historical details. Prior to his round the world voyage, Bougainville had served in Canada against the English; when the French were defeated, he returned home as a prisoner. In an attempt to begin to restore France's flagging colonial fortunes (relative to the ascendency of the English), he financed the settlement of what we now know as the Falkland Islands by Acadians (driven from Novia Scotia by the British). The first motive of his circumnavigation was to oversee the *end* of that venture – over his head Louis XV had agreed to hand the islands over to the Spanish. This was thus a personal defeat for Bougainville, and also a setback for France in her competition with European rivals. The hand-over is described very briefly in chapter three of Bougainville's *Voyage autour du monde*, a chapter which begins with thick fog, as does the *Supplement* – the sun comes out in the course of A. and B.'s discussion. Diderot does not mention the Iles Malouines, only the Magellan Straits and a story about birds happy to perch on men. The sunshine of Tahiti thus completely obscures the storms of the Falklands, where Bougainville is stuck for over two months. Bougainville, still determined to make France greater, despite the monarch's unwillingness to provide the necessary finance and France's lack of English-style adventure capitalists, had a number of profitable colonising ends in mind as he sailed around the globe – all ended in failure. Only the scientific or epistemological aspect of the journey bore fruit. It is perhaps unsurprising that the first report of his voyage (before his own account was published) was entitled 'Tahiti ou La Nouvelle-Cythère', and focused exclusively on Tahiti as the new island of love.[20] Bougainville in fact stayed only ten days in Tahiti, but no mention is made of any of the other ports of call in his long journey.[21] Venus, the erotic exotic, covers any public sense that at this stage France may be lagging well behind in the race to exploit colonies. Thus Van Den Abbeele's account gives credit to what some may have wished to believe at the time – that they had only to trace a line, and new territory would magically be theirs. In fact (as Bougainville knew only too well), new territory had to be held in the face of competition.

The term *economy* includes among its semantic values law (*nomos*) and home (*oikos*). The law of the economy is the circle (exchange, circulation,

20 Philibert Commerson (a naturalist who accompanied Bougainville), *Mercure de France*, November 1769, pp. 198–9 (extracts of his journal are reproduced in Bougainville, *Voyage autour du monde*, Paris, Cercle du Bibliophile, 1969, pp. 283–7). He names Tahiti 'Utopia', after More (as does Bougainville). He writes with respect to sexual relations: 'Every foreigner is allowed to participate in these happy mysteries; indeed it is one of the duties of hospitality to invite strangers to attend to them, so that the good Utopian is constantly enjoying either his own feelings of pleasure or the spectacle of others' (p. 284).

21 Even Tahiti had already been 'discovered' by the English one year earlier (and by the Portuguese even earlier).

return) – the circular return to the point of departure, the home. Derrida claims in *Given Time* that 'Oikonomia would always follow the path of Ulysses. The latter returns to the side of loved ones or to himself; he goes away only in view of *repatriating* himself, in order to return to the home from which the signal for departure is given and the part assigned, the side chosen, the lot divided, destiny commanded' (*Given Time*, p. 7). This theme also appears in Cixous's account of the 'masculine economy', an expression which includes within it the capitalist market economy. She writes in *The Newly Born Woman* that masculine exile is an exile which is only provisional, characterised by longing for reappropriation: homesickness, nostalgia. I shall return to this analysis in chapter eight. Discussing her childhood identifications, Cixous writes:

> I didn't like to catch myself being Ulysses, the artist of flight. The Winner: the one who was saved, the homecoming man! Always returning to himself – in spite of the most fantastic detours. The Loaner: loaning himself to women and never giving himself except to the ideal image of Ulysses, bringing his inalterable resistance home to his hot-shot little phallic rock. (p. 74)

The Ulyssean or Odyssean theme in Bougainville's voyage is clear, and like Ulysses he returns home more or less empty-handed. The economic gain of his voyage is nil, but there is a cultural or scientific profit. Diderot's B. sums up the the profit of the 'Voyage' as threefold: 'it affords us a better knowledge of our old globe [*domicile*] and its inhabitants, greater safety on the seas, which he sailed with sounding line in hand, and more correct information for the use of our map makers' (pp. 180–1). However, out of defeat, victory is snatched, and history (re)turns to myth. In a similar way the British will convert the ignominy of retreat at Dunkirk into 'the Dunkirk spirit', something quintessentially British, which becomes a reference point on countless future occasions, both in the political arena and in private exchanges. Here, Tahiti, the new Cythera, conveys the French philosophical spirit, but also metonymically the Gallic taste for pleasure – in fact, while Tahiti already knew sexual freedom, Diderot tells us that it was the French who introduced Eros. As the Tahitian patriarch proclaims: 'Our women and girls we possess in common; you have shared this privilege with us, and your coming has awakened in them a frenzy they have never known before' (p. 188).

Intérêt

One final victory is the discovery that even the most exotic peoples are in some ways just like us, a liberal bourgeois universalism which is typical of many eighteenth-century texts. A good example would be Voltaire's *Candide*; Barthes comments:

Such is the paradox of Voltairean travel: to manifest an immobility. There are of course other manners, other laws, other moralities than ours, and this is what the journey teaches; but this diversity belongs to the human essence and consequently finds its point of equilibrium very rapidly; it is enough to acknowledge it in order to be done with it: let man (that is, Occidental man) multiply himself a little, let the European philosopher be doubled by the Chinese sage, the ingenious Huron, and universal man will be created.[22]

While I do not agree with all the suspicious readings of *The Supplement* – some seem to me to homogenise the text excessively – I do consider that the stumbling-block for a reading which would wish to emphasise the text's respect for difference is the word *intérêt*. Asked by a French chaplain about emotions such as marital affection and paternal love,[23] the Tahitian Orou replies:

> 'We have put in their place another impulse which is more *universal*, power-ful and lasting – self-interest. Examine your conscience in all candour, put aside the hypocritical parade of virtue which is always on the lips of your companions, though not in their hearts, and tell me, if there is anywhere on the face of the earth a man who, if he were not held back by shame, would not prefer to lose his child – a husband who would not prefer to lose his wife – rather than lose his fortune and all the amenities of life?' (p. 211, my italics)[24]

Indeed, another reason (apart from the focus on specialisation and the division of labour) why *The Wealth of Nations* is the preferred point of reference for neoclassical economics is the famous 'Invisible Hand' theory that it is perceived advantage (*intérêt*), rather than benevolence, which leads to human co-operation (*The Wealth of Nations*, p. 26). One of the most quoted sentences in the work is the following: 'It is not from the benevolence of the butcher, the brewer, or the baker that we expect our dinner, but from their regard to their own interest' (p. 119). Therefore, markets need not be planned, but should be the result of numerous independent decisions made by self-interested individuals. Diderot insists on reading economic self-interest as the prime motor of all behaviour in any society. He dislikes utopias 'in which folly and passions, self-interest and prejudices, are not taken into account'.[25] His own 'utopia' allows for *l'intérêt* as a motivating passion. This

---

22 'The Last Happy Writer', *Critical Essays*, p. 88. For Barthes, 'the anti-Voltaire is indeed Rousseau', who sets history moving again (p. 89).

23 'L'amour paternel' is – intriguingly – rendered as 'maternal love' in the English translation (p. 210).

24 'Nous y avons suppléé par un autre, qui est tout autrement général, énergique et durable, l'intérêt [. . .] Dis-moi si, dans quelque contrée que ce soit, il y a un père, qui sans la honte qui le retient, n'aimât mieux perdre son enfant, un mari qui n'aimât mieux perdre sa femme, que sa fortune et l'aisance de toute sa vie.' This universalising speech echoes the title in its use of *suppléer*.

25 *Observations sur le Nakaz*, *Œuvres politiques*, ed. P. Vernière, Paris, Garnier, 1963, p. 365.

universalisation of the profit motive is a hallmark of capitalist ideology (as opponents such as Rousseau were well aware at the time). Diderot's Tahitians are not 100 per cent *homines economici* – their approach to the productive work of their society and the distribution of their output is contrary to most basic capitalist principles (private property, the work ethic, competition and so on). Critics have sometimes glossed over this, and argued that the Tahitians' approach to *reproductive* work (with woman as the proletariat) mirrors capitalist forms. I think that this requires stretching a point or two, and thus it reintroduces the question of how we read. Diderot's Tahitians both are the same *and* the other in economic terms – they are said to be ultimately motivated by *intérêt* rather than marital affection or paternal (NB) love, and yet they are indolent – working for pleasure, not profit, for subsistence, not for accumulation or *luxe*.[26] They have a rational and scientific interest in eugenics, and yet they hold all property in common, including their sexual partners. Diderot figures this in his comments on language: Orou and the old man (the two Tahitians who 'speak' to us directly) are said to speak like Europeans (up to a point). Diderot plays with our knowledge of his ventriloquism. He also refers to the difficulty of translating between two languages which do not share the same concepts (in this case, French and Tahitian) – the anthropologist's continuing problem.[27] This doubling, or explicit dubbing, may be a route away from the reverse discourse which rejects economism only to fall into the racism of primitivism.

Esclavage

The argument of the *Encyclopédie* articles relating to trade, and of Diderot's general emphasis on material progress (*contra* Rousseau) is an argument in favour of colonialism – Bougainville, Voltaire, Montesquieu, the collective voice of Mr Spectator and a thousand more go all the way in celebrating colonial trade (with the occasional parenthesis about the wicked Spanish who got it wrong).[28] The more than occasional parenthesis, the sticking-point

26 Diderot's *Encyclopédie* entry for 'Cacao' (Cocoa) is remarkable for its lengthy account of the details of botany, cultivation, manufacture, and so on, without any hint of concern over colonial exploitation. One comment on the quality of chocolate begins dispassionately, 'The Spanish, more industrious than the savages . . .'

27 This play of sameness and difference can be contrasted with the typical *petit-bourgeois* figure of identification which Barthes analyses in *Mythologies*, pp.165–6. Barthes writes: 'The *petit-bourgeois* is a man unable to imagine the Other', and gives a footnote reference to Marx's *The Eighteenth Brumaire*, where he comments on this restricted consciousness. Barthes argues that sameness is the general rule, but there is 'a figure for emergencies: exoticism. The Other becomes a pure object, a spectacle, a clown.' This highly illiberal stance takes its most extreme form in fascism.

28 The evocation of the Black Legend could be compared to the bourgeois strategy of inoculation, which Barthes describes in *Mythologies*: it 'consists in admitting the accidental evil of a class-bound institution the better to conceal its principal evil' (p. 164).

for most of the Enlightenment *philosophes* (and where they parted company from many merchants!), is over slavery. The *Encyclopédie* article 'Traite des nègres' ('The Slave Trade') is totally hostile to slavery. Diderot is famous for his call to armed revolt, which Benot links to Haiti's successful slave revolution. (Voltaire is rather more circumspect, and not completely sure that negroes are human, since they are so easily enslaved.)

Interestingly, the term *esclavage* turns up at a certain pressure point in the *Supplement*. Elsewhere in the text *esclavage* is used rhetorically to express the appalling nature of the French act, which is to put up a sign, saying 'This land belongs to us' on Tahiti. There is no doubt that slavery is resoundingly to be condemned. However, in a discussion of the mild penalties ('we attach little importance to all these lapses') to be inflicted on those who engage in sexual relations at times when they are not fertile, Orou, the wise Tahitian, remarks: 'We do have dissolute old women who go out at night without their black veils and take [*reçoivent*] men, even though nothing can come of it. If they are recognized or taken by surprise, the punishment is either exile to the north of the island or slavery' (pp. 209–10, translation modified).[29] Nowhere else in the text is there any suggestion that the Tahitians practise slavery; on the contrary, there are a number of statements condemning the act of treating a human being as a thing (*res*), rather than as a free *persona*. Orou proclaims, for instance, that the Roman Catholic laws enforcing marital fidelity are against nature 'because they assume that a thinking being, one that has feelings and a sense of freedom, can be the property of another being like himself [*semblable à lui*]' (p. 198). A person, according to Orou, 'ne saurait devenir un effet de commerce' ('can never be treated like a trader's stock of goods') (p. 198). Why is there this sudden reification of older women? Women who are menstruating wear grey veils, and are also forbidden to have sexual intercourse – the flow of blood (Irigaray's *sang rouge*) is taboo. But the total absence of the periodic flux, the menopause, is far more taboo – the woman who is not like the phallus (*sang blanc*, *semblable*), but who apes men in having the phallus.[30]

---

29 The eccentricity (and horror) of the suggestion of *esclavage* is such that even a skilful reader such as Peter France may simply skip over it: 'There are however rules against unproductive sexual practices – dissolute women who continue to receive men after they have passed the age of childbearing are exiled to another part of the island. None of this is very ferocious perhaps . . .' (*Diderot*, Oxford, Oxford University Press, 1983, p. 65).

30 Old women are frequently represented as possessing the wrong kind of knowledge. Derrida echoes Nietzsche's evocation of the cynicism of old women in *Spurs* – they know the (non-)truth about truth, the superficiality of depth, they know that castration does not take place. The Enlightenment may have been opposed to witch-hunts, but it waged a fierce campaign against midwives – 'sage-femmes' – whose wisdom is represented as prejudice and trickery, as opposed to men's medical science.

We could interpret this sudden eruption of social violence intratextually by examining the location of the remark – between a discussion of incest and one of jealousy. Men are never sterile in Tahiti (and in the *Encyclopédie* we learn from the voice of science that women are far more often infertile than men – of course)[31] – the only male transgressors of the law of reproductive sex are 'sons'; those who are too young and eager. Fathers are generous men – sleeping with their daughters as an act of charity, only if no other man can fertilise them – so says Orou in his account of incest. With respect to jealousy, we learn that it does not exist (and here there is an irresistible intertextual leap to Montaigne's 'On the Cannibals', and the fantasy of wives joyfully offering other women to their husbands – the reverse of Orou's hospitality). The absence of the incest taboo is one of the key elements distinguishing Diderot's Tahiti from a patriarchal economy where men exchange women, but there is a hint here that incest would not mean sons taking their father's women (with a touch of Gallic wit, Orou can gently scoff at the idea of a son preferring his old mother to a fresh young girl . . .), but give fathers a chance to act generously in husbanding a womb as yet infertile.[32] The same father can act hospitably in offering his wife and daughters to his guest, and the intertext gives the reader hope that the wife will reciprocate in procuring some choice partners for her husband. I am trying to suggest that the micro-context of this *esclavage* is rich in patriarchal anxiety and wish-fulfilment, even though the *Supplement* as a whole has some strikingly anti-patriarchal formulations.

Equally we could make another intertextual leap back to Bougainville, who *does* mention that the Tahitians practise slavery. Bougainville's account of Tahiti is temporally double: first we learn what he saw on his visit to Tahiti, which seems close to paradise. Then we are told about what he learns from his conversations with the Tahitian Aotourou on his return to Paris, when Tahiti begins to seem a far more structured and tyrannical society. There are two ways of reading this: one is that the rose-coloured spectacles of wishful ignorance are gradually removed as more detailed information is acquired from the native informant. The second might focus on Bougainville's insistence on the difficulty of communicating with Aotourou, because the two languages (Tahitian and French) are so different – the two peoples do not share the same set of concepts. This *is* a point which Diderot echoes. Aotourou can orientate himself in the streets of Paris, can enjoy opera (a notably passionate form) and can recognise generous people. However, he has problems with conventional intellectual conversation (*esprit?*) – to the extent that the arrogant Parisians think he (and

31 'Sterility more often comes from the woman's side than from the man's' ('Homme' ('Man'), p. 259).
32 Oedipus is safe here. There is an echo of the missing Oedipus in the *Encyclopédie* – a child blinded with a pin (a diminutive phallus). See my Afterword, pp. 184–5.

all Tahitians?) must be stupid. Perhaps he is *bête* like an animal or *infans* like a child – these are the centre's colonising clichés with respect to the other race, the monkey or the cannibal. Thus Bougainville's Paris-based knowledge of Tahitian slavery and inequality of wealth may be as much to do with *translation* as with the failings of his original insight. Montaigne too, we might note, suffers from the inadequacy of translation when he at last comes face to face with his noble savages.

The feminisation of commerce had to be represented as a positive feminisation (a civilisation) as opposed to the dissolute effeminacy of the over-perfumed aristocrat.[33] In the relative democratisation of conspicuous consumption (the enlargement of the domestic market which would have to accompany the expansion overseas) *luxe* must be distinguished from the irrational expenditure of the gambler. The *dépense* of the female body, its generosity in giving and receiving pleasure unbound by the economics of scarcity commonly believed to govern 'normal' male sexuality must be bound up in reproduction.[34] And, of course, the new celebration of the maternal woman (*Vénus féconde* as opposed to *Vénus galante*) enabled a new dynamics of sexual opposition – leaving space for a new masculinity, as femininity is enclosed in fecundity. Diderot's sudden outburst of violence (*esclavage!*) at the notion of post-menopausal women being sexually active evokes the spectre of the sexually predatory aristocrat, liberated by position from the confines of her sex. She prowls at night, stealing men's vital fluids without giving them any return on their investment (their deposit in the sperm bank of her sterile womb). *Dissolute*, indeed. We are reminded of the horrible power of the older woman in so many French novels from the *Liaisons dangereuses* to Sade (to Balzac) – of course she is usually punished for her usurpation.[35]

33 A troublesome figure for those in favour of trade in the eighteenth century was that of credit. Credit was most necessary to fund the various enterprises (particularly those of a colonial nature). And yet *she* is often represented as a whimsical woman, whose fickle fancy might abandon the honest project. (See, for example, *The Spectator* and Pocock, *The Machiavellian Moment*, e.g. pp. 448–57. This was the nightmare of speculation brought home to France by Law. Even in the nineteenth century stock-market speculation is not altogether free of this fantasmatic element, well illustrated in Zola's *Money*.

34 This is the domestication of the monstrous and enigmatic womb figured in the illustrations to the *Encyclopédie*. See Barthes, 'The Plates of the *Encyclopédie*', p. 36.

35 I should stress that I do not wish to generalise with respect to Diderot's many and varied texts. For example, the *Sequel to the Conversation* which follows *D'Alembert's Dream* presents powerful arguments in favour of non-reproductive sex – even if a chain of economic reasoning (and a series of supplements) is a significant feature. Furthermore, the motor force of that dialogue is Mlle de Lespinasse's interest in knowing more about the possibilities of mating between different species – the accepted wisdom is that where there is fruit of such intercourse then it is itself sterile (the example given is the mule). Dr Bordeu and she speculate on the possibility of science overcoming this barrier, and, by selective breeding (eugenics), producing

On a conceptual level, trade assumes equality (and a certain demo-cratisation of material progress), but in the real world of power politics, in the political economy, trade leads to enormous inequalities. By focusing on the slave trade as evil (a contingent aspect of colonial expansion which can be shown to be uneconomic) the *philosophes* can brush over other inequal-ities. Slavery is the sometimes literal, sometimes metaphorical underside of colonial expansion, of the new commercial dream. Diderot stands firm against the slave trade, and yet the term returns to haunt his writing, as if it clings like a shipwreck survivor to the hope of progress. *Esclavage* returns as the punishment for the woman who acts like a man (just at the moment when men are becoming civilised), and *esclavage* reminds us of the difficulty of translation, the projection of the 'other' race as well as the 'other' sex.

a race of centaurs, who would be a wonderful underclass – acting as footmen, for example (no doubt serving all kinds of purposes). Thus unreproductive sex becomes both reproductive and productive.

5

The eighteenth century III: the domestic economy. Rousseau's *La Nouvelle Héloïse* and Scott's *Millenium Hall*

This chapter will focus on eighteenth-century fiction from two angles: the economic and the sexual. There are numerous examples of aristocratic texts, firmly based in *ancien régime* society (whether this is viewed with a critical eye or not), and also numerous examples of 'bourgeois' novels produced by and helping to produce a changing world.[1] For the early modern noble *the world (le monde)* or *society* means a small elite circle of conspicuous consumption such as the gambling potlatch at Versailles.[2] It involves games of amorous conquest and the intellectual battle to *pénétrer* and *fixer* the other.[3] England leads the way in the expansion of the world, with its more closely packed social strata and economic growth, so that more people than ever before have the ability to indulge their desire to spend on fashionable luxury goods. In this chapter I shall, however, focus on two fictions which choose to conjure up a different kind of economy: Rousseau's *Julie, or La Nouvelle Héloïse* (1761) and Sarah Scott's *Millenium Hall* (1762). These novels have a great deal in common with respect to moral framework and tone, but have had radically different histories. Rousseau's best-seller has consistently retained a reputation as an important work, just as Rousseau's canonical (if controversial) status has not diminished since its publication. One of the reasons for reading Rousseau seriously is precisely because of Rousseau-ism.[4] The same cannot be said for Scott, whose works are mostly out of

---

1 Richardson is one obvious example; see Terry Eagleton, *The Rape of Clarissa*, Oxford, Basil Blackwell, 1982.

2 See Thomas Kavanagh, *Enlightenment and the Shadows of Chance*, Baltimore and London, Johns Hopkins University Press, 1993 for an analysis of gambling and the eighteenth-century French novel.

3 See Peter Brooks, *The Novel of Worldliness*, Princeton and London, Princeton University Press, 1969.

4 Derrida emphasises the legacy of Rousseau in *Of Grammatology*, both in general and with regard to Lévi-Strauss. Again, with respect to the gift, he writes: 'We will find a surer guide back to this archaic originarity, which we have left behind or allowed to become perverted, in a non-Marxist socialism, a liberal anti-capitalism or anti-mercantilism. That is the morality or the politics that organizes the structure, even

print. However, *Millenium Hall* has enjoyed an awakening of interest at a moment when archaeological work to rediscover lost women writers is recognised as important, and thus it is probably as much read amongst contemporary undergraduates as *La Nouvelle Héloïse*, now affection for long epistolary novels is on the wane. The coincidence between *Millenium Hall's* woman-centred universe and all-female community and contemporary interests and desires, even the interest in feminine economies, makes it a valuable gift from the past.

First of all I am going to try to set up a framework for distinguishing what I want to call utopian thinking from other kinds of thinking about social organisation. Then I shall turn to *La Nouvelle Héloïse* and finally *Millenium Hall*, to analyse certain passages in the light of the theoretical framework I have set up. I shall differ from a number of other critics who have treated this question in that I shall maintain that in discussing 'other' (or utopian) economies, questions of sexual difference are always at stake.

Utopian elements

Utopias are clearly of interest to my argument in general in so far as they are attempts to rethink questions of inequality in a disjunctive mode. Neither of these texts is a straightforward representation of utopia, but they have certain characteristics which are utopian or which illuminate utopian thinking and are therefore interesting to draw out. According to the Oxford English Dictionary, which refers, of course, to More, a utopia is an imaginary place with a perfect social and political system. Following such a definition, *La Nouvelle Héloïse* is not a utopia. A number of critics have, however, attempted to lay exceptional emphasis on the utopian traits of this novel (and indeed of other works by Rousseau).[5] Quite often there is something at stake in assimilating Rousseau to a utopian tradition, for instance, establishing a 'guilt by association' chain of 'totalitarian' precursors to the twentieth century – a chain of thinkers whose plans for social and

the theoretical *telos* of this essay. As for the formal characteristic of this profound identity between the theoretical and the ethical, we could invoke a Platonic or Aristotelian tradition. However, as for its content, one glimpses rather a Rousseauist schema. This is not only the model that will soon be reclaimed by [. . .] Lévi-Strauss; it is already Mauss's model, even if he does not refer to it as explicitly as Lévi-Strauss does' (*Given Time*, p. 66).

5 One example is James F. Jones, *La Nouvelle Héloïse*, Geneva and Paris, Librairie Droz, 1978. In a review of Jones, Felicity Baker has pointed out how Arcadian characteristics are more dominant in the novel than utopian ones (*Modern Language Review*, 75 (1980), 195–8). She argues that all three meanings (as identified by Panofsky) of Petrarch's *Et in Arcadia ego* are embraced by Rousseau's text: I used to live in Arcady; death is in Arcady also; Arcady may be restored to us in death (p. 198). I would argue that there are also important utopian elements in *La Nouvelle Héloïse*.

political reform appear to involve considerable control over and manipulation of people's lives. I regard these imaginary invocations of other economies positively, rather than as a mark of the totalitarian. One of the reasons for maintaining the term 'utopian' here (with due recognition of the elements which are not utopian) is to make a bridge between Rousseau and recent feminist theorisations of utopia as an enabling and transforming mode of writing. *La Nouvelle Héloïse* is not, it seems to me, complete and fixed, even though there are rhetorical moments when Clarens is said to be the peak of perfection. The seeds of uncertainty and change, the role of amorous passion, make the novel a dynamic experience for the reader in the way that feminists suggest utopias can be.

La Nouvelle Héloïse and *Millenium Hall* are not utopias in so far as in many respects they are firmly rooted in contemporary reality. While most utopias (and dystopias) do admittedly refer indirectly to contemporary reality in some way – if only contrastively – Rousseau explicitly locates his novel in a slightly modified version of eighteenth-century Switzerland and Scott her's in Cornwall. Not only is the geography only slightly modified, but social relations retain many structural features of the period. The aristocratic code of honour has a profound influence on the story of the young lovers in Rousseau's novel – it is an influence which is shown to be morally disastrous, and disaster is only averted by a kind of miracle. Here the novel falls into a more familiar eighteenth-century category of social critique. Scott's novel presents contemporary class relations with a less critical pen (and, in her case, we cannot make the link with an *œuvre* of political theory that we can for Rousseau), although one of the stories within the story of *Millenium Hall*, that of Miss Mancel, is very close to Rousseau in that it shows social pride destroying the happy union of two beings who are clearly well matched.[6]

Even more importantly, Clarens is shown to be not quite utopia in Rousseau's terms, because it is run by waged labour, both within the house and on the land. The key aspect of the economy of the just state, as Rousseau presents it in *The Social Contract*, is that there should be no market in labour.

---

6 The impoverished and parentless Miss Mancel is taken in by a female benefactor whose only fault is her pride. Although she can see that Miss Mancel has every noble virtue, she will not give way to her beloved grandson's desire to marry her. Despite Miss Mancel's love for the grandson, gratitude to Lady Lambton obliges her to fly his presence. In despair, Sir Edward more or less commits suicide in battle – to learn on his death-bed that Miss Mancel has been fortuitously reunited with her mother, and that her new-found wealth and status has prevailed upon his grandmother to agree to the match (*Millenium Hall*, London, Virago, 1986, pp. 86–107). Lady Lambton's pride and inability to recognise true quality has thus lost her both her grandson and the grateful beneficiary whose company she had cherished. Miss Mancel, although heart-broken, has a chance of a new life, joining with her dearest friend, Mrs Morgan, in founding 'Millenium Hall'.

Clarens, with its masters and servants (albeit good masters, beloved and loving servants), is far from the relative equality and freedom of Rousseau's just state. Millenium Hall also has its beloved and loving servants, and master–servant relations have much in common with those prevailing at Clarens – there is even a rustic ball (pp. 113–14) which is highly reminiscent of the *fêtes* at Clarens. One twist on Rousseau is Scott's sympathetic interest in physical disability. The housekeeper at Millenium Hall, who has 'distorted fingers' thanks to a fever, tells us:

> Few of my fellow-servants are better qualified; the cook cannot walk without crutches, the kitchen maid has but one eye, the dairy maid is almost stone deaf, and the housemaid has but one hand; and yet, perhaps, there is no family where the business is better done, for gratitude, and a conviction that this is the only house into which we can be received, makes us exert ourselves·to the utmost; and most people fail not from a deficiency of power, but of inclination. (p. 121)

It is typical of this kind of utopia that all members of society should be, and feel themselves to be, productive members of the economy – that they should work and take pleasure in work. We can distinguish between this and the nascent capitalist exploitation typical of the period in certain details. In the carpet factory set up by the ladies of Millenium Hall to provide employment in the neighbourhood, they pay 'great wages', and 'give more to the children and the aged, in proportion to the work they do, than to those who are more capable' (p. 201). This decision clearly arises more from the criterion of morality than from that of efficiency – which would not permit such cross-subsidisation, and would set a wage at no more than the marginal product of labour. Marx points out that the introduction of those who were previously unemployed into the labour market in a capitalist economy is a means of keeping wages low. There is a significant gap between the competition characteristic of a capitalist economy and the *emulation* encouraged in utopias – although both may be fuelled by human passions.

Both texts do have certain characteristics in common with most representations of utopia, of the perfectly just social system, and these are to be found in their detailed exploration of an economy of abundance via passion, reserve and the gift. Passion functions as a motor force which can be for the good or the bad; reserve is a form of regulation; and the gift, as we have seen, is an example of an interpersonal relation which can be a model for otherly economic relations. All utopias, all attempts at rethinking social and economic existence, have to deal with motivations (passions), regulation, and modalities of interpersonal and political relations.

The term 'utopia' is often used pejoratively both by those who wish to maintain the status quo and by those who wish to change it by 'scientific' revolution. The problem with 'scientific' revolutionary thinking (Marxism) is that it uses the same rational assumptions about human behaviour as does the account and defence of the status quo (capitalism) – a vice which enables its virtue, its ability to reveal the material and ideological violence underpinning the system. In other words, it is highly effective as an analysis of capitalism. But utopian thinking allows for the space of desire.[7] Utopian thinking necessitates a disjuncture with the present – that is one of the reasons (that it shows us another world but does not tell us how to get there) why it has been criticised by scientific socialism. My argument with respect to utopias is that, in discussing other economies, questions of sexual difference are always implicated, even though this may not be made explicit in the text.[8]

Utopias may be either static, regressive Golden Age nostalgia or dynamic projection. The crucial point about dynamic utopias is that they might effect a change in their readers: 'that imagining how things could be different is part of the process of transforming the present in the direction of a different future' (Whitford, *Luce Irigaray*, p. 19). This has been a central element in recent feminist thinking which valorises utopia: 'Utopia is process. It is found in neither past arcadias nor future Elysiums.'[9]

La Nouvelle Héloïse

Rousseau presents economic inequality as an evil, and shows in his *Discourse on Inequality* that it is a difference in wealth which is the fundamental inequality which leads to political and social inequality. In *The Social Contract* he argues that the just state requires relative economic equality. In *La Nouvelle Héloïse* he attempts to show the best possible relations between unequals, that is to say, relations inflected by *beneficence*, which is a certain kind of gift economy overlaying even the market relations between employers and employees at Clarens. Rousseau argues that sexual difference, however, does not signify inequality in any negative sense, that it is necessary, relatively natural and good.[10] But there are a number of tensions in his account

7 Barthes's writing on utopia is of considerable interest here; he points out that utopia is the sphere of desire while politics is the sphere of need, and that this desire is manifested in the fantasmatic imagining of the minutest details of everyday life. See Knight, 'Roland Barthes in Harmony: the writing of Utopia'.

8 It is interesting to juxtapose earlier utopias with certain contemporary strands of utopian thinking. Whitford brings Rousseau into her discussion of feminism and utopia in *Luce Irigaray*, for example, p. 190, pointing out both rhetorical and structural similarities.

9 Elaine Hoffman Baruch in R. Rohrlich, and E. H. Baruch (eds), *Women in Search of Utopia*, New York, Schocken Books, 1984, p. 207, cited by Whitford, p. 19.

10 See my *Justice and Difference in the Works of Rousseau* for an extended treatment of the interrelationship between beneficence (*bienfaisance*) and the code governing sexual difference (*pudeur*) in the works of Rousseau.

– not least a tension between what he prescribes (and what his characters prescribe) and what he, or they, show.

In contrast with a capitalising stress on efficiency, Rousseau privileges questions of equity: he posits a real (natural) abundance, but insists that the individual must be groomed, that moral behaviour must be artificially promoted, in order for social plenty to be achieved. Saint-Preux describes Clarens as follows: 'Everything breathes an air of plenty and propriety; nothing savours of pomp and luxury' (IV, 10, p. 301).[11] *L'abondance* or plenty is a relational term, indicating that supply exceeds demand; later Saint-Preux uses *richesse* in the same sense:

> There is no such thing as absolute wealth [*richesse*]. The word only signifies a relation of superabundance between a rich man's means and his desires. One man is rich with an acre of land; another is poor in the midst of his piles of gold. Disorder and fancy have no limits, and make more men poor than real needs ever do. (V, 2)[12]

Plenty is achieved largely because moral education has repressed desire to accumulate, rather than because efficient production and trade enable the luxurious living celebrated by Voltaire in 'The Man of the World'. Production is efficient at Clarens, but that in itself could never be a guarantee that the inhabitants would experience plenty, since a 'worldly' individual would want more (more exotic and more rare) goods than one estate (or indeed one country) could ever supply.[13] The scarcity of goods is what would give them their price, whereas at Clarens:

> Seeing that necessities are present in such abundance, and that nothing is superfluous, you begin to think that if something is not there it is because it was not wanted, and that if it were wanted then it too would be there in plenty: seeing goods constantly flowing out of the house with the help of the poor, you begin to say: this house is not big enough to hold all its wealth. (V, 2)

11 All page references will be to the abridged edition translated by J. H. McDowell, University Park and London, The Pennsylvania State University Press, 1968. On occasion her translation has been modified. In the paragraph preceding this remark, Saint-Preux remarks that everything at Clarens reminds him of his delightful Isle of Tinian.

12 Almost all of this key letter on the domestic economy of Clarens has been cut from the translation – reinforcing the assumed readerly preference for extra-marital matters of the heart.

13 'When I see that someone has aimed to have a great palace, I ask myself immediately why the palace isn't even larger. Why someone with fifty servants doesn't have a hundred. That fine silverware, why isn't it made of gold? The man who gilds his carriage, why doesn't he gild his panelling? If his panelling is covered with gold, why isn't his ceiling? The man who wanted to build a high tower was right in wanting to raise it to the sky; otherwise there was no point in doing it; the point where he had stopped would only have served to show the proof of his powerlessness at a greater distance.' (V, 2) And again, Saint-Preux comments with respect to Clarens: 'Add braid, paintings, a chandelier, gold, you would instantly impoverish everything.'

It has been suggested that the scarcity (market) model is a masculine one, arising from a fantasised paternal body, and the abundance (gift)
model is a feminine one, arising from a fantasised maternal body. I should
like briefly to reintroduce the terms 'masculine economy' and 'feminine
economy' taken from Cixous; I shall be returning to these at greater length
in my final chapter. Cixous deploys a problematic (as she is very ready to
acknowledge) gendered vocabulary to oppose what I have been calling
market economy practices and thinking to a gift-based 'feminine economy'.
She writes, for example:

> What does he want in return – the traditional man? And she? First of all,
> what *he* wants, whether on the level of cultural or of personal exchanges,
> whether it is a question of capital or of affectivity (or of love, of *jouissance*) –
> is that he gain supplementary masculinity: surplus-value of virility, authority,
> power, money or pleasure, all of which reenforce his phallocentric narcissism
> at the same time [. . .]
>
> How does she give? What are her dealings with saving and squandering,
> reserve, life, death? She too gives *for*. She too, in giving, gives herself –
> pleasure, happiness, increased value, enhanced self-image. But she doesn't
> try to 'recover her expenses'. She is able not to return to herself, never
> settling down, pouring out, going everywhere to the other [. . .]
>
> If there is a self proper to woman, paradoxically it is her capacity to
> disappropriate herself without self-interest.[14]

The first ('traditional man') is an economy of scarcity (driven by the profit
motive) and the second one ('she') of abundance (in which supply anticipates and exceeds demand). The principle of scarcity lies behind most economic thinking (classical, neoclassical, Marxist . . .) and indeed its extension
into interpersonal and even intrapsychic domains. The price mechanism
relies on relative scarcity. As Adam Smith points out with the famous water
and diamonds paradox, exchange value is not a function of use value alone,
but of scarcity. Scarcity, I should perhaps note, is often a figure for the costs
of production or the labour/capital required to produce a commodity. The
assumption of scarcity underpins the principles of rational economic behaviour. Economic thinking finds it very difficult to cope with a feminine
economy of abundance – which is frequently relegated to utopian discourse.
Contemporary theorisations of feminine economies – with their primary
focus on the interpersonal and intrapsychic rather than financial domains –
more readily suggest that abundance can be achieved by expanding supply
(of love, say), rather than controlling demand. The feminine economy is

14 *The Newly Born Woman*, trans. B. Wing, Manchester, Manchester University Press,
1986, p. .87, translation modified. See 'voice i . . .', *On Feminine Writing: A Boundary 2
Symposium*, ed. V. A. Conley and W. V. Spanos, *Boundary 2*, 12 (2) (1984), 51–67, for
an expression of Cixous's dissatisfaction with the sexed vocabulary which she nevertheless continues to use – albeit in a complex and slippery manner.

not a universalising principle (unlike the masculine economy) – it would exist in particular relations, although it could not be bounded by them, since it would be antithetical to limitation, property or propriety. Irigaray asks whether it is utopian to imagine 'a certain economy of abundance' in which:

> Use and exchange would be indistinguishable. The greatest value would be at the same time the least kept in reserve. Nature's resources would be expended without depletion, exchanged without labour, freely given, exempt from masculine transactions: enjoyment without a fee, well-being without pain, pleasure without possession. As for all the strategies and savings, the appropriations tantamount to theft and rape, the laborious accumulation of capital, how ironic all that would be. ('Commodities among Themselves', in *This Sex Which Is Not One*, p. 197)

For eighteenth-century and earlier thinkers who 'utopianly' privilege an economy of abundance, expansion of supply is usually associated with reduction of the desires which underpin subjective demand. Expansion of supply (say of foodstuffs) is often assumed as well because, as Thomas More makes explicit in his *Utopia*, a greater proportion of the population would be engaged in productive labour than in the writer's own society. When Julie and Wolmar contemplate their children's inheritance they have no desire to increase it in case of unforeseen problems ahead, for 'does not each person's labour supplement their share, and should not their industriousness enter into the calculation of their property?' (V, 2) However, even more importantly, desire for luxury, for more than your fellows, would be reduced by moral education, and thus a society in which only simple goods are available may be experienced as an economy of abundance if the members desire nothing more – the situation on which Voltaire pours scorn in 'The Man of the World'.

In Rousseau's writing there is a tension between his celebration of a certain feminine abundance and his fear of, and desire to contain, it. Rousseau makes periodic attempts in his assertions with respect to sexual difference to enclose woman (the model of abundance), making women the guardians of a fictional scarcity or making them pretend to be less generous than they really are.[15] This supply-side control is different from the moral education which leads men to restrict their desires relative to what they can realistically hope to attain. The difference is illustrated in *Emile*, in which the first four books are concerned with man's education for freedom – not economic freedom in Voltaire's or Adam Smith's free marketeers' sense,

15 The two major locations for these attempts are the *Letter to d'Alembert* and the fifth book of *Emile*. A number of commentators have remarked on Rousseau's wish to enclose women or hold them 'in reserve', for example, Derrida, in *Of Grammatology*; Sarah Kofman, in *Le Respect des femmes*, Paris, Galilée, 1982; Joel Schwartz, in *The Sexual Politics of Jean-Jacques Rousseau*, Chicago, The University of Chicago Press, 1984.

but freedom derived from an accepting of moral and social law. The fifth book, 'Sophie', and the unfinished sequel, 'Emile and Sophie', show woman brought to feel pleasure in the restrictions placed upon her. Likewise Julie, unlike most wives (Saint-Preux informs us), enjoys 'la retraite'; it is a sign of her virtue to 'enjoy being in the bosom of [her] family and shut herself away there of her own free will' (V, 2).

Market transactions are often referred to by the term 'commerce', which is something of a pressure point in Rousseau's thinking, and has both economic and sexual connotations. Economic commerce or the market is regarded negatively by Rousseau – in *La Nouvelle Héloïse*, apart from Clarens, he gives us an Arcadian image of the society of the Haut Valais, which is a largely self-sufficent, gift economy epitomised by its hospitality. But while the term 'commerce' in a sexual context is usually pejorative (*vil commerce*),[16] Rousseau's ideal of sexual relations is non-marketed and yet conducted on market principles of scarcity. And in the Haut Valais, as Saint-Preux relates with some embarrassment, women wait on their menfolk at table – enacting the master–servant inequality which I would argue (*contra* Rousseau's explicit statements) is inseparable from the absolute sexual difference of the Valais which he celebrates. It is typical that Rousseau will *show* what runs counter to the story he *wants to tell*.

In the case of Rousseau sexual difference enters the scene of otherly economic thinking in two ways. The first is that Rousseau appears to posit absolute and inflexible sexual difference (and hence, I would argue, built-in inequality) as a goal, whereas in general he presents dynamic and ultimately egalitarian relations as a goal. The second is that when he describes the role of women, where sexual difference is fixed, that role is one of reserve or *pudeur* (pudicity) – which contrasts with the generous, passionate expansiveness which motivates generosity. However, neither of these two positions is stable, as I hope to show through analysis of the text. Sexed traits float or slip from one sex to the other as the narrative progresses.[17] And, we might comment, reserve or regulation of passion should be combined with passionate expansion within one human subject – the attempt to segregate these roles along sexual lines cannot succeed.

Apart from these two conceptual crossings, there is a tendency for Rousseau's (or Saint-Preux's) writing to wander from the economic to the

16 The alliance of sex and commerce is usually taken as pejorative – although for antithetical reasons – either because sex is regarded as dirty relative to other kinds of commerce or because commerce is presumed to sully the purity of amorous sexual congress.

17 Rousseau's elaboration of a desired androgyny has been noted by a number of critics, for example Patrick Wald Lasowski in *Libertines*, Paris, Gallimard, 1980 or Robert J. Ellrich in 'Rousseau's Androgynous Dream', *French Forum*, 13 (1988), 319–38. Ellrich analyses some of Rousseau's minor fictions written within the decade around the composition of *La Nouvelle Héloïse*.

sexual in an errant, if not aberrant, fashion. One example is a section in Part V, Letter 2, where Saint-Preux has been describing the domestic economy of M. and Mme. de Wolmar to Edouard. Saint-Preux explains that despite her modest household budget, Julie delights in providing pleasure for her nearest and dearest. Gradually Saint-Preux's language hints at the (good) erotic as he repeats the term *plaisirs* without specifying the pleasures, and tells his reader: 'in her house you find the luxury of pleasures for the mind and the senses without sophistication or laxness'. To make a contrast with Julie's good pleasure of the senses, he slips metonymically from carriages with comfortable suspension (of which Julie approves) to carriages which are finely decorated, and then – rather surprisingly – to carriages decorated with obscene paintings. This bad erotic of the city becomes confused with the pleasures of Clarens, as Saint-Preux describes to his male friend his discussion of these obscene pictures with the virtuous Julie, telling him how he told her that it is women who outdo men in the lasciviousness of their decoration. This 'commerce' of conversation and of letters turns into pleasure even the actions of rich women who prefer to resemble prostitutes rather than the middle classes. Such a transformation is not untypical of *La Nouvelle Héloïse*. It remains, however, that the carriages with lewd decoration are almost an 'ungrammaticality' in the midst of the account of the domestic economy of Clarens.

There are two major aspects to *La Nouvelle Héloïse*: a love-story (Julie falls in love with her poor tutor, whose pseudonym will be Saint-Preux; they become secret lovers, but her aristocratic father forces her to marry his friend Wolmar), and an account of harmonious domestic existence (the descriptions of the Wolmar family life in their home, Clarens). The love-story appeals to many readers; the account of domestic harmony is often received more ambiguously.[18] For readers who identify strongly with a certain romantic myth it is inappropriate to devote so many pages to the details of the Wolmars' domestic economy: it is boring; how can Julie be happy when Wolmar was forced upon her? How can Wolmar invite his wife's former lover to live with them? How can Saint-Preux accept? Wolmar is sometimes turned by readers into a baddy in another sense, not just an old and cold unwanted spouse (compared to the hot young lover), but a manipulative, power-crazed totalitarian. This applies to his attempts, with Julie, to construct social harmony on their estate (relations with employees, for example) and to his attempts to remodel Julie's relationship with Saint-Preux so that love in the past becomes affection in the present.[19] I would

18 The moral themes were always, however, an integral part of the love-story for Rousseau; see Christopher Frayling, 'The Composition of *La Nouvelle Héloïse*', in *Reappraisals of Rousseau*, Manchester, Manchester University Press, 1980, pp. 181–214.

19 See Felicity Baker, 'La Scène du lac dans *La Nouvelle Héloïse*', *Le Préromantisme hypothèque ou hypothèse?*, Colloque de Clermont-Ferrand, 29–30 juin 1972, Actes et Colloques, 18, 129–52.

argue that the novel must be seen as a whole, and that one of the unifying features is that of the relationship between the guiding moral code of bene-ficence and amorous passion. It is in the vicissitudes of that relationship that we can see the strains in Rousseau's thinking.

Why is the novel so often misunderstood, as I would claim it is? Rousseau's repeated strategy is to make an absolute assertion (say, with respect to sexual difference) and then disturb it by other assertions almost immediately; both micro-context and macro-context (that is, the context of the body of Rousseau's works) rarely leave absolute oppositions undisturbed. But readers, caught up in a transferential relationship, projecting their own anxious desires on to the letters of the text, frequently pick out maxims to quote them in support of a position which does not hold in context. This keen excision can enable powerful readings which have their own interest as constructs, but disfigure Rousseau's more nuanced and complicated posi-tion. Fiction in general invites the reader's (counter-)transference, invites a filling of the gaps with material from the passionate text of the reader's history.[20] Paul de Man has suggested that 'Any book with a readable title page is, to some extent, autobiographical';[21] Peggy Kamuf glosses this as a placing of autobiography *between* writer and reader, writing and reading'.[22] *La Nouvelle Héloïse* in particular has aroused extraordinary identifications, enactments and projections – readers have fallen madly in love with author and/or characters as well as violently accusing them of fascist, or at least totalitarian, tendencies![23] In *La Nouvelle Héloïse* Rousseau presents a situ-ation in which 'teaching is not a purely cognitive, informative experience, it is also an emotional, erotic experience' (Felman, *Jacques Lacan*, p. 86) – Saint-Preux, a disciple of Plato, is not only shown to be Julie's teacher, but, more importantly, her pupil. Julie teaches (and learns from) a number of characters in the novel; her teaching is invariably suffused with loving.

20 See Shoshana Felman, *Jacques Lacan and the Adventure of Insight*, Cambridge, Mass. and London, Harvard University Press, 1987, chapter 4, 'Psychoanalysis and Education: Teaching Terminable and Interminable', for an account of the dynamics of trans-ference where knowledge and authority are at stake. Jacques Lacan asserts that 'The transference is an essential phenomenon, bound up with desire as the nodal phenom-enon of the human being – and it was discovered long before Freud. It was perfectly articulated [. . .] in a text in which the subject of love is discussed, namely, Plato's *Symposium* [. . .] As soon as the subject supposed to know exists somewhere [. . .] there is transference' (*The Four Fundamental Concepts*, trans. A. Sheridan, Harmondsworth, Penguin, 1977, pp. 231–2).

21 'Autobiography as De-facement', in his *The Rhetoric of Romanticism*, New York, Columbia University Press, 1984, p. 70.

22 *Signature Pieces*, Ithaca, NY and London, Cornell University Press, 1988, p. 124. Kamuf relates this to her work on *La Nouvelle Héloïse* in her *Fictions of Feminine Desire: Disclos-ures of Héloïse*, Lincoln, Neb., University of Nebraska Press, 1982.

23 Two examples of critics who find a disturbing totalitarian strain in *La Nouvelle Héloïse* are Jones, *La Nouvelle Héloïse* and Lester G. Crocker, *Jean-Jacques Rousseau*, New York, Macmillan, 1968–73.

Rousseau is often understood by his readers as a figure of authority, a subject supposed to know, someone to whom they can confess, a teacher and a lover. While this can have a positive dynamic, it can also (like analysis) degenerate into an enactment of conflict which is to some extent unwarranted by the actual situation of reading Rousseau's work.

A less extreme example (and I have chosen it for analysis because I respect the work as a whole) is Marc Eigeldinger's thesis that *La Nouvelle Héloïse* clearly privileges spiritual love over carnal love, that Rousseau unambiguously preaches the transcendence of the senses with his Empyrean or Elysean mythology.[24] Eigeldinger finds a number of convincing quotations; for example, Julie's line that 'true love is the most chaste of all bonds' (I, 50, p. 115). This can be read as a Platonic assertion that true love is chaste in the sense of being only spiritual and beyond the body. The microcontext is that our would-be virtuous young heroine, in a state of some sensitivity concerning her moral status, having recently lost her virginity to her social inferior, Saint-Preux, has just endured an evening in which he got drunk and spoke to her in what she considers to be a crude and offensive manner. Unsurprisingly, she wants to be reassured that he still respects her, and that he is not subconsciously regarding her as a 'fallen woman' – a view which seems to slip out when he has had too much to drink. She tells him that 'The heart does not follow, but guides the senses. It throws a delightful veil over their frenzies. No, the only possible obscenity lies in debauchery and its coarse language' (p. 115). This seems to me to be making a distinction between two kinds of sex (regulated and deregulated), rather than between spiritual and carnal love. Good sex which is part of a relatively durable pleasure needs regulation, spacing and disguise. Debauchery or unregulated indulgence will soon bring about disgust and cynicism. Here we can refer to a macro-context of Rousseau's general economy of pleasure, and to the many specific instances of this, such as Emile's tutor's advice to Sophie on the eve of her wedding to Emile, that she should regulate his sexual access to her to prevent early satiation and boredom. Although the virtuous man should be able to be moderate in his pleasures in order to increase his pleasure (as Rousseau attempted to put into practice with respect to his passion for coffee), it is frequently women who are allotted the task of control, and, realistically, in eighteenth-century society women have more to lose – Julie has been trained from an early age in such worldly wisdom.

Moving on from my debate with Eigeldinger, what is the conceptual difference between women's role with respect to sex and Rousseau's Epicurean control of his coffee habit?[25] In both cases we have relative natural

24 *Jean-Jacques Rousseau*, Neuchâtel, Editions de la Baconnière, 1978.
25 For Julie and 'l'art de jouir' as moderation or spacing see V, 2, pp. 541–2; for moderation with respect to coffee, see p. 552.

abundance: supply exceeds the ability to demand (to continue desiring). If he deprived himself of other goods, Rousseau could procure enough coffee to become addicted to and bored with it; he subscribes to the view wherein women have an almost endless capacity for sexual activity and can therefore supply sexual pleasure to men to the point at which men would die of exhaustion. But in the case of coffee it is the demander who voluntarily restricts his own consumption (thanks to his moral education) – and this is Rousseau's notion of moral liberty. In the case of sex, more classic economic thinking appears to prevail: suppliers restrict supply in order to increase the price. And a fixed sexual difference has been set up: women supply sex and men demand it, and the feminine pole is one of reserve.[26] This fixity cannot and does not work.

Both Julie and Saint-Preux (and Rousseau) make assertions with repect to absolute difference between the sexes – which are swiftly shown to be far from absolute. Julie's famous outburst to Saint-Preux on this subject (I, 46) is in the context that in his last letter he has teased her for being 'just like a woman' (in caring for inessentials); she responds: 'I'm proud that I'm like a woman', and 'I'm glad that I'm not like you/a man.' A couple of sentences later she demonstrates that the position which he was teasing her for adopting is identical to his own[27] . . . which fits in with their constant dream that they are utterly alike in thoughts, tastes, and so on. When a difference between them is revealed, it is usually that Julie is more sensible, more thoughtful, wiser – Saint-Preux is impetuous, over-emotional, subject to irrational fears. While that opposition could fit with certain stereotypes of sexual difference (women as wise and practical mothers, men as romantic children – and therefore poetic geniuses), it does not fit with other figures and relations in the novel, for instance, the cool and rational Wolmar and his almost paternal relation to his wife, Julie.

When, in letter 10 of part IV, Saint-Preux tells Edouard that sexual segregation is rightly the economic order of the day at Clarens, he presents a natural sexual difference in tastes as evidence: 'milk products and sugar are naturally preferred by the fair sex – they are like a symbol of the innocence and sweetness which are its loveliest ornament'. However, this is in the context that Saint-Preux himself has just eaten an enormous feminine meal of milk products and wafers, and the editor (Rousseau) has inserted an informative note defining 'des grus, de la céracée' as 'delicious milk

26 One of Rousseau's models of reserve is his Lucrèce (the Roman Lucretia, who was raped by Sextus Tarquinius); see my 'Lucretia's Silent Rhetoric', *The Oxford Literary Review*, 6 (1984), 70–86. Ellrich points out that her language is that of Rousseau when he withdraws from the world, resisting the argument of friends (particularly Diderot) who want him to 'prostitute' himself ('Rousseau's Androgynous Dream', p. 328).

27 'You reproach me for a mistake that I have not committed or that you commit as well as I' (I, 46, p. 108).

products', the 'delicious [*excellents*]' reminding those of us who have read his
Confessions of Rousseau's passion for milk products of all kinds. Saint-Preux
continues to confuse the issue by meditating on the different tastes of different nations, in which cause and effect of behaviour and diet oscillate, as
French social promiscuity causes women to lose their taste for milk and
men theirs for wine (behaviour causes a change in diet), while the Italian
diet causes a general effeminacy and softness (diet causes altered behaviour). (Edouard will learn, against these amazing generalisations, that not all
Italian women are effeminate and soft.) Julie's near-vegetarian diet – so
typically feminine – is modelled on Rousseau's own.

I should now like to shift focus from Rousseau's explicit modelling of
the economy of sexual difference in *La Nouvelle Héloïse* back to his account
of the managed economy of the Clarens estate. Saint-Preux describes the
method of M. and Mme de Wolmar as follows:

> Their maxim is to produce as much as they can from working the land, not
> to increase their profits, but to be able to feed more people. M. de Wolmar
> claims that the land yields in proportion to the number of hands which work
> on it; the better it is worked the more it yields; that excess produce enables
> you to work it more and better; the more men and cattle you put on it, the
> more surplus it provides to keep them. You don't know, he says, where this
> continuous and mutual increase of produce and workers will stop. On the
> contrary, neglected land loses its fertility [. . .] in any country where there is
> depopulation sooner or later people will be dying of starvation. (IV, 10)

As in More's *Utopia*, there is an emphasis on industry – on the need for
everyone to work. There is also, as a result, the crucial situation of abundance: supply exceeds demand both because so many people are engaged in
production, and because their industriousness is part of their moral liberty,
which means that they do not consume excessively, nor do they desire to
accumulate beyond their consumption needs. What is produced is consumed,
no profit is made: 'on ne travaille que pour jouir' ('We work only to enjoy
ourselves') (IV, 10, p. 304), and the community is largely self-sufficient (in
a somewhat utopian, in the sense of 'idealised', way).[28] Wolmar is here
preaching the doctrine of Increasing Returns to Scale.[29]

The issue of sexual difference underlies this economy in a fundamental way. It is not simply that Rousseau prescribes separate spheres (and
then permits Saint-Preux's tantalising, even titillating, peeks into the feminine domain), but that sexual difference is an essential part of the test, the

---

28 In Part V, Letter 2, Saint-Preux explains that Julie and Wolmar want to maintain,
rather than increase, their property, since they consider that they have enough to
meet their needs and those of their children, assuming that these children should not
live a life of idleness: 'the only treasure which they wish to add to their inheritance
is that of their example'.

29 See chapter six on *The Social Contract*.

standard, by which any society should be judged. For, according to Rousseau, absolute sexual difference is necessary for healthy reproduction. *The Social Contract* teaches us that the just state is one which enjoys population growth. And yet *La Nouvelle Héloïse* is remarkable for the way in which so many of its characters refuse to reproduce, in spite (or perhaps because) of the high value placed on the family.[30] Saint-Preux, Edouard and Laure all vow that they will never marry; Claire, as a young widow, refuses to remarry. Seven adults (Julie, Saint-Preux, Wolmar, Edouard, Laure, Claire, M. d'Orbe) produce three children between them. Furthermore, moral bonds are privileged over those of biology, friendship and tutelage over parenthood. Saint-Preux, and not their blood father, Wolmar, will be tutor to Julie's children.

At Clarens, servants are carefully chosen and 'formed'; they are paid the going rate plus bonuses for length of service and for excellent work. The relation between masters and servants, which is figured in terms of parents and children, is judged offensive (to egalitarian sensibilities) by some readers. The *forming* of servants can be read as training in servanthood or it can be seen as a process of moral (and physical) education. It is important to note that parent–child terminology is not a direct reference to the blood-tie, but rather to the code of beneficence and hence to moral education: 'Mme de Wolmar does not believe that money is sufficient to repay the effort someone has made on her behalf, she considers that she owes a service to someone who has done one for her.' Thus beneficence supplements the waged relationship. And the factor which is paramount for Rousseau is the *intention* or affective charge.

In Part V, letter 7, Saint-Preux describes the grape-harvest; work becomes *fête*. Masters work and play alongside waged employees:

> How delightful to see such good and wise managers make working the land the instrument of their beneficence, their amusement, their enjoyment, dispensing the gifts of providence with both hands; using the goods overflowing from their barns, their cellars, their attics to feed up all who surround them – men and beasts; accumulating abundance and joy around them, and making the work which enriches them into a continual festivity.

La fête des vendanges entails temporary equality between master and servant; Jean Starobinski comments: 'The festival expresses, in the "existential" realm of emotion, what the *Social Contract* formulates in the theoretical realm of

---

30 Of course, this could be turned around – it could be claimed that it is androgyny, which is quite marked for instance in the representation of Saint-Preux, which is implicated in the failure to reproduce. Ellrich suggests that for Rousseau androgyny is guilt-inducing and linked to sterility, citing *Narcisse* as an example ('Rousseau's Androgynous Dream', p. 325). However, I would argue that Rousseau's androgyny is creative in a number of different ways, *and* that the fantasy of absolute sexual difference and sexual fertility is quite simply unsustainable, even on the level of Rousseau's representations.

law.'[31] There is equality of being, if not of having (whereas in *The Social Contract* there is both): 'each person is "alienated" in the gaze of others, and each is restored to himself by means of universal "recognition"' (p. 97). The communality of the *fête* also relates intertextually to *Utopia* – not only the sharing of food, but also the emphasis on the public and visible rather than the private and secret. *La Nouvelle Héloïse*'s rootedness in eighteenth-century society means that, unlike *Utopia*, private property is the order of the day – although not amongst the elect (Julie, Wolmar, Claire, Saint-Preux, Edouard and the children), who have a certain structural resemblance to the top tier in Plato's *Republic*, the Guardians. But in any case, as Starobinski shows, on the level of *être* there is transparency.

Starobinski also points out, however, that the masters have the choice whether or not to descend to the level of their employees, whereas the hired helps cannot choose to rise to the level of their masters. Rousseau does have Saint-Preux make such a comment, and Wolmar, in describing his past adventures, remarks that it is easy for someone who is well born to try out inferior situations. On the one hand, Rousseau is being realistic about contemporary conditions (who pays whom). On the other hand, while Saint-Preux states that the servants cannot choose to treat their masters as equals – in the sense of behaving *badly* or intrusively – he also says that the moral environment at Clarens is such that the servants are enabled to behave *as well as* their masters – virtuously, beneficently, and so on (IV, 10).

In *La Nouvelle Héloïse* certain factors are deliberately made to relate to contemporary reality: Julie's father acts according to the outdated, but still powerful, aristocratic code of honour, and prevents Julie from marrying the commoner, Saint-Preux. The Wolmar family do have servants – although we could refer to them as waged employees under enlightened management. Alongside these inegalitarian features, the entire novel is concerned with the question of benign moral influence. Emblematically, when Julie and Saint-Preux are lovers, they miss a rare chance of a private rendezvous, in order to help another young couple in trouble. Saint-Preux attempts to buy the young man's release from the army; his money is refused, but the release is granted the next morning in exchange for his beneficent *intention*. Once Julie is married, she and Wolmar become engaged in a variety of different kinds of beneficence – to passing beggars, to people living in their locality, to employees, to family and intimate friends.

The passionate source of Julie's beneficence is pity – and yet it is also pity which 'lost' her (made her lose her virginity to Saint-Preux). In Rousseau's strict code governing feminine behaviour (indeed, identity), expansive movement out towards others has to be constantly checked and

---

31 *Jean-Jacques Rousseau: Transparency and Obstruction*, trans. A. Goldhammer, Chicago, University of Chicago Press, 1988, p. 96.

contained. In general, passion has to be regulated by all human subjects (this is Rousseau's definition of moral liberty), and the positive virtue of beneficence must always be subordinated to the negative duty of justice, i.e. to universal considerations – this is why employees (like any other moral beings) must not 'generously' turn a blind eye to others' misdemeanours if these are likely to harm a third party. However, there is a significant difference between the reserve which women are told they should adopt and the reserve of men.

The significant male characters in the novel (Wolmar, Saint-Preux, Edouard) love and lose and live on as virtuous men. But their virtue is shown to be founded on the immolation of the women they love. Edouard is helped by Saint-Preux to free himself from the love of the wicked Marquise (who is dead by the end of the novel) by turning to love the former prostitute Laure (V, 12). As, by the social standards of the day, she would be a most unsuitable wife for an aristocrat, Saint-Preux – encouraged by Wolmar – repays Edouard for his benefactions by persuading the unhappy Laure to take the veil (a living death, as Rousseau tends to present it). Laure's return to virtue is demonstrated in that 'her constitution will make her enjoy her sacrifice more than the rank which she must refuse' (p. 373). Edouard comments that he will now devote his life to friendship.

In many ways Laure resembles Julie – a proximity which Julie (alone) has the generosity to acknowledge (V, 13). Julie dies *apparently* a martyr to maternal love, but sees her death as a saving grace, since she could not bear the strain of her husband Wolmar inviting her lover Saint-Preux to live with them. She writes in her death-bed letter to Saint-Preux: 'We dreamed of rejoining each other. That reunion was not good. It is Heaven's blessing to have prevented it, thereby, without a doubt, preventing misfortune' (VI, 12, p. 405). She was indeed the one who would have had to bear the strain, the tension between the passion Wolmar wants her to show (hospitality, friendship, beneficence are all forms of passionate expansion) and the reserve expected of her as wife and mother (not tempting Saint-Preux). Already in Part IV, Letter 16, Julie had written to Wolmar 'you sport cruelly [*vous jouissez durement*] with your wife's virtue' (p. 332). The transparency of *fête* cannot be reconciled with *pudeur*.

It is in the immolation of Laure and Julie that Rousseau reveals a strain in his utopian underpinnings. Is the answer to be more utopian still? Contemporary feminist theorisations of utopia emphasise that utopias should not be static, but rather in process. In Part IV, Letter 11, Wolmar repeats Julie's death-bed words: 'Is man made for permanency? No, when you have gained everything you must lose something; if only the pleasure in possession which wears itself out.' The readerly transference could be said to effect a change in the reader – and while some readers hate the experience, others love it. I would argue that a gift economy is shown not to hold up

where absolute sexual difference is supposed to be sustained. The characteristics normatively attached to each sex are those which have a long
history of being so attached; for example, men should be rational, while
women are more emotional. Thus Rousseau's masculine models (Wolmar,
the legislator and the tutor) seem to be no more than rational thinkers and
planners, while Julie is often read as all love (loving and beloved). And yet
this polar opposition (the conceptual equivalent of the physical segregation
of the sexes preached in the *Letter to d'Alembert*) does not quite fit the representations Rousseau constructs. *La Nouvelle Héloïse* mingles masculine and
feminine forms, treatise and love-story (which are separated in *Emile*).[32]
Masculine and feminine traits are not clearly located in male and female
characters. Furthermore, Rousseau's preferred response to the economic
inequality which so disturbed him – beneficence – is itself an androgynous
combination of reason and passion. Rousseau's beneficence is not rational
market calculation (the masculine economy), but neither is it unthought
superabundant generosity (the polar extreme of the feminine economy). It
is an attempt to combine rational regulation with passionate expansion in
the human subject: in the benefactor and in the beneficiary. Rather than
adopting Rousseauian man as the utopian model for men and women (one
liberal strategy when reading, say, the first four books of *Emile*), I would
argue that traits attributed to each sex should be held in play for both
sexes[33] – as they are to some extent in *La Nouvelle Héloïse contra* some of
the explicit statements. In other words, the economy of abundance could
only be sustained by passion and reserve, eros and thanatos, shown by all.
What Rousseau describes is thus to be treated as at least as important as
what he prescribes.

Millenium Hall

Like *La Nouvelle Héloïse, Millenium Hall* combines utopian elements with
an adherence to much which relates to contemporary material reality –
including class structures.[34] *Millenium Hall* differs sharply from *La Nouvelle*

32 See my 'From the Philosophy of Man to the Fiction of Woman: Rousseau's *Emile*',
   Romance Studies, 18 (1991), 75–87.
33 I would like to relate this to the structure of bisexuality which Cixous describes in
   The Newly Born Woman, not the 'fantasy of a complete being, which replaces the fear
   of castration' (p. 84) but 'the location within oneself of the presence of both sexes,
   evident and insistent in different ways according to the individual, the nonexclusion
   of difference or of a sex, and starting with this "permission" one gives oneself, the
   multiplication of the effects of desire's inscription on every part of the body and the
   other body' (p. 85).
34 It is likely that Scott did not hold such radical political and economic views as Rousseau,
   and was unworried by the institution of wage labour. While Saint-Preux follows his
   creator in proclaiming that any master–servant relationship is unnatural, Scott's narrator only echoes these words (in a 'prequel' episode in a later novel, *The History of*

Héloïse in the history of its reception. Published just a year or two after *La Nouvelle Héloïse*, this novel of ideas did not arouse such passions, but was moderately popular, and had gone through four editions by 1778.[35] However, unlike the other texts on which I have focused so far, *Millenium Hall* did not become part of the canon – in common with the vast majority of writing by women of the early modern period. It has aroused a little interest over the last few decades as the great archaeological work of rediscovering some of our lost Mothers has gradually been undertaken – and it could yet replace *La Nouvelle Héloïse* on the syllabus, if not in the canon. Recent readers have tended either to celebrate the utopian elements of the novel or critique what are perceived as more conservative (and anti-utopian) elements.[36] In *The Progress of Romance* (1785), Clara Reeve commends *Millenium Hall* as suitable reading for young persons – apparently because it preaches the particularly female virtues of self-abnegation, dedication to chastity and so on (see Spencer's introduction, pp. x–xi). However, this detail alone would seriously misrepresent what I would claim to be the radical force of this extraordinary novel. First of all, like *La Nouvelle Héloïse* the novel is a mixture of beneficence with touches of a more utopian economy of abundance. Second, and unlike Rousseau's Clarens (or Diderot's

Sir George Ellison, London, A. Millar, 1766) when referring to the institution of slavery. Mr Ellison (the narrator of *Millenium Hall*) finds himself a slave-owner as a result of his first marriage: 'perhaps few have more severely lamented their being enslaved by marriage than he did his being thus become the enslaver of others' (p. 18). He insists (to his Jamaican planter wife's fury and scorn) that 'the present difference is merely adventitious, not natural', and devotes most of his married life to improving the lot of his slaves (and, by example, that of many on the island). According to Mr Ellison (here in agreement with Rousseau), slavery is introduced 'at the expense of humanity; the master becomes a tyrant, for human nature always abuses a power which it has no right to exert; and the slave's mind being as heavily fettered as his body, he grows sordid and abject' (p. 37). Where Ellison's attitude differs from Rousseau's is in his contrast between Jamaica and England, which he represents as 'conspicuously generous, frank and merciful, because it is free; no subordination exists there, but what is for the benefit of the lower as well as the higher ranks; all live in a state of reciprocal services, the great and the poor are linked in compact' (p. 38). It is difficult to know Scott's own views here – while the lengthy passages on slavery suggest that she did indeed hold it in abhorrence, *Millenium Hall* is a little less optimistic about the freedom of England.

35 See Jane Spencer's introduction to the Virago edition, 1986, p. viii. Much of the information in this introduction is also to be found in Walter M. Crittenden's introduction to the novel, New York, Bookman Associates, 1955 – but I refer to the later edition as it is more readily available.

36 In the dozen or so articles which I have discovered relating to *Millenium Hall* there seems little inclination to perceive utopias as inherently repressive, as has been the case in some work on *La Nouvelle Héloïse*. I suspect that that may relate to traditional and recent feminist revalorisations of utopian writing, since unsurprisingly, unlike much of what is written on *La Nouvelle Héloïse*, work on Scott tends to come from an explicitly feminist subject postion.

Tahiti), Millenium Hall is an exemplary all-female community. In some ways it is a literary response to Mary Astell's *A Serious Proposal to the Ladies for the Advancement of their True and Greatest Interest* (3rd corrected edn, 1696), which proposes the setting up of communities, like secular convents dedicated to education, for unmarried gentlewomen. This is radical enough in its assertion of the pleasures of the single condition for women. However, in *Millenium Hall* women's sexual reserve combined with economic expansiveness is also a model for the world, as the frame of Mr Ellison's letter makes clear.[37] In a later novel, indeed, Mr Ellison is shown putting into practice some of what he learnt at Millenium Hall. This is presented as completely in accordance with the teachings of religion – and yet, dominant British religious doctrine asserts that woman's salvation lies in her role as wife and mother.[38] Peter Earle quotes Defoe's Roxana (in the slippery text of the same name) to illustrate the general point that marriage could in fact mean 'giving up liberty, estate, authority, and everything, to the man, and the woman was indeed a mere woman ever after, that is to say, a slave' (Earle, *The Making of the English Middle Class*, p. 158). Scott illustrates this fate in the story of Mrs Morgan, who is not even allowed to entertain her dearest friend Miss Mancel once she is married. She thus does not underestimate material power, although she does emphasise the potential power of a wife's influence, particularly when the wife is superior in understanding to the husband, as is the case with Mrs Morgan herself, her mother and her stepmother. (Indeed it is hard to find a male character in *Millenium Hall* who is not outshone by women he encounters for better or for worse.) I shall first consider Scott's exploration of an economy of abundance, and then move to analyse her exorbitant insistence on sexual reserve.

37 Vivien Jones points out, in an analysis of an obituary for a Mrs Barclay (1794) and a passage from Edmund Burke's *Philosophical Enquiry into the Origin of our Ideas of the Sublime and the Beautiful* (1757), that even in such diverse texts it is abundantly clear how feminine virtues are generally subordinated to masculine ones. See the introduction to *Women in the Eighteenth Century*, London and New York, Routledge, 1990, pp. 1–4. Burke's 'softer virtues' (associated with the maternal sphere) include 'compassion, kindness and liberality', while his sublime (paternal) virtues include 'fortitude, justice, wisdom'. However, Scott refuses to separate these virtues: her ladies combine them all. Rousseau's ethical theory too insists on the necessity of combining justice with generosity, lest justice be too harsh (provoking revolt) or generosity unjust.

38 There is a distinction to be made here between Britain and Catholic countries in which monasteries and nunneries provide a regular alternative model of virtue. Leonore Davidoff and Catherine Hall discuss the religious emphasis on the necessity of women's dependence in 'Doctrines of Femininity' in their *Family Fortunes*, London, Hutchinson, 1987. They remark: 'Lack of attachment to a family would mean that women were exposed to being "surplus", with no meaning to their lives, and with the additional dangers of uncontained sexuality' (p. 114). A wife's financial dependency on her husband was enshrined in common law. See, for example, 'The Legal Status of Women' and 'Relations Between the Sexes' in Peter Earle, *The Making of the English Middle Class*, London, Methuen, 1989, pp. 158–60, 198–204.

In general, *Millenium Hall* is characterised by an economy of abundance, and scarcity is disdained:

> As these ladies have no taste but what is directed by good sense, nothing found a place here from being only uncommon, for they think few things are very rare but because they are little desirable; and indeed it is plain they are free from that littleness of mind, which makes people value a thing the more for its being possessed by no one but themselves. (p. 12)

This comment applies to the choice of plants in the garden at Millenium Hall, and thus relates both metaphorically and synecdochically to the entire project of the community. (This is another point in common with *La Nouvelle Héloïse*.) The eighteenth century saw an agricultural revolution when plants and animals began to be bred and cross-bred selectively for certain (marketable) qualities. At the same time, certain 'groceries' from colonised territories (such as tobacco or sugar) began to be imported in very much larger quantities than ever before (suggesting a certain democratisation of consumption), and thus ever more exotic imports became ever more highly valued as marks of distinction.

Mr Ellison suggests that the ladies are imitating their Creator (in setting up the community for needy gentlewomen), and thus must partake of his felicity. Mrs Maynard (a latecomer) responds:

> I will not [. . .] give up my share of the felicity you so justly imagine these ladies must enjoy, though I have no part in what occasions it. When I reflect on all the blessings they impart, and see how happiness flows, as it were, in an uninterrupted current from their hands and lips, I am overwhelmed with gratitude to the Almighty disposer of my fate, for having so mercifully thrown me into such a scene of felicity, where every hour yields true heart-felt joy, and fills me with thanksgiving to him who enables them thus to dispense inumerable blessings, and so greatly rewards them already by the joyful consciousness of having obeyed him. (p. 70)

This economimesis may be compared to images not only of God, but to other solar economies (such as that of the superabundant generosity of the Sun King to which Derrida refers at the beginning of *Given Time*)[39]. Mrs Maynard (like the gentlemen) can take pleasure in the spectacle of beneficence, even if she is not a prime mover. Such pleasure, which will be celebrated by Rousseau in his *Rêveries*, is one of the pretexts for Mr Ellison's long letter describing Millenium Hall (that is to say, the novel itself). He claims that he could not fail to communicate the pleasure he received from the sight of that 'society', but has 'a view beyond the pleasure which a mind like yours must receive from the contemplation of so much virtue' (p. 1). This view is that his friend should judge 'whether, by being made public

---

39 Mme de Maintenon, the Sun King's mistress, and her views on the education of girls are an interesting intertext of *Millenium Hall*.

[this account] may be conducive to your great end of benefiting the world' (p. 2).[40] Visual pleasure is not, of course, necessarily innocent: Rousseau suggests the proximity of pity, the motor passion of beneficence, and amorous passion (which are both aroused by the imagination). Scott illustrates this in the image of the grieving and beautiful child Miss Mancel at her aunt's death-bed, seen both by a virtuous old man and by the rake Mr Hintman (pp. 25 ff.). A suspicious contemporary eye may see another danger: that the male observer and judge are deemed necessary to validate what otherwise would have little value.[41] However, it seems to me that nothing in the novel confirms the opinion (widely held at the time) that observation succeeded by reasoned judgement is a male prerogative. The novel is not the portrait of one exceptional woman, but, unusually, introduces a whole series of women who are, or (thanks to other women) become wise judges in whatever sphere they inhabit. Crucially, their powers of observation, analysis and judgement are, however, informed by pity and generosity, rather than being spuriously dispassionate (which, Rousseau informs us, usually means self-interested).

Tahiti has to be interpreted to the world by the Frenchman B. in his dialogue with another Frenchman, A., and B. repeats the words of native informants (the old man and, more particularly, Orou). Diderot's fiction uses this ethnographical structure with a light, ironic and undeceived touch. This kind of mediation may be a more appropriate model for understanding the structure of *Millenium Hall* – not only to suggest a degree of incommensurability between the two societies (a difficulty of translation), but also a lack of burning desire to evangelise on the part of the happy society, an awareness of the risk of contact alongside benevolent intentions towards the outside world. The all-female Millenium Hall is interpreted by an anonymous man writing to another anonymous man (the publisher), and, in a closer parallel, the letter recounts his dialogues with a third man, Lamont, who plays the role of worldly prejudice finally overcome by the evidence of another kind of society. The chief native informant is Mrs Maynard, but as anthropologists truly desirous to learn, the two men also interrogate a number of the beneficiaries of Millenium Hall.

As well as the elements of superabundance, there are less radical traces of rationality and frugality which relate to the economics of beneficence.

---

40 Pleasure in the spectacle of beneficence or in listening to the narrative of beneficence is the mark of goodness; it does not require particular virtue. The project of educating society as a writer–benefactor would, however, require particular qualities – Mr Ellison hopes merely to be the transparent medium by which the ladies' example is transmitted, at the same time enabling their reserve to be respected.

41 This is the view of Vincent Carretta, in 'Utopia Limited: Sarah Scott's *Millenium Hall* and the *History of Sir George Ellison*', *The Age of Johnson: A Scholarly Annual*, 5 (1992), 303–25.

Each act of beneficence is made to do as much good as possible: the ladies are 'economists even in their charities' (pp. 111–12). Mrs Maynard stresses the importance of industry 'to all stations, as the basis of almost every virtue' (p. 67). What may seem even less radical is the degree of social stratification which persists in spite of some dynamic (meritocratic) possibilities. Not only are most of the children to be educated in a way which may be enlightened for the time, but with a degree of pragmatism as to their future social status (whether and how they will be earning their livings), but also exceptional individuals who seem to be educated and have qualities beyond their station tend to emerge ultimately as quality stock too.

Nevertheless, as well as the trope of benefactors' emulation of God, in *Millenium Hall* we see beneficiaries striving to emulate their benefactors. Emulation is a much-used term in the eighteenth century. Frequently it is a question of the lower orders 'aping' their betters – particularly for the conservative opponents of progress. In *Milllenium Hall*, as in *La Nouvelle Héloïse*, emulation is regarded in a positive light as a means of encouraging people to imitate *morally* better behaviour (or, occasionally, physically or intellectually improving behaviour). In other texts, emulation is often a question of imitating higher levels of consumption – and thus relates to the debates over the market. Those *in favour of* an expansion of trade come increasingly to realise in the course of the eighteenth century that exports are not the only way of accelerating economic growth.[42] Neil McKendrick argues that it is the imports of cheap calico and muslins from India that first reveals the elasticity of demand: the propulsive power (and economic advantages to the nation) of envy, emulation, the love of luxury and a host of other qualities previously regarded as vices (*The Birth of a Consumer Society*, p. 14). Mandeville notoriously expresses it in the subtitle of *The Fable of the Bees: Private Vices, Public Benefits*. When he produces the final version of that work in 1724 he is the target of much hostile criticism, but it is a view which is to receive ever more positive attention from economists.

Women are often the targets of accusations of *aping*, and it is worth noting that it is the sudden availability of cheaper fabrics for women's dresses which, it is suggested, first revealed the elasticity of demand. In *Millenium Hall* we are given an account of the perils of *aping* (in a bad education) which we can contrast with positive emulation (good education):

> The first thing a girl is taught is to hide her sentiments, to contradict the thoughts of her heart, and tell all the civil lies which custom has sanctified, with as much affection and conceit as her mother; and when she has acquired

42 See McKendrick, Brewer and Plumb, *The Birth of a Consumer Society*, for an account of the consumer revolution in eighteenth-century England, including, for example, the use of advertising. Hoh-Cheung Mui and Lorna H. Mui, in *Shops and Shopkeeping in Eighteenth-Century England*, London, Routledge, 1989, analyse in detail the development of the retail sector in that period.

all the folly and impertinence of a riper age, and apes the woman more ungracefully than a monkey does a fine gentleman, the parents congratulate themselves with the extremest complacency on the charming education they have given their daughter. (p. 181)

Mr Ellison, in *The History of Sir George Ellison*, explains Lamont's views on women (and hence his initial difficulty in understanding Millenium Hall): 'the persons who so much excelled him in reason as well as virtue, were women, were of that weak sex, which he had hitherto considered only as play-things for men; a race somewhat superior to monkeys' (I, 106–7, also quoted in Spencer's introduction, pp. xiv–xv).

In Millenium Hall, the ladies encourage all their beneficiaries to learn to be benefactors in their turn. When Mr Ellison questions one of the old women supported by the ladies, she explains how each old woman helps the others, and how they also help their younger neighbours, for instance, with child-care: 'The ladies settled all these matters at first, and told us, that as they, to please God, assisted us, we must in order to please him serve others; and that to make us happy they would put us in a way, poor as we are, to do good to many' (p. 13). While the emphasis on pleasing God may seem a touch authoritarian, there is also an emphasis on personal pleasure. Scott, like Rousseau, is firmly of the persuasion that doing good is almost always pleasurable for the benefactor – the trick is to make it pleasurable for the beneficiary. One of the ladies, Miss Mancel, tells Lamont that, far from wishing people to be slaves to one another:

> 'I would only make you friends. Those who are really such are continually endeavouring to serve and oblige each other; this reciprocal communication of benefits should be universal, and then we might with reason be fond of this world.'
> 'But,' said Lamont, 'this reciprocal communication is impossible; what service can a poor man do me? I may relieve him, but how can he return the obligation?'
> 'It is he,' answered Miss Mancel,'who first conferred it, in giving you an opportunity of relieving him. The pleasure he has afforded you, is as far superior to the gratification you have procured him, as it is more blessed to give than to receive [. . .] But do not think the poor can make no adequate return. The greatest pleasure this world can give us is that of being beloved, but how should we expect to obtain love without deserving it?' (pp. 62–3)

The ladies' beneficiaries are much happier because they do not simply receive charity (generous as their reception is), but are enabled to *emulate* the ladies and to be benefactors themselves.

This emulation requires the freedom of beneficiaries: beneficiaries who feel enslaved by their benefactors tend to rebel against them (they have unsuspectingly been subject to a market transaction). As at Clarens in *La Nouvelle Héloïse*, the beautiful grounds of Millenium Hall are a text which echoes the moral lessons of the work. Aesthetic pleasure and moral pleasure are conjoined: beautiful effects are derived with frugal care and in the service of utility. A pretty temple is in reality a pigeon-house (p. 59). In the grounds of both estates 'perfect equality in nature's bounty seems enjoyed by the whole creation' (*Millenium Hall*, p. 17). Because wild animals are left free and unmolested, they welcome the approach of humans. Nevertheless, the ladies are not vegetarians, and the hare, fish, deer and so on which flourish on their estate help them to achieve that self-sufficiency typical of utopias – this detail may, of course, be received less happily today. The estate is almost independent of the world outside. Like the animals on the estate, benefactors, and more importantly, beneficiaries, benefit from a general freedom: 'all burdensome forms are expelled [. . .] no-one is obliged to stay a minute longer in company than she chooses' (p. 68).

Carretta, a rare sceptical commentator on *Millenium Hall*, chooses as epigraph to his essay: 'But still I am puzzled; what we behold is certainly an inclosure, how can that be without a confinement to those that are within it?' This is a typical naive question from Lamont, who plays the part of the man made foolish by his worldly 'wisdom' alongside the more adequate judge (or pupil), Ellison. Carretta, however, sees this question as insightful – in his analysis the house and garden for dwarfs and giants to which Lamont is referring is a microcosm for the estate, and both represent a strategy of containment. Other commentators have also argued (as I would) that the home for the 'monsters' (p. 205) is both important and somehow emblematic, but have not viewed this in such a negative light. Linda Dunne, for example, claims that the monsters represent female sexuality in a much more positive way than other similar images of a later period may do.[43]

Before posing the question quoted above, Lamont had typically distinguished himself by assuming that the enclosure he has seen contains lions and tigers, and expressing his enthusiasm for viewing these fashionable, exotic and rare creatures. Miss Mancel responds with a diatribe against

43 'Mothers and Monsters in Sarah Robinson Scott's *Millenium Hall*', in *Utopian and Science Fiction by Women*, ed. Jane L. Donawerth and Carol A. Kolmerten, New York, Syracuse University Press, 1994, pp. 54–72. Commentators tend to pick up the term *monsters* to refer to these vertically challenged or challenging individuals: it is a term which at once may seem offensive but also conjures up a chain of interesting associations. One of these is the association with *monstrare*, 'to show' – although the etymology of monster is to be traced back to *monere*, 'to warn' (monsters as divine portents). Another is the use of 'monster' to refer to impossible hybrids such as centaurs or sphinxes. Mlle de Lespinasse famously remarks in *D'Alembert's Dream* (quoted and discussed in Elizabeth de Fontenay, *Diderot*, p. 116): 'Perhaps men are nothing but a freakish variety [*monstre*] of women, or women only a freakish variety [*monstre*] of men' (*Rameau's Nephew and Other Works*, p. 135). This relates to the idea mooted in medical circles at the time (and by Dr Bordeu in *D'Alembert's Dream*) that male and female sexual organs and secondary sexed characteristics were inversions or differently sized versions of each other.

man's whimsical tyranny over animals in general, and, in particular, his imprisonment and enslavement of exotic pets. The enclosure they see is the opposite of what Lamont assumes, since the dwarfs and giants it contains have been freed from the tyranny of being displayed as rare beasts. They have been liberated into a private domain where they can control, not only their own movements, but also those of visitors. This has a clear parallel with the lot of society women, released from display and show, into their own space in Millenium Hall. This freedom within boundaries (the bounds created by the larger society which surrounds Millenium Hall, and which those leaving the Hall necessarily enter) is not total freedom. Rousseau and Scott would both argue that, in any case, there is no total freedom, since any form of living with others creates certain obligations, and affection is a kind of dependency. However, I would not agree with Carretta that this is 'freedom through subordination' (p. 314), and would take more literally Scott's claim both that 'They [the dwarfs and giants] are entirely mistresses of their house' (p. 22), and that they were persuaded to lay aside pretensions of superiority – not, I would suggest, in order to learn subordination, but to learn the pleasures of equality and reciprocity. The former 'monsters' become happy (if selective) hosts, able to present their benefactors with gifts of the finest flowers, and to entertain other guests elegantly with fruit and wine and conversation.

Sexual reserve

Clara Reeve, in one of the earliest works of English literary criticism, *The Progress of Romance*, commends *Millenium Hall*, but is less tolerant of *La Nouvelle Héloïse*, because it arouses dangerous passions which ought to be checked.[44] *Millenium Hall* is so utterly rigorous in its checking of heterosexual passions that its very reserve could seem excessive. Male persons are allowed into the society of Millenium Hall as guests (of course, the ladies are perfectly hospitable) or as other beneficiaries, where the distance between benefactor and beneficiary is deemed to be so great that amorous passion cannot intervene. When the ladies make music, they are joined by 'the shepherd who had charmed us in the field [. . .]; a venerable looking man, who is their steward, playing on the violincello, a lame youth on the French horn, another, who seemed very near blind, on the bassoon, and two on the fiddle' (p. 10). For the best of reasons, the ladies prefer disabled

---

44 Introduction by Suzi Halimi, Paris, Editions d'Aujourd'hui, 1980, II, pp. 13–19. Clara Reeve also wrote a work on women's education (*Plans of Education; with Remarks on the Systems of other Writers*, London, T. Hookham and J. Carpenter, 1792) which was probably influenced by *Millenium Hall*. See Barbara Brandon Schnorrenberg, 'A Paradise like Eve's. Three Eighteenth-Century English Female Utopias', *Women's Studies: An Interdisciplinary Journal*, 9, 1982, 263–73.

servants (p. 120) of either sex, and this can be (and has been) read meta-phorically as an inclusion of all who are marginalised by contemporary society, and thus a reiteration of the marginalisation of women. Neverthe-less, it hardly even seems necessary to invoke psychoanalysis in order to suggest the ladies' preference that men who are constantly in their presence should somehow be 'castrated' by marked old age or physical disability. The one *lapsus* in the account is the shepherd – conventionally essential for an Arcadia, because Arcadia was classically associated with love. Thus the visitors' first animal (rather than vegetable) clue that they are entering an 'earthly paradise' (p. 6) is the shepherd (p. 4). And yet towards the end of the letter–novel the writer–narrator knows better, eros has been banished, and he tells us that:

> These ladies are epicures in rural pleasures and enjoy them in the utmost excess to which they can be carried. All that romance ever represented in the plains of Arcadia are much inferior to the charms of Millenium Hall, except the want of shepherds be judged a deficiency that nothing else can compens-ate; there indeed they fall short of what romantic writers represent, and have formed a female Arcadia. (p. 179)

The banishing of eros (the conjuring away of the shepherd) can be read as a conservative adherence to the feminine virtue of chastity. And yet it has already been remarked (in the cases of *The Republic* and *La Nouvelle Héloïse*, for example) that utopias frequently choose to regulate passions. The friend-ship between the ladies easily matches the morally best features of love between the sexes. There is no regret at the loss of biological motherhood, as maternal beneficence is clearly preferable; in an anti-filiative gesture, parenthood is to be earned.

What is most severely punished in the novel is any assault on a woman's chastity; this is shown most clearly in the stories told by Mrs Maynard of the lives led by the ladies prior to their arrival at the Hall. There are three examples of vulnerable women abused: Miss Mancel, the innocent beneficiary, Miss Jones, who acts foolishly because of her poor education, and Lady Emilia (Miss Selvyn's mother), who falls through a mixture of pity and love.

Miss Mancel is brought up from the age of ten by a 'benefactor' – in order to be his mistress when she is old enough. Her story begins with a scene calculated to arouse pity in the hardest heart, and a tragic nar-rative to reinforce the effect of the spectacle. Unfortunately, in accordance with Rousseau's genealogy of passions, pity is very close to amorous pas-sion. Gifts from a man to a beautiful and abandoned young girl can be interpreted generously, but, as in this case, may simply be investments in his future pleasure. Scott establishes a rigorous pattern with respect to such malefactors: he dies just as he is about to reap what he regards as his reward. There are many examples of this kind of false beneficence in eighteenth-century fiction, such as that of Marivaux's Climal in *La Vie de Marianne*. Rousseau recounts in his *Confessions* how he himself was tempted by just such a scheme. His friend Carrio 'unearthed a little girl of eleven or twelve, whom her wretched mother wanted to sell [. . .] My pity was stirred at the sight of this child. She was fair and as gentle as a lamb' (Book VII, p. 302). Together he and Carrio pay for her upkeep and for music lessons, which cost very little; 'but as we had to wait till she was mature [ripe], we had to sow a great deal before we could reap' (p. 303). (It is interesting to note the mixture of economic and agricultural/sexual metaphors.) While Miss Mancel's 'benefactor' anticipates his profit with ever more relish as he sees her more and as she grows older, in Rousseau's (and his friend's) case:

> Insensibly my heart grew fond of little Anzoletta, but with a paternal affection in which my senses played so little part that as it increased the possibility of sensuality entering into my feelings for her steadily diminished – I felt that I should be as horrifed at approaching this child, once she was old enough, as at committing the crime of incest.

Typically Rousseau argues that the innocent pleasures he experienced were probably just as sweet as the erotic ones he had anticipated. In any case, he is removed from Venice before Anzoletta is fully grown, and so the reader learns no more of her fate.

Scott's Miss Jones is not treated with such calculated design, but her seduction is attempted by a rake, Lord Robert, who regards girls who act without proper caution as 'lawful prize' (p. 163). He is cheated of that particular prize when she seeks advice from her wiser friend, Miss Selvyn. Lord Robert gets his final comeuppance when he falls deeply in love with Miss Selvyn, whom he respects as a transparently virtuous woman. She rejects his marriage proposal and reminds him of his behaviour with Miss Jones, pointing out that such an opportunistic theft of virginity would be no better (indeed worse) than robbing a man of his money because he failed to lock it up securely enough (p. 164).

The case of Lady Emilia is the strictest application of Scott's principle. Lady Emilia and Lord Peyton consummate their marriage in advance of the ceremony, on the eve of his departure to the army. On reflection, Lady Emilia decides to punish both him and herself (and, in conventional terms, the child which is the fruit of her lapse) by refusing to marry him, since she no longer believes that he can respect her. They remain close friends, and eventually mother and daughter (Miss Selvyn) are reunited. It is as if love between the sexes can only be maintained by means of a certain distance. (A parallel could again be made with *La Nouvelle Héloïse*.) Equally parental love is much challenged in the life histories of the five ladies (Mrs Maynard does not tell her own story). Lady Emilia enjoys a true maternal bond with her daughter because it was forged without any knowledge (on Miss Selvyn's part) of a biological relation, and without any legal obligation.

Lasting love, sustainable through proximity as well as distance, seems largely to rest in relations between women. At the beginning of the novel-letter, Mr Ellison refers to the community at Millenium Hall as a family (p. 1). What is interesting is how the text redefines the 'family' and the range of social and biological bonds it involves. In the eighteenth century, as already suggested, the family was at once a key *locus* for women and equally, very often, the site of their subjection both to parents and to spouses. The subjection of women to patriarchal power can prove highly damaging to mother–daughter relations, as Irigaray, amongst others, has pointed out. I have suggested elsewhere that Rousseau conjoins benefactor and father in a number of apostrophes in *La Nouvelle Héloïse* and other texts, less in order to imply that benefactors behave like fathers than that fathers should behave like benefactors. In *Millenium Hall* the emphasis is more on mother–daughter relations – biological maternity is consistently displaced by moral maternity in which any initial natural inequality develops into reciprocity. In patriarchal society women are commodities, and any goods they own may become their husbands' property – just as they themselves are their husbands' property. In *Millenium Hall* women are not commodities and have chosen to hold all their property in common – a *model for* marital relations rather than *modelled on* marital relations.

Lillian Faderman refers to *Millenium Hall* as 'the most complete fictional blueprint for conducting a romantic friendship'.[45] George F. Haggerty goes somewhat further and praises it as a 'lesbian narrative in action'.[46] He argues that Scott reinfuses the maternal with the erotic. It seems to me that to label the narrative as lesbian or to suggest (as Haggerty does) that the ladies' old steward (and close friend) is textually marked as gay is an interesting strategic gesture which functions beneficially in two ways. The first is to foreground the issue of lesbian histories, how they might have been experienced and written and how they can now be investigated. The second is to make the reader examine more closely the differences in the text. It seems to me, however, that the *erotic* as conventionally understood has a dangerous edge which Scott tends to reject. When lovers governed by eros are separated, then conventionally (romantically) they indulge in foolish behaviour – a classic example is Scott's Sir Edward Lambton, whose despair at being parted from Miss Mancel leads him to act recklessly on the battle-field, and thus (appropriately, Scott suggests) brings about his death and prevents the lovers' reunion. Saint-Preux too is tempted by suicide when

45 *Surpassing the Love of Men*, New York, Morrow, 1981, p. 103. Faderman does not analyse the novel in any detail.

46 '"Romantic Friendship" and Patriarchal Narrative in Sarah Scott's *Millenium Hall*', *Genders*, 13 (1992), 108–22.

parted from Julie. Mrs Morgan's love for Miss Mancel and Miss Mancel's love for Mrs Morgan, by contrast, is tempered by reason – when the two are separated, each individually (sadly) makes the best of her life as duty dictates. To call this love erotic may be pulling it into an inappropriate semantic field. It is deep, long-lasting, the most important relationship in both their lives; it is passionate, but without any touch of insanity, of violent loss of self, of eros as the poets depict it. No doubt the relationships of Millenium Hall have their place in a lesbian continuum, but they do not represent the whole of that continuum. Scott also suggests that men and women can (and should) enjoy lifelong love which is free of eros, but it is clearly more difficult, she implies, for men to govern their passions (partly because of obvious material differences in men's and women's situations). Miss Trentham and her cousin, Mr Alworth, enjoy a relationship which could be modelled on the women–women relations Scott prefers: 'They were continually together and never happy but when they were so.' It was 'an affection calm and rational [. . .] totally free from that turbulency and wildness which had always appeared to them the true characteristics of love' (p. 186). However, their marriage is called off when Mr Alworth experiences an overwhelming and irrational passion for a coquette – who makes him experience 'the continual transition from pleasure to pain' (p. 189), which some might define as the erotic.

Utopias, economies of abundance, beneficence – all these structures have a problematic relation to eros. All have a need to regulate sexual relations. For the Scott of *Millenium Hall*, the necessary qualities of generous passion and just reason are primarily located in women (in spite of all society does to make women apes) – although men, in the shape of George Ellison, are presumed to be educable. Society's injustices to women, not only in the poor education it offers them, but in the inequity of the marital contract, militate against marriage and hence (for Scott) procreation – alongside any woman-centered preferences for female company. Thus we have a utopia which not only regulates eros but banishes biological reproduction – although the community grows apace, since so many wish to join it from the unhappy world outside. As I have noted, Rousseau scatters the necessary qualities between men and women, but his division of responsibility makes intercourse difficult – and his heterosexual community slow to reproduce. Simply introducing men into utopia is not sufficent. The hopeful answer lies in transformation – in the relation between reader and text, observer and spectacle.

Twentieth-century writings are more ready to celebrate the liberating effects of the erotic for women. While this is particularly a feature of the period following the significant increase in women's control over their fertility other than by abstinence, the erotic which is celebrated is not necessarily a conventional heterosexual one. Derrida opens *Given Time* with a quotation from a letter from Mme de Maintenon. She writes that the King takes all her time – leaving only 'the rest' for Saint-Cyr – when she would like to give it *all* to Saint-Cyr. Saint-Cyr is the educational foundation for impoverished young girls which she set up – an example which inspired Scott in her life and in the writing of *Millenium Hall*. Derrida reads the sentence primarily wilfully as an expression of an *impossible* desire – love being to give what one does not have[47] – and of the paradox of time. He reads it secondarily as the opening on to a daily economy of leisures and charities. I would argue that *La Nouvelle Héloïse* clearly expresses that unthinkable desire alongside the workaday domestic economy. *Millenium Hall* seems to be less about 'the infinite sigh of unsatisfied desire' (*Given Time*, p. 4), but I would argue that that erotic has been opened up *over time*. It is women's desire to turn from the King, the Lord and Master, and establish a women's space (a new *oikos*) which has created rereadings of *Millenium Hall* not only as a novel of good work(s), but as a lover's dream.

47 Derrida cites Lacan's formulation that to love is to give what one does not have (p. 2), thus Mme de Maintenon's paradoxical expression is part of a different economy and a different logic.

6

The eighteenth century IV: a state without a market. Rousseau's *Social Contract*

What is interesting about Rousseau in the context thus far established is *the way in which* he resists the move towards the market across a range of different texts. Resistance in itself could, of course, mean conservative support for the feudal status quo ante. Against those who promote the freedom of the market, Rousseau would point out that analytical equality (the assumption of equality as a fact rather than as a goal) sustains real inequality. Rousseau is not alone in his form of resistance, but is a pre-eminent figure – not only at the time, but in his later influence. In this chapter, I shall be discussing a few of the other resisting writers, if only to avoid the trap of representing Rousseau as somehow unique and utterly alone, as some of his rhetorical statements imply. However, I shall be less concerned to establish a panoramic view than to analyse a key text in some detail – *The Social Contract* (1762). This deservedly has a special place in the canon of political theory for its formulation of an egalitarian contractual basis for the just society, and the consequences of that kind of contract where sovereign and people coincide (as opposed to the more common contract of submission found in Hobbes or Locke). Here I shall be focusing on the interstices of that text and with reading it not only between the lines, but also inter-textually, in order to highlight the political economy of the just state.[1]

Against the grain: Enlightenment and the gift

The first question to ask here is to what extent do eighteenth-century writers, and Rousseau in particular, hypothesise a non-market economy in their political writings? And, if they do, does it exist somewhere (historically or geographically) other than capitalism, or than market economies (e.g. in feudal or tribal societies) – or does it exist alongside, in the interstices, of the

---

1 Rousseau claims that the form of government determines the kind of society and the character of individuals within the state, but also the reverse. Equally, the political structure shapes the economy, *and* vice versa.

market and of thinking in market terms? Rousseau and other Enlightenment thinkers insistently look back (for instance, to Sparta or to Rome) and
look to other places and peoples (for instance, North American Indians or
Peruvians[2]) in order to present examples of other economies. But to what
extent is this gesture a rhetorical trope? The brief definition of a gift economy
in the strict sense which opposes it to the market is that goods or services
(or psychic energy) are given with no thought of return, not even *reconnaissance*. The argument over whether a gift economy could exist, or whether,
even if it does not, the utopian possibility should be maintained as a horizon,
is a lengthy one. As I have suggested, there may be a median position
between a 'feminine economy', the most radical kind of gift economy, and
the market – this median position is beneficence. On the whole, Rousseau
is concerned with the code of beneficence rather than with 'the gift', and
yet there are elements of superabundant generosity in certain of his texts.

Some utopias are characterised by the total absence of private property.
In his 'The Utopian System' (1794), Thomas Reid distinguishes between
property-owning societies which necessarily tend towards inequality and
those (speculative) societies like that of Thomas More in which all property
is held in common.[3] He gives as one of the disadvantages of the latter,
that there is no opportunity to practise virtue (understood as struggle) for
instance, for the rich to practise generosity. Unlike some other writers, he
does not, I should add, present this as by any means a conclusive argument
against common ownership. Indeed, he argues that what he calls the utopian
system is the form of political system best adapted to the improvement and
happiness of men. (However, since he emphasises the speculative quality of
utopia, it may well be the case that he views its function primarily as that
of a critique of existing ills – which is one traditional view of utopias.) In
spite of the claim that private generosity is inhibited by common ownership
and state provision of crucial services such as education, it is possible to see
this kind of utopia as a gift economy on the social scale, in the sense that
it is an economy of abundance.

Some theorisations of gift exchange or non-market economies focus
on the exchange (or lack of exchange) of products, but I think that it can
be more fruitful specifically to involve the question of labour. For one
thing, many political theorists (including Plato, More and Rousseau) who

2 See Françoise de Graffigny, *Letters from a Peruvian Woman*, trans. D. Kornacker, New
York, The Modern Language Association of America, [1747] 1993, for a popular fictional
image of Peru (this novel went through thirty editions in the thirty years which
followed its first publication). Montaigne's essay 'On Coaches' is one of the several
sources.

3 *Practical Ethics*, ed. K. Haakonssen, Princeton and London, Princeton University Press,
1990, pp. 277–99. This is an unusual paper both in terms of the general Anglo–Scottish
eighteenth-century fondness for property, and in terms of Reid's traditional reputation for 'common sense'! I am grateful to Roger Gallie for drawing it to my attention.

have attempted to lay down the principles of a just state have suggested that one prerequisite is to abolish the market in labour, which in itself acts as a strict control on the accumulation of wealth. An additional reason for involving labour is that even today, in an advanced capitalist economy, a great deal of labour is not marketed – in particular, women's labour. I would suggest that the fact that historically women have been expected to function in a non-market economy, if not exclusively, at least at the same time as engaging in paid work, has had a major influence on the social construction of femininity. While that oppressive construction of femininity is not to be confused with a feminine economy, there may well be interesting areas of interference, as I suggested in chapter one. As regards the affluent classes of the eighteenth century (including many of Rousseau's benefactors), there was, of course, a greater market in domestic services (cleaning, laundry, cooking, child-care – even breast-feeding – and so on) than there is today. Rousseau places a higher premium on the time-consuming gift of a service than on the more common gift of an object or the even easier gift of money. Such a hierarchy in beneficence is less obvious today, when the impersonal gift may be more highly prized; it would be interesting to speculate how this reversal in values relates (if at all) to the fact that feminine domestic services are frequently unwaged, or sometimes low-waged on the black economy. A further reason for focusing on the (lack of a) market in labour is the fact that it is the ubiquity of waged labour, the worker being dispossessed of the means of production, which is the mark of capitalism.

The eighteenth century has been represented in this book as the location of a gradual shift from thinking which focuses on the grooming of the moral individual and which represents just society as the moral individual writ large, to the thinking which underpins the rise of capitalism. For much of the century both kinds of thinking coexist, and the question is hotly debated. Eighteenth-century French thinkers who insist on regulating commerce in the light of moral considerations include, for example, Jean Morelly and the Abbé de Mably.[4] In his *Code de la nature* (1755),[5] Morelly argues

4 Almost nothing is known of Morelly. In fact for fifty years the *Code de la nature* was attributed to Diderot, and there are still doubts over whether or not the seven works understood to be by Morelly are indeed all by this mysterious individual. However, he has been claimed as a forebear by a range of successors (Babeuf, Fourier, Tocqueville, amongst others). The Abbé Gabriel Bonnot de Mably (1709–85) was the brother of the philosopher Condillac, and of the M. de Mably who hired Rousseau as tutor to his children. Rousseau mentions him several times in his *Confessions*. At first Rousseau was glad to discuss his work with the Abbé, with whom he shared many ideas, an admiration for the simplicity of the Greeks and Romans and a disapproval of modern decadence and luxury (see pp. 263, 266, 276, 379, 473, for their early friendship). Later, however, they become enemies, as the Abbé feared that Rousseau was inciting revolution, and Rousseau saw in the Abbé's *Entretiens de Phocion sur le rapport de la morale avec la politique* (1763) nothing but 'a barefaced and shameless compilation from my own writings' (p. 574).
5 Introduction by V. P. Volguine, Paris, Editions Sociales, 1953.

from natural abundance to relative economic equality – in other words, like
Rousseau, he is positing normative (rather than analytic) equality: '[Nature]
passed on undivided the ownership of the land which produces her gifts,
and to each and every one she allows the use of her benefactions. The
world is a table which has an abundance for all guests, and all the dishes
are theirs' (p. 23).[6] We may note his deployment of the vocabulary of
generosity. He claims further that, if man were properly educated:

> Extravagant desires would not have been aroused in him by the fear of
> lacking help, of lacking what was either necessary or useful. If fathers wisely
> set aside any notion of private property; if any competitiveness were pre-
> vented or kept out by the access to goods held in common, would it be
> possible for man to imagine seizing by force or trickery something that had
> never been withheld from him? (p. 35)

In his *Doutes proposés aux philosophes économistes* (1768), the Abbé de Mably
refers to the Guardians of Plato's *Republic*, to the ancient Spartans and to
the North and South American Indians – all of whom, he claims, had no
private property – as models of happiness. He also uses the example of
the state established by the Jesuits in Paraguay in 1604, which Reid too
describes as a kind of utopia; this was a subject for much topical debate, as
the Jesuits were expelled from all Portuguese territories during the 1750s.[7]
'La communauté des biens' is preferable for the Abbé not only because
equality is natural, but because of the social qualities it engenders. He denies
that property is necessary to spur men on to work, and argues that, on the
contrary, it promotes idleness, brutality and all manner of other vices.

Rousseau

It is sometimes assumed that Rousseau is far from antipathetic to market
commerce on the grounds of his Genevan artisan's background. Even his
background is not, however, so simple. His father was indeed a watch-
maker, but he experienced his apprenticeship to an engraver at the age
of 13 as bondage; and he later worked as a servant, a secretary, a tutor,
and principally as a music copyist. His common-law wife, Thérèse, was
a laundry-maid. Marxist critics have also sometimes over-simplistically
allocated Rousseau a petty-bourgeois class position and then identified his

---

6 Joseph Schumpeter, a twentieth-century economist who typically wishes to deny that
economic analysis is ideological, distinguishes between normative equality (what
is right according to certain moral thinkers) and analytical equality in his *tour de
force* study the *History of Economic Analysis*, Oxford, Oxford University Press, 1954.
Schumpeter makes this distinction, for instance, with respect to the Natural Law
philosophers (pp. 55–6).

7 In *The Supplement to Bougainville's 'Voyage'* we have the other perspective: anti-clerical
hostility leads to the absolute rejection of the idea that Jesuits could have done anything other than brutally exploited any indigenous peoples whom they encountered.

writings with that position. The comparison of Rousseau with Adam Smith is very helpful, it seems to me, in order to clarify the real differences between Rousseau's writings and the rising bourgeois ideology. Rousseau's location at a particular pressure-point in history when economic thinking, and the ideology of capitalism, was about to become dominant, a moment when arbitrary and fixed authority was being challenged, but often in the name of (economic) progress dependent on an expanding market, no doubt contributes to certain conflicts in his writing. I would argue that Rousseau not only challenges mercantile values in social and emotional relationships (a stance which is fairly common; it can be found, for example, in Montaigne writing on friendship, or in Molière's portrayal of the misanthropist), but also advocates a non-market economy in general. While ultimately gift economy thinking might be relegated to certain domains, it is worth considering Rousseau's grand hypothesis of a state based on non-market principles – which we find in *The Social Contract* and the relevant Rousseauian intertexts. Rousseau clearly draws on classical theorists such as Seneca for elements of a code of beneficence in interpersonal relationships, and adds to those sources both an emotional and a political dimension.[8] More radically it can be argued that there are traces of a feminine economy in Rousseau's writings.

The Social Contract

In *The Social Contract* Rousseau establishes, in the words of the subtitle, *principles* of political right (or justice);[9] he does not describe a just state – if only because any given state would be, he argues, particular to a given place and people, their history and traditions. And so – although I would want to argue that utopian texts are of particular interest for a theorisation of a feminine economy – it is inaccurate to describe *The Social Contract* as a utopian text in the strict sense of the term (which presupposes details of an 'other' place).[10] However, it exists in a special relationship with utopian

---

8 A longer elaboration of Rousseau and beneficence which is relevant here is my *Justice and Difference in the works of Rousseau*, Cambridge, Cambridge University Press, 1993.

9 The difficult expression *droit politique* is rendered by both Maurice Cranston and Christopher Betts in their respective translations of *The Social Contract* as 'political right'. Cranston glosses this as 'a semi-technical expression to designate the general abstract study of law and government' (Preface, Harmondsworth, Penguin, 1968, p. 26).

10 See R. A. Leigh, *Rousseau and the Problem of Tolerance in the Eighteenth Century*, Oxford, Oxford University Press, 1979. Judith N. Shklar highlights Rousseau's depiction of Sparta and of Neufchatel as two antithetical utopias in his writing: one banishes the family in favour of the state to facilitate military virtue and the other is based on the domestic unit. See *Men and Citizens*, Cambridge, Cambridge University Press, 2nd edn, 1985.

texts (by Rousseau or others) – which may partly explain why it is so often incorrectly described as one.

The first readers of *The Social Contract*, it has been suggested, responded to Rousseau less as a political scientist than as the author of the enormously popular *La Nouvelle Héloïse*. As I have tried to suggest, this is a semi-utopian novel of fine feeling (*sensibilité*) and emotional union, of benefaction and self-sacrifice. The first readers responded with tears, sighs, effusive letters and pledges. While we may have lost that particularly violent responsiveness, I would argue that, nevertheless, Rousseau's writing in general is read in the light of a powerful imaginary author figure who fascinates or repels the reader with his emotionalism, rhetorical extravagances, crimes (real or imputed) and virtues (also real or imputed). In Rousseau, positivism or economic thinking is clearly subordinated to moral thinking, and the 'return gift' which seems appropriate to the text is rational thinking which is in the service of an emotional response.

What are the principles underlying the just state? I shall focus on three of these which relate to the economy: the restriction on private property (enabling rough economic equality); the restriction of the market in labour (achieved via household self-sufficiency) and hence of division of labour and specialisation and of trade in general; the reduction of taxation – preventing (at least waged) representation. I shall deal with each of these in turn, and then move on to the question of sexual difference and how this is (strangely) related to the measuring of the success of the just state.

Rousseau argues that the origin of such a state must consist in a gesture whereby each member of the community gives himself and all his resources and possessions to the state – only in that way can it be brought into being.[11] (I am holding to Rousseau's 'he/man language' as the mark of the distance between us – which necessitates a deliberate responsive gesture on my part.) Only by virtue of such an initial gift can any citizen accede to being a lawful proprietor as opposed to a *de facto* possessor of goods: 'Each member of the community gives himself to it at the moment it is brought into being just as he is – he himself, and all his resources, including all his goods' (Book I, Chapter 9, p. 65). This inaugural gesture is a gift of self, which Baker convincingly theorises as a *deposit*; and yet Rousseau may be using the language of gift as an important and necessary fiction. At the moment of alienation, the citizen-in-process cannot or must not imagine any potential reversion. This alienation has also been interpreted

11 See *The Social Contract*, Book I, Chapter 6, where Rousseau refers to 'the total alienation by each associate of himself and all his rights to the whole community' (p. 60).
See F. Baker, 'Remarques sur la notion de dépôt', *Annales Jean-Jacques Rousseau*, 37
(1968), 57–93, and 'La Route contraire', in *Reappraisals of Rousseau*, ed. S. Harvey,
M. Hobson, D. Kelley and S. B. Taylor, Manchester, Manchester University Press,
1980, pp. 132–62.

as an *exchange* – of natural rights for civil ones. However, Roger Masters points out that

> In *Contrat social*, I, iv, Rousseau defines the verb 'to alienate' as 'to give or to sell', and explicitly rejects a sale or exchange of natural rights as the foundation of civil society; the alienation required in the 'essential clause' of the social contract is a free gift, without reserve.[12]

The social contract has been interpreted as a move to protect private property because it is a legitimation (and it does enable a distinction between 'mine' and 'thine', enabling beneficence; it is less radical than More's *Utopia*). But it is important to contrast the principle of the founding of the just state with the founding of the unjust state as Rousseau figures it in the opening paragraph of the second part of his *Discourse on Inequality*: a man who encloses some land states 'this belongs to me', and manages to convince his naive audience to believe him. The unjust state is founded *with an individual possessive speech-act* in order to protect the unequal distribution of wealth which has grown up *de facto* as the state of nature has degenerated. The unjust state establishes a duplicitous equality or sameness before the law (we all respect each other's property) in order to mask a real and growing inequality or difference (some people have far more property to be respected than others).[13] The founding of the just state *with a general alienation* leaves open the possibility of any redistribution of wealth with the proviso that material inequality be minimised to the point where a market in labour is impossible. This proviso is justified in a series of arguments not only in *The Social Contract* but elsewhere; for example, in the earlier *Discourse on Political Economy* Rousseau is already claiming that it is crucial to prevent accumulation, since laws are only effective where poverty and wealth are equally excluded: 'The full force of the law is felt only by those in between; laws are equally powerless against the rich man's wealth and the poor man's destitution [. . .] one breaks the net, the other passes through it' (p. 21). It is hard to see how this can be perceived as anything other than an attack on property as property is generally understood (let alone as it existed in eighteenth-century France) – although quotations from Rousseau where he claims that he is defending property are sometimes used to back up the opposite case. The crucial point to understand in these quotations is that Rousseau regards property which has not been distributed by the state as theft; whereas Locke, presenting market relations

---

12 *The Political Philosophy of Rousseau*, Princeton, Princeton University Press, 1968, p. 315, note 60.

13 Paul de Man tackles this question in his essay on the *Discourse on Inequality*, in his *Allegories of Reading*, New Haven, Yale University Press, 1979, pp. 135–59. The deceit inaugurated with 'this belongs to me', which benefits the speaker and not the recipient, must not be confused with the benign fictions promulgated by the legislator, which are all to the benefit of the people.

between individuals as the natural order of things, claims that men already have rights such as property in the state of nature. Since, therefore, legitimate property must derive from the state, according to Rousseau, and since the state can only survive through a relative equality, Rousseau is defending the only legitimate form of property. He asserts:

> The social pact, far from destroying natural equality, substitutes, on the contrary, a moral and lawful equality for whatever physical inequality that nature may have imposed on mankind; so that however unequal in strength and intelligence, men become equal by covenant and by right. [A footnote in the original reads:] Under a bad government, this equality is only an appearance and an illusion; it serves only to keep the poor in their wretchedness and sustain the rich in their usurpation. In truth, laws are always useful to those with possessions and harmful to those who have nothing; from which it follows that the social state is advantageous to men only when all possess something and none has too much. (*The Social Contract* Book I, Chapter 9, p. 68)

Like Thomas More in his *Utopia* and Plato in his *Republic*, Rousseau emphasises the importance of everyone working and of preventing a market in labour both on the grounds that this is morally desirable in itself and that it is the only way to achieve even approximate equality.[14] However, he suggests bringing about a reduction in trade by promoting household self-sufficiency rather than the non-market exchange between households advocated by More. This means that the only division of labour is the sexual division of labour within the household. Within the household, of course, the usual assumption of harmonious gift exchange is made. Rousseau's opposition to the division of labour is very important in the light of Adam Smith's insistence that specialisation is the key to commercial progress (the famous pin factory). Marx will bear out Smith's point in his analysis of the laws of motion of capital; and indeed, the efficiency and hence advisability of specialisation goes almost unquestioned today.

Rousseau is against taxation: 'I believe that compulsory service is less contrary to liberty than is taxation' (Book III, Chapter 15, p. 140). This is partly because citizens would in general have low incomes, if any, and little wealth. He perceives taxation as an attack on the poor – as it indeed was in contemporary France. He advocates taxes on wealth or luxury as a desperate measure if the state has failed to prevent inequality from gradually

---

14 Rousseau declares: 'As for equality, this word must not be taken to imply that degrees of power and wealth should be absolutely the same for all [. . .] where wealth is concerned, that no citizen shall be rich enough to buy another and none so poor as to be forced to sell himself' (Book II, Chapter 11, p. 96). See my article 'Dreams of the End of Markets: The Model of Women's Work in Plato, More and Rousseau', *Paragraph*, 15 (1992), 248–60, for expansion of these points.

installing itself.[15] A public purse (preferably in the form of land) could be established by the Legislator immediately after the social pact establishes the state, and thenceforth there would be little need to raise revenue as long as administrators were virtuous and economy was deployed correctly (that is, as common people understand it): '[this] is perhaps the origin of the usual sense of the word *economy*, since it is commonly understood to mean the wise management of what one has, rather than the means of acquiring what one does not have' (*Political Economy*, p. 29).[16] Rousseau is also opposed to taxation because he is against representation. His notorious stance against representation has been understood largely in terms of a desire for unmediated presence.[17] However, it should also be related to his opposition to a market in labour. He argues that it is wrong to pay taxes in order to be represented by professional legislators or soldiers,[18] that public work should be more important and time-consuming than private domestic concerns. 'It is the bustle of commerce and the crafts, it is the avid thirst for profit, it is effeminacy and the love of comfort [*la mollesse et l'amour des commodités*] that commute personal service for money' (Book III, Chapter 15). The term *la mollesse*, with its implications for Rousseau of effeminacy, brings us to a certain anxiety – and to a point at which the reader can do some work herself.

The sexual division of labour is related to Rousseau's concern with population growth. 'The strength which is derived from the size of your population is more real than that which comes from wealth, and is more sure to have the desired effect.'[19] In Book III, Chapter 9 of *The Social Contract*, 'The Signs of Good Government', Rousseau reveals that healthy population growth is the paramount sign of a just state. Rousseau returns to this a number of times in his fragments of political writing, such as those gathered

15 In *Political Economy*, he strongly argues (against Montesquieu) that if general taxation should become necessary, then it should not be indirect (i.e. on goods), but be a progressive direct tax: 'other things being equal, a man having ten times the wealth of another man should pay ten times as much in tax' (p. 34). As he continues the argument, he concludes that other things are not equal, since at this stage inequality must have asserted itself and a market in labour must have emerged – and therefore an equitable tax burden would work on a compound ratio (p. 36). It really is hard to see why Rousseau is sometimes claimed to be a defender of the interests of the propertied classes.

16 This would allow, for example, the establishing of public grain stores so that grain could be distributed in years of poor harvest (*Political Economy*, p. 30). Rousseau is, of course, opposed to those such as Quesnay and the physiocrats who wanted free trade in corn.

17 Key critics maintaining this position (in rather different ways) are Starobinski and Derrida.

18 This could be related to debates in England, where the Country opposition to the pre-eminence of trade is tied up with hostility to a standing professional army as opposed to traditional militias. Pocock writes in this respect that Adam Smith's focus on division of labour as the motor of historical change must be seen against 'what the classic and civic tradition presented as the crucial and disastrous instance of specialization of social function' (*The Machiavellian Moment*, p. 499).

19 *Projet de Constitution pour la Corse*, *Œuvres complètes*, III, p. 904.

together under the heading *Du bonheur public* ('On Public Happiness'): 'The family showing off its children will say: this is how I am thriving' (*Œuvres complètes*, III, p. 511). Here he accepts the family–state analogy which elsewhere, in terms of the internal economy of the family, he rejects so strongly. The family's pleasure, pride and well-being is, like that of the state, demonstrated in its abundance of children. The encouragement of reproduction is a crucial task for the Legislator – and setting everyone to work in fact contributes to that end. Work in agriculture is particularly beneficial, according to Rousseau, because it not only produces food, but also helps produce citizens. In his projected *Constitution for Corsica*, while emphasising that different political and economic arrangements are suitable for different environments, he asserts that farming not only feeds the population, but also encourages virility in men and pudic fertility in women, as well as instilling a patriotic taste for freedom:

> A preference for agriculture is not only advantageous to population growth in increasing men's subsistence, but also in bestowing a character and way of life on the body of the nation which makes for a greater number of births. In any country, country dwellers have more children than townsfolk do, either because the simplicity of rustic life encourages better formed bodies or because persistent hard work prevents disorder and vice. For, all things equal, the chastest women, those whose senses are the least enflamed by the experience of pleasure, have more children than the rest, and it is no less sure that men who are worn out by debauchery, the certain fruit of idleness, are less fit for reproduction than those whose hard work has made them more continent. (*Projet de Constitution pour la Corse*, pp. 904–5)

One of the problems for the present reader in Rousseau's theories is that he *states* (but does not *show*) that survival of the individual and of society necessitates a commerce (between men and women) which can only take place if sexual difference is fixed.[20] Rousseau's concern with the increase of population is shared by a number of thinkers from the seventeenth century onwards – there is near unanimity in the first half of the eighteenth century that a numerous and increasing population is a symptom and cause of wealth, or indeed that it is wealth in itself.[21] Smith himself

---

20 The case is most clearly made in Rousseau's *Lettre à d'Alembert* (1758) in *Politics and the Arts: Rousseau's Letter to d'Alembert*, trans. A. Bloom, New York, Cornell University Press, 1960, where Rousseau concludes that the sexes should live apart most of the time, otherwise men will become like women, gradually losing their health and vigour as well as their morals.

21 One influential work is *L'Ami des hommes, ou Traité de la population*, Avignon, 1756, by Victor Riquetti, Marquis de Mirabeau. He writes: 'Agriculture and population are thus necessarily and intimately linked, and form together the main priority, from which all others arise' (p. 4). However, Rousseau differs from Mirabeau in many other respects: Mirabeau asserts that man is naturally sociable, and that 'the first law of society is the division of property, and this is the foundation of all other laws: let no one cite against me the example of savage peoples' (p. 3).

asserts that 'The most decisive mark of the prosperity of any country is the increase of the number of its inhabitants' (*The Wealth of Nations*, pp. 87–8). This concern can be related to a belief in Increasing Returns to Scale, a belief which will be increasingly challenged from the mid-eighteenth century by thinkers such as Quesnay who suggest that the population has a worrying tendency to increase beyond the means of subsistence (a view we tend to bond to the name of Malthus).[22] The two factors of production which obsess eighteenth-century thinkers are land and labour (roughly, population). Rousseau, a notorious opponent of luxury, is not, of course, concerned with increasing per capita wealth. However, his populationist stance – allied to the view that the population must be evenly distributed and not concentrated in conurbations – is interestingly infected by economic theories. Many utopian thinkers posit population control as a necessity, since – as Rousseau holds – the ideal State should not be too large in size. Rousseau's contradictory aim of a population held at a manageable size to màintain justice in the state, and insistence that an increasing population is the measure of the justice of the State suggests perhaps his notorious historical pessimism (progress carries the seeds of destruction within itself), but also a certain sexual obsession.

In any case, Rousseau's chain of thinking obsessively returns to the assertion of a need for a marked sexual difference. In Rousseau's hypothetical just State, men and women would be distinguished by the content of their tasks, by their social behaviour and so on. There is a greater degree of sexual differentiation than in More's *Utopia*, for example, where there is some difference between men's and women's crafts, but far less than in More's own society. And there is an even lesser degree of sexual differentiation in the society of the Guardians in Plato's *Republic* – although it must be admitted that in his just State Plato does abolish amorous passion altogether.[23] But crucially, as in the *Republic* and in *Utopia*, in Rousseau's just State neither sex would market their labour, and hence it would not be possible to say of it, as Delphy has said of the modern economy, that while most men are engaged in the capitalist mode of production, most women are *also* engaged in a feudal (or even slave) mode of production.[24] Both sexes would be engaged in production for gift exchange within the household. Of course, if men controlled distribution within the household, that could lead to disturbing inequalities of consumption. But like his precursors,

22 Schumpeter, in his *History of Economic Analysis*, hails Turgot as the outstanding analyst in this respect, since he approximates to the modern view that, all other factors held constant, returns will tend first to increase and then, decline with the scale of any one factor.

23 See Leo Strauss, *The City and the Man*, Chicago, Rand McNally, 1964. See also Masters, *The Political Philosophy of Rousseau*; he suggests that Rousseau 'puts his finger on an essential characteristic of the *Republic*, namely its abstraction of *eros* or love from the political realm' (p. 22).

24 See *Close to Home*, trans. D. Leonard, London, Hutchinson, 1984.

Plato and More, Rousseau insists on the importance of simplicity of diet, dress and entertainment being positively valorised thanks to the force of socially educated public opinion – thus, in theory, inequality of that kind would not arise. Thus although in *The Social Contract* Rousseau prescribes as an absolute necessity a great degree of sexual differentiation, he does not follow other Enlightenment thinkers (such as Adam Smith) down a path – the social division of labour which requires and is required by commerce – which has been associated with a structural and material distinction between men and women.

Rousseau's theoretical writings are notorious for their strict codes of sexual difference; they prescribe the location of femininity (pudicity) in women and masculinity in men and the establishing of separate spheres. But at the same time I should like to argue that all of Rousseau's writing incessantly enacts and conjures up a sexual difference which cannot function on that model of biological exclusion – for his divine legislator to be human he must be suffused with femininity; the political economy must be a domestic economy, if not a feminine economy.[25] It is our attention to the descriptive as well as the prescriptive mode in Rousseau's writing which is our return gift.

Rousseau's hypothetical legislator is a model of generosity, the most self-sacrificing, the most self-effacing of all Rousseau's imaginary model benefactors; he is nothing but the answer to the needs and interests of the people – like the ideal Mother. Interestingly, many liberal as well as conservative readers of Rousseau have perceived the Legislator as utterly sinister – a model for whichever historical leader they most detest.[26] There is little textual justification for this, as many other readers have pointed out.[27] I

25 See Shklar, *Men and Citizens*, for an analysis of Rousseau's 'Images of Authority'. Shklar suggests that they all have a tendency to be divine rather than human, and she finds the Legislator the 'most wooden' (that is, least human) of the three (p. 155). She points out the creative role of the Legislator, and that his voice must speak directly to the heart (p. 157), but does not focus on the sexual politics of Rousseau's distribution of properties.

26 See J. L. Talmon, *The Origins of Totalitarian Democracy*, London, Secker & Warburg, 1952, and Ralph Leigh's response, 'Liberté et autorité dans le *Contrat social*', in *Jean-Jacques Rousseau et son œuvre*, Paris, Klincksieck 1963 pp. 249–64. In *Rousseau and the Republic of Virtue*, Ithaca, NY and London, Cornell University Press, 1986, Carol Blum slides from suggesting that Rousseau is a model for Robespierre to implying that Rousseau creates this murderous persona by the way in which he invokes virtue. In his biography (*Jean-Jacques Rousseau*, Paris, Tallandier, 1988–89), Raymond Trousson charts some of the extreme reactions to the living and the dead Rousseau. A very recent example is that of Conor Cruise O' Brien, who wrote in *The Independent Magazine* (12 December 1992): 'My villain has long been Jean Jacques [*sic*] Rousseau, and a most satisfactory villain he is [. . .] This is no inconsequential villain, but one built on true satanic scale' (p. 62).

27 See, for example, Jean Starobinski's review of Lester G. Crocker's *Jean-Jacques Rousseau: A New Interpretative Analysis of His Life and Work*, 'Rousseau and Modern Tyranny', trans. P. France, *The New York Review*, 29 November 1973, 20–5.

would suggest that it is a violent emotional reaction which is similar to a hatred of the imaginary Mother for her lack of need/desire for us and for her gift of milk, which produces, for instance, fantasies of being smothered, fantasies which Rousseau himself reproduces textually over and over again. Readers – perhaps unsurprisingly – tend to repeat Rousseau's textual gestures, both aggressive–sadistic ones and amorous–generous ones.

While the Legislator is certainly qualified as male, and evokes a chain of mythicised male precursors such as Moses or Lycurgus, he has many motherly traits. He creates his people, and this creation cannot be a late second birth. Like the maternal voice of Nature in the *Discourse on Inequality*, he has to speak directly to the soul. Rousseau defines the Legislator as no more than the condition of possibility of the people's achieving virtue, and one of his few detailed stipulations about this shadowy figure is that his only power must be moral, i.e. that he must not wield either financial or political power. He has 'a task which is beyond human powers and a non-existent authority for its execution' (Book II, Chapter 7, p. 86). The legislator must give abundantly without expecting return – his gifts do not function according to an economy of scarcity. Is it appropriate that he should be perceived purely in a paternal mode, a mode which we identify as one of interdiction? He is a Law-giver, and yet his success is to be judged by his not laying down laws, and by his people growing to resemble him – impossible though that is – by a growth *towards* a kind of pre-Oedipal identification and union which would never be reached and which would be the end of beneficence.

Rousseau's writing refuses the market in the name of beneficence – this in itself makes Rousseau's texts the *locus* of a significant displacement in the context of the eighteenth century and later. His model of beneficence, culled in part from classical texts, can, however, easily be read as a masculine one – and one which reserves femininity for the home – in the one acceptable fixed division of labour. And yet Rousseau chooses to tell his reader (preferably a woman) that his earliest memories are of being in the place of his mother on his father's lap. The most generous gift a feminine reader can make to Rousseau is to treat his texts as he dreamed of being treated, to gaze on them in the feminine guise which Rousseau was later to adopt for his comfort. I would argue that Rousseau's rational theory of beneficence can only be sustained by his dream of generosity, a dream of a feminine economy.

For Rousseau, economic structures should be understood morally and affect moral domains; he resists the tendency which will become dominant, that is, to analyse the economy in terms of efficiency above all. Rousseau's refusal of commerce is thus a general one. And despite his insistence on the need for sexual difference, his economy in many ways brings men and women closer together than they will be in the commercial world to come.

7

Bataille: pre-text or post-script

This chapter is a brief excursion into the work of Georges Bataille, both as a significant pre-text to structuralist and poststructuralist thinking on the gift, and as an example of a text transformed by the gift of rereading. His work on economy (advocating a consideration of general rather than only restricted economy) is an important pre-text for contemporary work on feminine economies, but his tone and content may be seen as masculinist, if not misogynist. Barthes, Derrida and Kristeva amongst others have nevertheless chosen to read Bataille generously.[1] I want merely to introduce the wild anthropology of Bataille and the work which has been written in its wake. While this theorisation of symbolic exchange can be and is subsumed under the heading of the gift, it would not necessarily be recognised by moral philosophy's speculation on altruism. What Bataille's *dépense* (*unthinking expenditure*) or sacrifice primarily share with the gift is their oppostion to, or exclusion from, the economic. Bataille's writing, which can easily be judged as misogynistic in its pornographic turn, is also precisely the kind of avant-gardist limit text which may be considered as shaking the symbolic order – and a deconstructive reading can find a certain feminine in Bataille.[2]

1 Other examples include Baudrillard, Philippe Sollers, or Susan Rubin Suleiman. See Barthes, J.-L. Baudry, D. Hollier, J.-L. Houdebine, J. Kristeva, M. Pleynet, P. Sollers and F. Wahl, *Bataille*, Paris, U.G.E. 10/18, 1973; Sollers, 'Le toit', in *L'Écriture et l'expérience des limites*, Paris, Seuil, 1968, pp. 105–38; Rubin Suleiman, 'Pornography, Transgression and the Avant-Garde: Bataille's *Story of the Eye*', in *The Poetics of Gender*, ed. Nancy K. Miller, New York, Columbia University Press, 1986, pp. 117–36, or, a more critical reading, 'Bataille in the Street. The Search for Virility in the 1930s', in *Bataille: Writing the Sacred*, ed. C. Bailey Gill, London and New York, Routledge, 1995, pp. 26–45. In 'Pornography, Transgression and the Avant-Garde', Rubin Suleiman analyses two poles of reading response to Bataille: a (feminist) critique of the pornographic content of his work and an avant-gardist celebration of the formal qualities of his work.

2 I shall be reading Bataille in the most productively generous way possible – taking as a cue the seminal, if not disseminal, readings by Barthes and Derrida. See Barthes, 'The Metaphor of the Eye', in *Critical Essays*, pp. 239–47 and Derrida, 'From Restricted to General Economy', in *Writing and Difference*, pp. 251–77.

In 'The Notion of Expenditure'[3] Bataille emphasises the restricted nature of theory which focuses on production and consumption, conservation and reproduction. He opposes the finite questions of need and utility to infinite free expenditure. He forcefully argues for a principle of loss (or non-productive expenditure), which must be taken into account. His examples include jewels; blood sacrifice (etymologically 'the production of sacred things'); games and gambling; and poetry (a form of sacrifice). According to Bataille, it is wrong to see the primitive origins of economy in barter, but classical economics at a particular historical conjuncture 'had no reason to assume, in fact, that a means of acquisition such as exchange might have as its origin not the need to acquire that it satisfies today, but the contrary need, the need to destroy and lose' (p. 121). For Bataille the model is not barter, but potlatch as described by Mauss, a model which he describes as anal. 'The hatred of expenditure [or economy in the vulgar sense] is the *raison d'être* of and the justification for the bourgeoisie; it is at the same time the principle of its horrifying hypocrisy [its validation of domination]' (pp. 124–5). Bataille's 'general economy' will have a strong influence on concepts developed by a number of later thinkers, including Baudrillard's 'symbolic exchange';[4] however, Baudrillard does question Bataille's key example of solar energy as superabundant generosity; Baudrillard claims that 'the sun gives nothing, it is necessary to nourish it continually with human blood in order that it shine. It is necessary to challenge the gods through sacrifice in order that they respond with profusion' ('When Bataille Attacked', p. 61). For Baudrillard a crucial aspect of the archaic gift is reversibility.

In *Eroticism*,[5] Bataille distinguishes between reproductive sex, on the one hand, which is common to both man and the animals, which has a natural goal, and which reveals the discontinuity between individuals, and eroticism, on the other hand, which involves a mental relationship with death, a common sense of vertigo at the edge of that abyss. Thus, paradoxically, eroticism, the domain of violence and violation, to some extent dissolves the discontinuity between subjects. Bataille presents economy, the profane world of work and of taboos, as man's way of saying 'no' to nature's constant luxurious waste of resources (including human lives). However, according to Bataille, we also need *sacred* time, festivals of prodigal consumption.

In his 'Introduction to Economics I. Because the World is Round', Geoff Bennington carefully analyses Bataille's *The Accursed Share* to reveal that 'there is no general economy except as the economy of restricted

3 First published in 1933, reprinted as an introduction to *La Part maudite*, Paris, Minuit, 1967; in *Visions of Excess*, pp. 116–29.
4 See, for instance, 'When Bataille Attacked the Metaphysical Principle of Economy' (first published in 1976), trans. D. J. Miller in the *Canadian Journal of Political and Social Theory*, 11 (1987), 57–62.
5 First published in 1957; trans. M. Dalwood, London, John Calder, 1962.

economy' (p. 48) and thus 'there is only ever exchange and signification' (p. 53).[6] These formulations recall Lyotard, and also a crucial moment in Derrida (pronounced with respect to the gift in *Given Time I*). Yet Derrida has a poetic counterpoint to such pronouncements, an (on the) other hand *presenting* the gift.

There have indeed been a range of readings of Bataille: Derrida reads him in terms of sovereignty; Barthes in terms of metaphor or metonymy; Rubin Suleiman in terms of pornography and Kristeva in terms of abjection.[7] Bataille will be presented here largely via abjection, and as an analysis of abjection as much as an experience[8] of abjection (from inside and from without) – perhaps a 'working through'. The abject is a slippery concept to engage with if you treat Kristeva's series of cautions and provisos seriously. Abjection is immediately defined as a revolt of being (as a twisted braid of affects and thoughts), a revolt against a threat from an exorbitant 'something' (not a thing) inside or outside the subject, something close but unassimilable, which both fascinates and frightens or disgusts desire. When commentators (even the most distinguished commentators) refer to the abject in passing, they tend to simplify it as the other or that which has been (successfully) expelled. For example, Naomi Schor writes: 'Otherness in Beauvoir's scheme of things is utter negativity; it is the realm of what Kristeva has called the abject.'[9] And yet Kristeva defines the abject with a series of neither/nors which are perhaps unsurprising in a psychoanalytical and poststructuralist context, but nevertheless make it hard to conceptualise: neither subject nor object, neither within nor without . . . And when you move to middle ground, since, neither within nor without, the abject must exist on the border *between* inside and outside – you generate fresh

6 *Bataille*, ed. C. Bailey Gill, London and New York, Routledge, 1995, pp. 46–57.

7 Kristeva refers to Bataille at a number of points in almost any one of her works. With respect to abjection, see *Powers of Horror*, trans. L. S. Roudiez, New York, Columbia University Press, 1982 (pp. 56, 64, 138, 207, 208). She quotes him both as an anthropologist writing on abjection and as a producer of literature (alongside Baudelaire, Lautréamont, Kafka and the Sartre of *Nausea*), which is 'the ultimate coding of our crises' (p. 208). She has also written essays on him in Barthes *et al*, *Bataille*, and in *Tales of Love*. One article which brings Kristeva and Bataille together is Catherine Marchak's 'The Joy of Transgression: Bataille and Kristeva', *Philosophy Today*, (Winter 1990), 354–63.

8 Bataille himself plays with the (auto)biographical question in a range of ways – for example in 'Part 2. Coincidences', in *Story of the Eye*, trans. J. Neugroschal, Harmondsworth, Penguin, 1982, pp. 69–74 and in *W.C.*, Preface to *Story of the Eye* from *Le Petit* (1943), *ibid.*, pp. 75–8.

9 'This Essentialism Which Is Not One: Coming to Grips with Irigaray', in *Engaging with Irigaray* ed. C. Burke, N. Schor and M. Whitford, New York, Columbia University Press, 1994, pp. 57–78 (p. 65). See also Judith Butler, *Gender Trouble*, London, Routledge, 1990: 'The "abject" designates that which has been expelled from the body, discharged as excrement, literally rendered "Other"' (p. 133). I should like to thank Paul Hegarty for drawing this example to my attention.

neither/ nors: neither accepting a frontier nor breaching it. It is possible to think this paradox (especially if you are familiar with psychoanalysis, with poststructuralism), but it must be as a kind of permeable, necessary but impossible, non-space. Perhaps 'the in-between', *l'entre-deux* (*Powers of Horror*, p. 4)? While the abject is neither subject nor object, it does have a relation to both subject and object. The abject is not the *objet 'a'*[10] – the 'a' (*autre*) becomes *ab-*, not only or not even other and desired, but not quite other and *also* rejected. There is a fresh importance to *-jet* or *-ject*, the thrown or cast out: it is the fallen 'object' drawing me towards the collapse of meaning, soliciting a discharge, a spasm, a cry (pp. 1–2, the translation renders *chu* as 'jettisoned' rather than 'fallen').[11] It is also the pre-object (or semi-object, transitional object) of primary repression, dating from a moment when the ability to distinguish or separate is there, but prior to the distinction between subject and object, prior to the separation from the mother (which requires a struggle, a violent bodily encounter, a *corps à corps*, the mother repulses and is repulsive), prior to imitation. The *corps à corps* conjures up Irigaray's work of that name, which particularly refers to the difficult relationship between mother and daughter. Kristeva says of Joyce's Molly, that the abjection arises from the distanced writer making the body speak of what escapes words: 'turns out to be the hand to hand struggle [*le corps à corps*] of one woman with another, her mother of course, the absolute because primeval seat of the impossible – of the excluded, the outside-of-meaning, the abject' (p. 22). Irigaray too is concerned with the difficulty for the daughter to symbolise the relation to the mother, although she may be more optimistic about the possibility of change.

Bataille's interest for me lies in his potential to disturb economies of sexual difference – although at a price (which Kristeva regards as unsurprising, if not inevitable). I shall begin by attempting to summarise his account of sovereignty (and Derrida's commentary on it), and then move on to his fiction. At the same time I want to keep hanging Cixous's footnote to a statement about the persistence of hierarchical binaries:

> All Derrida's work traversing–detecting the history of philosophy is devoted to bringing this to light. In Plato, Hegel, and Nietzsche, the same process continues: repression, repudiation, distancing of woman; a murder that is mixed up with history as the manifestation and representation of masculine power. (*The Newly Born Woman*, p. 130)

10 Here I differ from Elizabeth Grosz's helpful elucidation of the concept in *Sexual Subversions*, Sydney, Allen and Unwin, 1989. See *Powers of Horror*, p. 1; *Pouvoirs de l'horreur*, Paris, Seuil, 1980, p. 9 (the point is less clear in the English translation).
11 This is reminiscent of Bataille's writings on extreme eroticism. Kristeva states: 'jouissance alone causes the abject to exist as such. One does not know it, one does not desire it, one joys in it [*on en jouit*]. Violently and painfully. A passion.' (*Powers of Horror*, p. 9).

Cixous comments specifically on Bataille:

> Why did this comedy, whose final act is the master's flirtation with death,
> make Bataille laugh so hard, as he amused himself by pushing Hegel to
> the edge of the abyss that a civilized man keeps himself from falling into?
> This abyss that functions as a metaphor both of death and of the feminine
> sex. (p. 80)

The comedy to which she refers is the conditionality of masculine desire:
'the fragility of a desire that must (pretend to) kill its object. Fantasizing
rape or making the transition to the act of rape. And plenty of women,
sensing what is at stake here, consent to play the part of object . . .' (p. 80).
Irigaray, too, suggests that history is founded on the death (such as the
matricide of Clytemnestra by Orestes) or the incarceration (Hegel's chosen
example of Antigone) of a woman. Irigaray's concern with the repeated
sacrifice of the woman and of women gives her a different approach to
sacrifice than that of theorists of the gift such as Bataille and Baudrillard.
For Bataille, sacrifice returns *things* to the *sacred*: 'sacrifice restores to the
sacred world that which servile use has degraded, rendered profane'.[12] For
Irigaray this repugnance for the material thing-ness of things is itself bound
up with the sacrifice (in a pejorative sense) of women, often intimately
associated with materiality. In the final analysis it may be that Bataille's
structure is founded on a sacrifice which is the sacrifice of a woman (the
mother) even if, or because, he himself is also that woman. Kristeva, however, while agreeing that writers of 'limit texts' try to maintain their fragile
hold on the symbolic through violent racism or misogyny, sees this as part
of the process of exploration of the fascinating but lethal abject, the other
within/without themselves. She writes, in *Powers of Horror*:

> The fact that 'something of the maternal' turns out to motivate that un-
> certainty I call abjection, makes it clear that literary writing involves the
> essential struggle which any writer (male or female) engages in with what
> he names his demon, only in order to signal that it is the reverse or lining
> of his very being, that it is the other (sex) which works on and possesses him.
> (p. 208, translation modified)

Sovereignty

Sovereignty is a term used in the first half of this century – notably by
Bataille – in an attempt to think something other than the economy of *homo
economicus*. Sovereign man is declared to be above all free – unlike *homo
economicus*, whom he represents as animal and servile. Thus certain aspects
of the Bataillean text might encourage a reading not as abject, but rather as
heroic transgression, and Kristeva argues that transgression is a modality of

---

12 *The Accursed Share*, trans. R. Hurley, New York, Zone Books, 1988, volume I, p. 55.

negation, whereas abjection is a question of *exclusion* (*Powers of Horror*, p. 6). Kristeva argues with respect to Dostoievski's *The Possessed* that Stavroguine is less abject than the cynical Verkhovenski because 'his immoralism admits of laughter and refusal, something artistic, a cynical and gratuitous expenditure that obviously becomes capitalized for the benefit of private narcissism but does not serve an arbitrary, exterminating power' (p. 19). In 'From Restricted to General Economy', Derrida asks whether Bataille's *sovereignty* is a translation (and displacement) of Hegel's *Herrschaft* (p. 254), a term which indicates that you are not attached to any being, nor to life itself – unlike the slave, the one who won't wager his life, who wants to preserve it. You need to rise above life and look death in the face in order to be free. However, the difference between *Herrschaft* (mastery) and sovereignty (the displacement which Bataille attempts to effect) is that mastery has a meaning; wagering life is one stage in the constitution of meaning. Hegelianism, Derrida tells us, seeks to reappropriate all negativity 'as it works the "putting at stake" into an *investment*, as it *amortizes* absolute expenditure; and as it gives meaning to death, thereby simultaneously blinding itself to the baselessness of the nonmeaning from which the basis of meaning is drawn, and in which this basis of meaning is exhausted' ('From Restricted to General Economy', *Writing and Difference*, p. 257).[13] Bataille *exceeds* this meaning by laughter (non-meaning) which is both more and less than the dialectic. Laughter opens up the sacred for Bataille. He laughs at himself because (like Hegel's master) he still needs life so that he can enjoy himself – there is always an element of simulation of risk, of comedy. In this respect he reminds the reader of Derrida's analysis of Nietzsche's woman artist who is sceptical both about castration and about anti-castration; and thus suspends the relation to castration (*Spurs*, pp. 59–61). For Bataille, there has to be a subterfuge because you have to experience death as a living consciousness, and thus there is a need for spectacle, for representation – to escape from animality by the *fiction* of death (the fiction of the woman's death?).

Homo economicus has an ordered linear temporality: past, present, future tenses – all with their place in his economy (for example, taking responsibility for past debts, investment for the future). The moment of

13 The desire to *account* for everything (economism) could be related to a certain theoretical imperialism as well (even structuralism), something highlighted, for instance, in Shoshana Felman's analysis of the figure of the governess in *The Turn of the Screw* (just to show it's not only males who adopt this model of masculinity): where she seeks mastery through interpretation, and is blinded by knowledge, through grasping the answer to the enigma, where she finds the phallus as general equivalent (including to the mast of a ship . . .). See *Literature and Psychoanalysis*, ed. S. Felman, Baltimore, Johns Hopkins University Press, 1982, pp. 94–207. In a capitalist economy everything valuable must be understood as work, men's work (women's work not being real work – not because of its content, which is variable, but because of the relations of production within which it takes place).

sovereignty, Derrida explains, slips between two presences: 'It does not give itself [*ne se donne pas*], but is *stolen* [*se vole*]' (p. 263). Indeed, just as there is no time of sovereignty, so sovereignty has no identity, has no power over itself or others – in order not to command (in other words, be enslaved), 'it must expend itself without reserve, lose itself, lose consciousness, lose all memory of itself and all the interiority of itself' (p. 265). Sovereign man must actively forget (following Nietzsche) and not seek recognition. According to both Barthes[14] and Derrida, Bataille (like Nietzsche's woman) is profoundly superficial. All concepts associated with general writing are there not to signify but to make meaning slip. He inaugurates a potlatch of signs 'that burns, consumes and wastes words in the gay affirmation of death: a sacrifice and a challenge' (p. 274).

Pierre–pieuvre; Peter and the prostitute, or rocks and fish

In this section I shall explore Bataille's fiction in terms of one saturated set of images typically linked with the feminine and the masculine, as suggested in the subtitle. In the next section I shall briefly discuss one of his most famous obsessions, the eye.

The narrator of Bataille's *My Mother* is called Pierre; the pseudonym under which Bataille first published *Mme Edwarda* is Pierre Angélique.[15] The narrator is called as well as named: the first word of the novel is ' "Pierre!" ', the mother's gentle but insistent voice, calling her son from his bed. Pierre is a common name, but also (and biblically) a common noun: rock or stone, the foundation of the Church, the line of Holy Fathers. Thus, through Peter the Rock, we come to the male as hard (man), and to the man as the inaugurator of the Symbolic Order. Woman, on the other hand, or the woman's *sexe* (her sex, her sexual organs) is compared in both works to a *pieuvre*. Mme Edwarda asks the narrator ' "Do you want to see my rags?" ' As she opens her slit (*fente*), the narrator tells us: 'And so Edwarda's "rags" were staring me in the face, pink and hairy, full of life like a repulsive octopus.'[16] In *My Mother*, the narrator imagines in advance his encounter

---

14 '*Histoire de l'œil* is not a "profound" work: everything is given on the surface and without hierarchy' ('The Metaphor of the Eye', p. 242).

15 *Angélique* reminds us of Bataille's penchant for the saintly *and* for the bisexual or ambivalently sexed (Hansi in *My Mother*, Simone and Marcelle in *Story of the Eye*). The same names, or variations upon them, ciculate between texts and sexes. Mme Edwarda echoes Edouard in *The Dead Man* and perhaps Sir Edmund in *Story of the Eye*. Bataille published some poetry under the title *L'Archangélique* in 1944. His pleasure in a perverse onomastics is displayed in his careful explanation of the pseudonym Lord Auch (author of *Story of the Eye*) as an evocation of God going to the toilet, *aux chiottes* (W.C., p. 76).

16 Bataille, *Madame Edwarda* (1937), in *Œuvres complètes*, Paris, Gallimard, 1971, III, pp. 20–1; *My Mother; Madame Edwarda; The Dead Man*, trans. A. Wainhouse, London,

with his mother's lover Réa: 'I was delirious: I saw her taking all her clothes off at the first hint; and my mother, forced to flee by her vulgarity, would abandon me to this octopus, who resembled the "girls" who filled my imagination thanks to my father's obscene pictures' (p. 57). The *pieuvre*, the monster octopus (*poulpe*), is figuratively, according to the French dictionary *Le Petit Robert*, 'Someone who is insatiable in their demands, who never releases their prey'. If we stopped here, we would find classical misogyny which could be termed in a sophisticated-sounding fashion 'abjection', and yet keep us fixed in sexual opposition. Mme Edwarda refers to her genitals as rags, fragments of material – but for the narrator they are not (and she is not) sufficiently close to the passivity of clothing or fabric – they are full of life, like a powerful and terrifying octopus, mobile, briny, repulsive – ready to suck him in, maybe to immobilise him with their tentacles. This could be analysed as a phobic moment: an inverted metaphor in which my empty, incorporating mouth threatens me from outside, like the horse for Little Hans, or the dog for the little girl analysed by Anna Freud (*Powers of Horror*, p. 52).[17] Kristeva argues that the scopic investment in such hallucinatory objects frequently ends up in writing.[18]

Pierre also fears the activity of Réa, stripping off, putting his mother to flight with her lewdness. He thus sees his mother's gift of Réa to him (or of him to Réa) as her abandoning him to an insatiable octopus, to something like the pornographic images which spilled from the shelves of his dead father's study. 'The absence, or the failure, of paternal function to

Marion Boyars, [1989] 1995. Unfortunately these translations are strikingly inaccurate, for instance, ' "Comme j'ai joui!" ' (p. 21) is rendered as ' "Oh, listen, fellow! The fun I've had . . ." ' (p. 150). David Macey gives the more accurate translation: 'I came, I came', in his important analysis of Bataille's influence on Lacan in *Lacan in Contexts*, London, Verso, 1988, p. 205. I shall provide all the translations of *My Mother* and *Mme Edwarda*, but give page references to the English editions.

17 See also Bataille's article 'Mouth' in his *Critical Dictionary* in *Encyclopaedia Acephalica*, trans. I. White *et al.*, London, Atlas Press, 1995.

18 'To speak of hallucination in connection with such an unstable "object" suggests at once that there is a visual cathexis in the phobic mirage – and at least a speculative cathexis in the abject. Elusive, fleeting, and baffling as it is, that non-object can be grasped only as a sign. It is through the intermediary of a *representation*, hence a *seeing*, that it holds together. A visual hallucination that, in the final analysis, gathers up the others (those that are auditory, tactile, etc.) and, as it bursts into a symbolicity that is normally calm and neutral, represents the subject's desire. For the absent object, there is a sign. For the desire of that want, there is a visual hallucination. More than that, a cathexis of looking, in parallel with the symbolic domination taking the place of narcissism, often leads to voyeuristic "side effects" of phobia. Voyeurism is a structural necessity in the constitution of object relation, showing up every time the object shifts towards the abject; it becomes true perversion only if there is a failure to symbolize the subject/object instability. Voyeurism accompanies the writing of abjection. When that writing stops, voyeurism becomes a perversion' (*Powers of Horror*, p. 46).

establish a unitary bent between subject and object' (*Powers of Horror*, p. 49); the 'foreclosure of paternal function' (p. 50), the failure of symbolic law, are recurrent themes in Kristeva's analysis of modalities of abjection. In *My Mother* the alcoholic father whose death occurs on the second page of the novel is revealed to have been repeatedly abused by the mother. In *W.C.*, Bataille tells us 'What upset me more [i.e. more than masturbating next to his mother's corpse] was: seeing my father shit a great number of times. He would get out of his blind paralytic's bed' (*Story of the Eye*, p. 76), and then asserts: 'My father having conceived me when blind (absolutely blind), I cannot tear out my eyes like Oedipus' (p. 77). Bataille thus insists that he (his protagonist) can commit incest without being punished; his father is so feeble that he cannot even pronounce a prohibition. Furthermore, he has seen his father's nakedness. The father is always already castrated – absolutely blind at the moment of conception – thus the son will be sovereign. Kristeva informs us that the parental gift (here most obviously Réa, but also the pornographic images as legacy) as sign of their desire provokes nausea (*Powers of Horror*, p. 10), but as 'I' only exist in the desire of the (m)other, 'I' am expelled with the vomit; this is the abject, 'a repulsive gift' (p. 9).

However, I wish to argue that Bataille's writings need not be read as fixing us in a kind of sexual opposition, and that this lack of definition brings him closer to Kristeva's analysis of abjection. His theory of eroticism is a theory of fusion, of melting, of a temporary breaking down of the discontinuities which are a feature of human existence.[19] The fiction is, furthermore, more radical than the theory. The theory still asserts (hankers after) a starting-point in male activity and female passivity – although that is not the end point. The theory, for example, refers to *mise à nu*, stripping naked, as a miniature *mise à mort* (as orgasm is a small death). We imagine the (female) subject being stripped, a necessary ritual, sacrificial degredation (and only mysticism's hairbreadth's away from traditional sexual roles). In the fiction it is a different story. In *Mme Edwarda* the story begins with the words: 'At a street corner, despair, a dirty, intoxicating despair, undid me [*me décomposa*] (perhaps because I'd seen two furtive "girls" on the stairs leading to a toilet). At such times, the desire to vomit myself up comes to me. I need to strip naked or strip the girls I lust after' (p. 148), and the narrator begins to drink Pernod, moving from bar to bar. Pernod, as a white or colourless liquid, is easily inserted into the Bataillean chain of eroticised fluids. As Barthes suggests, Bataille is at once obsessed by bodily and other fluids, and by the dryness of the sun – which then melts back into the series of flows. The abject collapse of the frontier between inside and

---

19 'The transition from the normal state to that of erotic desire presupposes a partial dissolution of the person as he exists in the realm of discontinuity' (*Eroticism*, p. 17).

out encourages an obsessional fixation on urine, blood, excrement, sperm, and so on (*Powers of Horror*, p. 65). Ultimately, Kristeva argues, this is a search for the fascinating and terrifying inside of the mother's body, which the abject subject desires to incorporate, and thus be able fantasmatically to give birth to her or himself – a birth which Kristeva compares to an abortion. In the quotation from *Mme Edwarda* an equivalence is set up between the man stripping himself or his stripping the girls (prostitutes) he lusts for – this is already a shift from an absolute active–passive polarity. The drunken narrator does begin to remove his own clothes in the streets, but then puts his underwear back on to enter a brothel. Contrary to his stripping fantasy, Mme Edwarda is already, casually, naked, and in the passage I cited above insists on bringing him face to face with her naked *sexe* (more nakedness than he wants). He is reduced to stammering like a child: 'Why are you doing that?' and she responds, 'You see [. . .] I'm GOD [. . .]' She forces him to *look*, and then to kiss – and he hears the sound of the sea: 'I thought I could hear the sound of the sea, the same sound that you hear when you put your ear to a large shell [. . .] as if Edwarda and I were lost on a windy night by the sea' (p. 150). Madame Edwarda's sex shifts from rags, to a material description (*velues et roses*), to the octopus, to the mark of her divinity, to an open wound,[20] to a shell giving the sound of the sea – the familiar French *la mer*. Textual, soft, decaying, velvety–hairy, pink, full of life, monstrously powerful and *petrifying*, divine, open and bleeding, waves and wind on the maternal sea-shore. And the brittle hardness of the shell[21] is not the furthest shift of the female sex towards Pierre. As Mme Edwarda dresses and leads the narrator outside, she blends into the triumphal arch of the Porte Saint-Denis: hole and stone ('Her presence had about it the unintelligible simplicity of a stone [*pierre*]' p. 152). The black hole which is femininity is also the black stone of the monolithic monument.

To return to *My Mother*, if we ever left it/her, Pierre's paternal-driven fantasy of a desirable, yet terrifying and repulsive, octopus is, we are told, *puérile* day-dreaming, an attempt to combine pleasure and horror – the sensation of *étranglement* (strangling/suffocation) which is preferred by so many of Bataille's characters. His mother could never be put to flight by

---

20 Coming so soon after Mme Edwarda's claim to divinity, the open wound has to remind the reader of Christ's stigmata. I should also like to make a link to what Kristeva says of the analyst: 'One must keep open the wound where he or she who enters into the analytic adventure is located – a wound that the professional establishment, along with the cynicism of the times and of institutions, will soon manage to close up [. . .] For the unstabilized subject who comes out of that – like a crucified person opening up the stigmata of its desiring body to a speech that structures only on condition that it let go – any signifying or human phenomenon, insofar as it *is*, appears in its being as abjection' (*Powers of Horror*, p. 27).

21 In the *Critical Dictionary* edited by Bataille, Jacques Baron contributes an article in praise of 'Crustaceans', where he writes of a shrimp, 'She is also a woman' (p. 39).

lewd behaviour; her goal throughout the story is to make her son face her own erotic self – and finally to have him merge with that eroticism. An act of incest which almost transcends incest, so successful is Hélène in submerging herself as reproduction beneath herself as desire and mastery – even though Pierre will never call her anything but 'maman' to her face, and 'ma mère' to his reader.

The maternal sex is represented for Freud by, amongst other things, the Medusa's head, the many snakes threatening castration; the apotropaic response of being turned to stone is an erection. In French, readers not only have the pleasures of *la mer/la mère*, but also of *la méduse*, the common noun derived from the Gorgon, meaning a jellyfish, that pale, soft, squashy sea-creature, seemingly less threatening than an octopus, but with a sting in its tail. These images and oppositions are not necessarily regressive in and of themselves; they are material to be reworked. The effect depends on the various contexts in which they appear: not only the context of production, but also that of receptions. The opposition between men (as hewers) of stone and women as creatures of the sea is a traditional topos still explored in a range of works today – including radical feminist works. One example would be Joan Slonczewski's *A Door into Ocean*.[22] This is part of the Women's Press Science Fiction series which aims 'to present exciting and provocative feminist images of the future that will offer an alternative vision of science and technology, and challenge male domination of the science fiction tradition itself'. *A Door into Ocean* depicts, on the one hand, the Valans, governed at a distance by the Patriarch, who controls a militaristic, highly structured empire. Their traders exploit natives on other planets, as Europeans exploited indigenous peoples from the early days of colonialism. On the other hand, the Sharers of Shora, an ocean moon, are an all-female community who have no leaders, no clothes, no crime, who respect all other life-forms and have a highly developed bioscience which promotes life rather than death. The Valan economy is dominated by hard, lifeless things, in particular, precious stones, which even dominate their names (Spinel, Beryl). The Sharers live in temporary silk houses on living rafts on their ocean moon. They enjoy eating octopuses and other sea-creatures – but respect them, too.

Bataille's texts do not effect a denial of sexual difference, rather they set difference afloat. The (frequently sexist) metaphors or *objects* which circulate in his fiction are related both by condensation and displacement. In *My Mother*, Pierre is circulated between women in almost a reversal of the hom(m)o-sexual economy – his name begins to conjure up precious stones (*pierres précieuses*), reminding us of what Bataille wrote about jewels: 'In the unconscious, jewels, like excrement, are cursed matter that

22 London, The Women's Press, 1987.

flows from a wound: they are a part of oneself destined for open sacrifice (they serve, in fact, as sumptuous gifts charged with sexual love)' ('The Notion of Expenditure', p. 119). Pierre could be seen as that accursed matter that flowed from his mother's wound; destined for open sacrifice, he is a sumptuous gift charged with sexual love – given first to Réa, then to Hansi (both his mother's lovers) and then to herself. Speaking of his conception (when she was raped by his father), she says to him: 'Pierre! you are not [your father's] son but the fruit of anguish [. . .] You come from terror [. . .] Pierre, I came for hours on end, my back arched amongst the rotting leaves: you were born of all that pleasure' (My Mother, pp. 72–3).

The eye

So does Bataille have a more significant relation to the feminine than the use of beautiful women ('innocent' girls) as characters who lead the plunge into debauchery and degredation (such as Simone in Story of the Eye)? Derrida analyses both Bataille and Nietzsche in terms of what, in Spurs, he calls the feminine: 'That which will not be pinned down by truth is, in truth – feminine' (Spurs, p. 55). Bataille is often associated with solar metaphors, and his argument for the natural necessity to spend without reserve, to waste, to consume, traces a path back to the sun's glorious expenditure of energy.[23] The sun appears to be a masculine image par excellence. And yet Barthes shows how Bataillean metaphor series cross and interrupt each other:

> What is 'dryer' than the sun? Yet it suffices that in the metaphoric field which Bataille traces like an haruspex, the sun should be a disc, then a globe, for light to flow from it and thereby join, through the notion of a soft luminosity or a urinary liquefaction of the sky, the theme of eye, egg, and testicle. ('The Metaphor of the Eye', p. 241)

No single term can be assigned pre-eminence, Barthes argues; the genital or phallic (the father urinating) has no more privilege than the father's blind eye, which, I would add, becomes in the metaphoric chain the dish of cat's milk, metonymically related to the female genitals. The gaze of the female sex ('Edwarda's "rags" were staring me in the face') reminds us of Story of the Eye (first published in 1928, final version, 1967) in which it is literalised. Simone asks Sir Edmund to remove Don Aminado's eye and slides it 'into her slobbery flesh, in the midst of the fur'. The narrator tells us 'in Simone's hairy vagina, I saw the wan blue eye of Marcelle, gazing at me through tears of urine' (Story of the Eye, p. 67). In Bataille's eroticism what is transgressed is sex, Barthes tells us.

---

23 Kristeva's essay on Bataille in Tales of Love is entitled 'Bataille and the Sun, or the Guilty Text' [Bataille solaire, ou le texte coupable], pp. 365–71.

For us the eye is strongly associated with Enlightenment and with masculinity (though also with love). The eighteenth century took divine all-seeingness and made it human: man, the rational observer, the scientist, shakes off blind prejudice and superstition and sees clearly, lucidly, from the Dark Ages into Enlightenment. The eye is active, darting glances as the sun beams out its rays.[24] Woman, a spectacle, is the passive recipient of the gaze. The hand is the instrument of the eye.[25] The eye is emblematic of potency. This is one dominant set of associations for the eye. Bataille takes the eye and displaces it: in the blazing heat of the sun Simone bites into a raw bull's ball; the matador approaches another bull, waving his scarlet cloth; Simone, with a blood-red face, fits the second 'pale globule' into her vulva; the bull's horn plunges into the matador's right eye; Simone orgasms and her nose bleeds; the matador is carried away, his eye dangling from his head (*Story of the Eye*, p. 53). Later Simone will insert another man's eye into her vulva. The non-place of castration becomes the site of the woman's incorporation of the testicle and the eye. When a man gazes at a male victim's eye in that place, he sees a female victim's eye. In *Eroticism*, Bataille quotes Rimbaud, whom he calls one of the most violent poets. Bataille relates poetry to eroticism, in that both lead to the momentary confusing of otherwise distinct objects: 'It leads us to eternity, it leads us to death, and through death to continuity. Poetry is eternity; the sun matched with the sea' (p. 25). It is interesting to note that in this twice quoted example the two distinct objects which are brought to indistinction are the sea/*la mer* and the sun. In *My Mother*, as Kristeva emphasises in *Tales of Love*, Bataille poetically equates the sun, death and the mother (or incest) as things which you cannot gaze steadily upon.

Against the succession of rounded, moist and whitish objects which circulate in *Story of the Eye*, I could set hard, sharp, pointed objects: pins, daggers, nail-scissors (which cut out the priest's eye), the horn of a bull, nails, thorns. I would like to sketch an imaginary of the pin (the emblem of division of labour, and thus of the market), which could be related to Derrida's spur. In a simple morphology the pin would be phallic, but diminutive multiplied phalluses suggest castration (as do the snakes on the Medusa's head). In any case, *Spurs* brilliantly demonstrates the reversibility of any sexual morphology: the ship is a container, but also a prow cleaving the waves, billowing sails, covering veils – *le/la voile*.

24 In Bataille's essay 'Eye' in *Visions of Excess*, pp. 17–19, he writes of the horror and seductiveness of eyes and of the terrifying eye in the sky. He also quotes Stevenson: the eye is a cannibal delicacy. Part of this essay is also reproduced as one of four in Bataille's *Critical Dictionary*: other contributions are by Robert Desnos and Marcel Griaule and one is anonymous.
25 See Barthes, 'The Plates of the *Encyclopedia*' in *New Critical Essays*.

With respect to Bataille's language, we might note the traits of repetition and the frequent gaps, the fragmentary nature of much of his fiction. Certain verbs (in particular *rire* or *étrangler*) are repeated obsessively. It thus has a tendency towards that of the *borderline* structure described by Kristeva: 'abstract, composed of stereotypes which cannot fail to seem deliberate: it aims at precision, self-reflexivity, a detailed understanding – traits which immediately bring obsessional discourse to mind' (*Powers of Horror*, p. 49, translation modified). However, it does not quite reach the pathological limit-point she describes of *morcellement* ('breaking up') and reduction to a 'pure' signifier (p. 49) because, finally, it is writing.

In guise of a conclusion

To summarise, I would suggest that Bataille's texts are a privileged example of what, for Kristeva, is a universal structure for all societies and all subjects, male and female. Their value lies in encoding our crises (*Powers of Horror*, p. 208), in symbolising abjection, through working on the borderline – on permeable thresholds such as laughter/despair, drinking/vomiting or coming/dying, sex/violence. But of course the necessity, yet fragility of their hold on the symbolic, on clear distinctions, does produce a reading effect of horror. In a way it is more comfortable to see the *pieuvre* as the product of the imagination of the *male* pervert/avant-garde artist, crazily projecting his *mother* on to other women.[26] We can separate ourselves off from that. We are more troubled (and I am thinking of the French *troublées*) by the anguished juxtaposition and attempted fusion of seemingly distinct entities (Kristeva suggests obscenity and philosophy as examples)[27] – since that evokes on some level what are problems for us all: sexual difference, loss of meaning, death. Bataille's potlatch of signs makes meaning slip – as Derrida writes of Nietzsche's woman: 'The gift, which is the essential predicate of woman, appeared in the undecidable oscillation of to give oneself/ to give oneself for, give/take, let take/appropriate. Its value or price is that of poison' (*Spurs*, p. 121).

26 For example, Kelly Oliver, who has written extensively on Kristeva, glosses *Powers of Horror* as a story only about men and their mothers. She writes, for instance: 'The child, the male child, feels rage against his mother because her carrying him in her womb compromises his identity', and then specifies that in *Powers of Horror* the child 'is always the male child' ('Nietzsche's Abjection', in *Nietzsche and the Feminine*, ed. P. J. Burgard, Charlottesville, University Press of Virginia, 1994, pp. 53–67, p. 55). This statement overlooks details such as Kristeva's use of the example of the little girl with the dog phobia analysed by Anna Freud. Rubin-Suleiman also claims that 'in [Kristeva's] model, the avant-garde is by definition male' ('Mothers and the Avant-Garde: A Case of Mistaken Identity?' *Avant Garde*, 4 (1990), 135–46, p. 135).
27 See *Histoires d'amour*, Paris, Denoël, 1983, pp. 457–8 and 461 for *troublés*.

8

The question of the gift in the late twentieth century: Cixous, Derrida, Irigaray

The question of the gift has been of continuous interest in certain contexts, such as that of ethnography. However, in this chapter I shall be focusing on one recent surge of interest in that intersection of disciplines which may loosely be referred to as poststructuralism. The three thinkers who will be analysed here are Hélène Cixous, Jacques Derrida and Luce Irigaray. Cixous is primarily a novelist and playwright as well as a (literary) theorist; Derrida a philosopher; Irigaray a psychoanalyst and philosopher. First I shall discuss the characterisation of market exchange, and then I shall turn to the sexualisation of the debate. Eighteenth-century and earlier anti-mercantile positions were deeply and unashamedly ethical. In poststructuralist debates the privileging of avant-garde linguistic experimentation and the choice to deconstruct the counter-tradition as well as the dominant tradition may seem inimical to ethics and, indeed, politics.[1] However, I would emphasise a strong ethical and political re-turn – after a process of dismantling and questioning – in all three writers. This ultimately brings them, via the impossible gift, to something closer to the eighteenth century notion of beneficence.

The market economy

All the thinkers mentioned above are in broad agreement in their critique of the market economy. I shall focus chiefly on the work of Cixous and then Irigaray, who have both been at pains to analyse the economy as masculine in every domain, whether financial, social, linguistic or psychic.

---

1 See, for example, Terry Eagleton's objections ('Marx is a metaphysician, and so is Schopenhauer, and so is Ronald Reagan. Has anything been gained by this manoeuvre?', Eagleton, *Walter Benjamin, or Towards a Revolutionary Criticism*, London, Verso Press, 1981, p. 140) and Spivak's response: 'Not all ways of understanding the world and acting upon it are *equally* metaphysical or phonocentric. If, on the other hand, there *is* something shared by élite (Reagan), colonial authority, subaltern and mediator (Eagleton/Subaltern Studies) that we would rather not acknowledge, any elegant solution devised by means of such a refusal would merely mark a site of desire' (*In Other Worlds*, New York and London, Routledge, 1988, p. 215).

This slippage from the production and distribution of goods and services within society to the psychic organisation of individuals (the phallic economy driven by castration anxiety) is perhaps easier to achieve in French, where the term *économie* is more happily used in a metaphorical sense, to refer to the way in which something is organised, than it is in English.

Cixous suggests that for some time there have existed two distinct economies (masculine and feminine), and yet that such a situation is not essential, but rather subject to change:

> Nothing allows us to rule out the possibility of radical transformations of behaviours, mentalities, roles, political economy – whose effects on libidinal economy are unthinkable – today. Let us simultaneously imagine a general change in all the structures of training, education, supervision – hence in the structures of reproduction of ideological results. And let us imagine a real liberation of sexuality, that is to say, a transformation of each one's relationship to his or her body (and to the other body), an approximation to the vast, material, organic, sensuous universe that we are. This cannot be accomplished, of course, without political transformations that are equally radical. (Imagine!) Then 'femininity' and 'masculinity' would inscribe quite differently their effects of difference, their economy, their relationship to expenditure, to lack, to the gift. (*The Newly Born Woman*, p. 83)[2]

The masculine economy is one of appropriation which can usefully be related to capitalism, although it is not identical to it. It presupposes some kind of allocation of property rights (mine and thine) and assumes that individuals behave rationally, calculating to bring about desired outcomes on the basis of mathematical probabilities, using as much data as it has been economic to acquire (another calculation). The desired outcome is taken to be maximum profit (profit defined as revenue minus expenditure), in other words, the accumulation of property. Hence investment, the temporary relinquishing of property, follows from the calculation that in the longer term more property will accrue to the investing individual, which will compensate for the short-term diminished consumption possibilities. This economic behaviour occurs in many situations. *Homo economicus* is not identical to the bourgeois or the capitalist, for although the bourgeois or capitalist must be *homo economicus*, this latter can also be found in other modes of production and, indeed, amongst the proletariat. *Homo economicus* is rational, calculating, and quantifying (following the laws of probability), accumulating, profit-maximising man. He knows how to use means to an

---

2 Cixous's choice of terms suggests an engagement with the work of Louis Althusser on ideological State apparatuses. A comparison could also be made with Kristeva's article 'Woman Can Never Be Defined' in *New French Feminisms*, ed. E. Marks and I. de Courtivron, Brighton, Harvester Press, 1981, pp. 137–41. See my 'Can Woman Ever Be Defined? A Question from French Feminism', in *Women Teaching French*, ed. A. Cady, Loughborough, Studies in European Culture and Society, 5, 1991, pp. 29–37.

end; he looks ahead. He is found in a range of times and places – although we should beware his tendency to universalise, his identification of all others as (more or less deviant) analogues of himself. He is associated with all the forms of the *propre*.

There is a dramatic representation of a homosocial economy in which women are the objects of exchange in Cixous's play *Portrait of Dora*.[3] Dora's very name conjures up both a truncated Pandora, an archetypal Eve, and the giving associated with a feminine economy.[4] But Dora is given her name (and told what she is?) by Freud. She could be said to be an object of exchange circulated between Freud, her father (Herr B.) and Herr K.; for example, her father gives tacit permission for Herr K.'s relationship with her in return for Herr K. turning a blind eye to Herr B.'s affair with his wife.[5] The attempted reduction of the various women to commensurable objects (and screens or substitutes, one for another) is suggested in Cixous's play by a number of details, including the similar 'presents' they are given. Dora says that her 'generous' father never buys her a piece of jewellery without buying one for her mother and one for Frau K. The items of jewellery and the jewel-cases in which they are kept are redolent with sexual significance both in Freud's analysis and in Cixous's play. When Dora tells how Herr K. gave her a valuable jewellery-box, Freud asks if she were not tempted to give him something in return. Such are the transactions of the masculine economy, and Dora indeed will ask, 'Do you think you can buy me? Do you think you can sell me?' These questions seem to be addressed to her father, but one of the features of Cixous's play is deliberate ambiguity over the addressees of many of the lines – this enables their strikingly polysemic quality to be even greater. Freud is one of the great sources of our contemporary ability to multiply meanings, but it can be argued from a feminist position that Freudian interpretation has a tendency to return to monologue and to monolithic meaning – for instance, the phallus as a positive content (the answer to a riddle) rather than as a sliding signifier. Cixous's feminine writing deliberately keeps meaning floating, and sex may turn to cakes or sewing as well as oral pleasure or manual dexterity turning into sex. This is a *form* of refusal of the proper.

Cixous describes the masculine schema of (sexual) difference as inequality, making an analogy between macro- and micro-processes, between the socio-political and the psychic; on both levels, man wants profit beyond consumption (or consummation) thus:

3 *Théâtre*, Paris: Editions des femmes, 1986; *Portrait of Dora*, trans. A. Barrows, London, John Calder, [1976] 1979.
4 For Dora's generosity see Mairéad Hanrahan, 'Cixous's *Portrait de Dora*: The Play of Whose Voice?', forthcoming.
5 For more analysis of the case history, as opposed to the play, see *In Dora's Case*, ed. C. Bernheimer and C. Kahane, London, Virago, 1985.

In the (Hegelian) schema of recognition, there is no place for the other, for an equal other, for a whole and living woman. She must recognize and recuntnize[6] the male partner, and in the time it takes to do this, she must disappear, leaving him to gain Imaginary profit, to win Imaginary victory. The good woman, therefore, is the one who 'resists' long enough for him to feel both his power over her and his desire (I mean one who 'exists'), and not too much, to give him the pleasure of enjoying, without too many obstacles, the return to himself which he, grown greater – reassured in his own eyes, is making [. . .]

All history is inseparable from economy in the limited sense of the word, that of a certain kind of savings. Man's return – the relationship linking him profitably to man's being, conserving it. This economy, as a law of appropriation, is a phallocentric production. The opposition appropriate/inappropriate, proper/improper, clean/unclean, mine/not mine (the valorization of the selfsame), organizes the opposition identity/difference [. . .]

And one becomes aware that the Empire of the Selfsame is erected from a fear that, in fact, is typically masculine: the fear of expropriation, of separation, of losing the attribute. In other words, the threat of castration has an impact. (The Newly Born Woman, pp. 79–80, translation modified)

Homo economicus is logical, and believes in opposition (mutually exclusive opposites). The belief in sexual opposition is particularly relevant here, as Cixous has suggested and as Derrida points out:

When sexual difference is determined by opposition in the dialectical sense (according to the Hegelian movement of speculative dialectics which remains so powerful even beyond Hegel's text), one appears to set off 'the war between the sexes'; but one precipitates the end, with victory going to the masculine sex. The determination of sexual difference in opposition is destined, designed, in truth, for truth; it is so in order to erase sexual difference. The dialectical opposition neutralizes or supersedes [Hegel's term Aufhebung carries with it both the sense of conserving and negating. No

6 One of the problems with translating (contemporary theoretical) texts is the strain of attempting to displace wordplay from one tongue to another. In French the syllable con occurs commonly and in a wide range of words such as connaissance (knowledge) or reconnaissance (recognition or gratitude). However, as a word in its own right it is a term of abuse also used to designate the female genitals. While the syllable occurs so often in innocuous contexts that speakers will not usually be conscious of using it, it is true that, unlike spoken English, where word boundaries are usually much more significant than syllable boundaries, in spoken French syllables are relatively more significant, as word boundaries are relatively less apparent than in English. In the seventeenth century les précieuses (bluestockings) struggled to avoid syllabes sales (dirty syllables), rather as Victorians covered piano-legs – or so we are told. Cixous gently plays with this linguistic legacy whereby female genitals are a dirty word, and ladies have to disembody themselves in order to be respected or to stake a claim to having a mind or soul – and are then mocked for their pains. The English translation is much more strident and striking than the French original, but I have left it unchanged, since it does communicate a certain charge.

adequate translation of the term in English has yet been found] the difference. However, according to a surreptitious operation that must be flushed
out, one insures phallocentric mastery under the cover of neutralization every
time. ('Choreographies', p. 175)[7]

In Irigaray's account of the masculine libidinal economy, which seems
to me to accord quite closely with Cixous's detailing of the 'Empire du
Propre' (the Empire of the Proper or the Realm of the Selfsame), desire and
consummation are frequently subordinated to consumption, and more is
better – the Don Juan economy of $1 + 1 + 1 \ldots$ Man attempts to take
everything (even infinity) unto and into himself, but this act of appropriation leaves him anxious. He loses his desired (self-)definition by attempting
to swallow up too much. The endless consumption of another (woman)
makes him lose his precious measure, his prized ability to calculate. And so
he keeps on naming the other, marking her, defining her. Fearing to fall
into the chaos of the abyss, he names her the abyss. The fear aroused by
the introjection brings about a projection, the construction of an imaginary
Woman, decked with fixed attributes and concepts, part-objects, debris which
he doesn't care to keep inside himself – or which he keeps better by fastening them to this fetish Woman.

According to Irigaray, man takes spatiality from woman, and:

> In exchange – but it isn't a real exchange – he buys her a house, even shuts
> her up in it, places limits on her that are the opposite of the unlimited site
> in which he unwittingly situates her. He contains or envelops her with walls
> while enveloping himself and his things with her flesh. The nature of these
> envelopes is not the same: on the one hand, invisibly alive, but with barely
> perceivable limits; on the other, visibly limiting or sheltering, but at the risk
> of being prison-like or murderous if the threshold is not left open. (*An Ethics
> of Sexual Difference*, p. 11)

This is an example of the masculine economy – an apparent exchange
revealed as one-sided imposition, because there is only ever one and the
same subject of the sentence or of the so-called 'exchange'. *He* gives to her
(or buys for her) and *he* takes from her. In this passage, Irigaray, in typical
fashion, has shifted from an abstract point (that man's category of space is
grounded in the feminine, which he figures simultaneously as a container
and as the infinite) to what could be a more specific and concrete point

---

7 In 'From Restricted to General Economy' Derrida warns against taking Hegel's
self-evidence too lightly: 'Misconstrued, treated lightly, Hegelianism only extends its
historical domination, finally unfolding its immense enveloping resources without
obstacle' (p. 251). Irigaray is one of the feminists who has addressed the heavy burden
of Hegelianism. See, for example, *Sexes and Genealogies*, trans. G. C. Gill, New York,
Columbia University Press, 1993, pp. 1–2, 110 ff.; *Speculum*, pp. 214–26; *An Ethics of
Sexual Difference*, pp. 107–8, 117 ff; *Thinking the Difference*, trans. K. Montin, London,
Athlone Press, 1994, pp. 65 ff. See also Whitford, *Luce Irigaray*, pp. 118–22.

(that traditionally men have often provided houses for their womenfolk, and that women have been to some extent confined in their homes), then back to a more abstract and poetic mode of discourse. Irigaray is playing on the fact that the body has historically underpinned (as a kind of substratum) a great deal of economic, socio-political and philosophical discourse. In Irigaray this is made visible in an often uncomfortable way – uncomfortable, because the reader is accustomed to gliding over bodily references in serious writing as no more than ornaments. The female body has frequently been represented as flesh *par excellence*, and thus the necessary (though not always welcome) covering for the masculine mind or soul. In the passage above the reader may be reminded of fantasies of the return to the womb as original home or of masculine fantasies of being trapped inside the female body during intercourse, while remembering that it is women who are more often literally restricted in their freedom to move.

I shall briefly touch on two further examples of Irigaray's body language – that of orgasm and that of defecation. In *Le Corps-à-corps avec la mère* (*The Bodily Encounter With the Mother*)[8] she distinguishes between *l'orgasme*, phallic orgasm which women too can 'achieve' (p. 68), indeed enjoy – but whose dynamics are economic; and feminine *jouissance* which is of a different order, that of an endless marine rhythm (p. 49).[9] Proper economies assume finite resources (limited supplies), whereas free goods (or even public goods) are notoriously difficult to price; how do we price something which is infinite and non-excludable? Tumescence/detumescence or erection/ejaculation models assume finitude and lead to energy crises. Now just as when the gift is understood as if within contemporary phallic linguistic economies, it appears that Irigaray and Cixous are simply celebrating a form of female self-sacrifice which has long been exploited under patriarchy, so these claims about *jouissance* could appear to fit nicely into masculine fantasies about female sexual insatiability (nymphomania being a disease which only affects women, you know). This is to understand *inter* as unable to mean anything but burial.

The second example is that of defecation: Irigaray sometimes refers to the present masculine economy as an anal economy. In *Speculum*, she analyses the Freudian equation excrement, child, penis, which sets up an anal symbolic, from which, however, the woman must detach herself in

---

8 Montreal, les éditions de la pleine lune, 1981. The first essay of this work is translated as 'Body Against Body: In Relation to the Mother' in *Sexes and Genealogies*, pp. 7–22.
9 This might be related to Lacan's distinction in *Encore* between the 'bête' 'stupid or animal' masculine *jouissance* and feminine *jouissance*, which is beyond symbolisation – however, Irigaray does not wish feminine jouissance to be frozen, as in Bernini's famous statue of Saint Theresa, in a mute visibility. For Irigaray, masculine orgasm is no more *bête* than canny – and all the more inadequate for that. See 'God and the *Jouissance* of The Woman' and 'A Love Letter', in *Feminine Sexuality*, ed. J. Mitchell and J. Rose, trans. J. Rose, London and Basingstoke, Macmillan, 1982, pp. 137–61.

the sense that she must let go of the child and the penis as she does her excrement (pp. 74–6). And yet the Freudian account does not let her take pleasure in anal drives. 'Everything is for the best: woman enters into the (re)production line with not the slightest desire to retain any auto-erotic satisfaction, any narcissism, any affirmation of her own will, any wish to capitalize upon her products' (p. 75). In *An Ethics of Sexual Difference*, Irigaray presents love of sameness as a kind of ontology of the anal 'or else a triumph of the absorption of the other into the self in the intestine'. Love is transmuted into products and tools (p. 101) and:

> Centuries will perhaps have been needed for man to interpret the meaning of his work(s): the endless construction of a number of substitutes for his prenatal home [. . .] Again and again, taking from the feminine the tissue or texture of spatiality. (*An Ethics of Sexual Difference*, p. 11)

Women's exclusion from the anal is also an exclusion from the commercial – which, in a market economy, facilitates not paying or underpaying women's work. While Irigaray questions the capitalist economy as a whole, she does not, therefore, celebrate the unpriced labour of women, either in the domestic or the intellectual sphere, as a gift economy. Rather she sees it as exploitation, in terms not so different from those of Christine Delphy.[10] Delphy would differentiate herself from Irigaray rather as Marx differentiated himself from the German Idealist tradition or from Utopian Socialism – arguing that Irigaray mistakes cause for effect. However, it is not so obvious to me that causal antecedence is clearly decided in Irigaray's writing.

Irigaray is concerned on a number of occasions, for example in her exchanges with Marx, such as 'Women on the Market' (in *This Sex Which Is Not One*), and briefly in *Elemental Passions*,[11] with the commodification of women under patriarchy, and with strategies which are inaccessible to commodification:

> Who knows that the possibility of exchange is born from two lips remaining half-open?
>
> Exchange between men is sealed by the gift of a virgin. And the rite of breaking and entering, of raping and stealing the hymen, represents a denial of what was always already offered: exchange within woman and between women. A commerce without an object, without salesmen, without a society or an established order, which is denied in the setting up of the fetish and of currency. But without the prerequisite openness, without those lips always leaving a passage from inside to outside, from outside to inside, and staying

---

10 See, for example 'The Cost of Words' in *Je, tu, nous*, trans. A. Martin, London, 1993. Delphy refers to Irigaray in 'Proto-Feminism and Anti-Feminism', in *French Feminist Thought*, ed. T. Moi, pp. 80–109.

11 *Elemental Passions*, trans. J. Collie and J. Still, London, Athlone Press, [1982] 1992.

in between as well, the place of exchange would not be secure. (*Elemental Passions*, p. 64)

Irigaray draws on the familiar Lévi-Straussian representation of society founded on men exchanging women; what she notoriously calls a hom(m)o-sexual economy.[12] This is a term not dissimilar to Eve Kosofsky Sedgwick's 'homosocial',[13] but with the additional sense, which is very important for Irigaray, of monosexuality, and probably a play on anality – since Irigaray argues that anal sadistic drives are not accessible for women at present, and that this alienates them from the anal pleasure which men derive from intercourse.[14] Classical (non-Marxist) theories of the economy emphasise the freedom of the market: no one is compelled to buy or sell; agents participate willingly in transactions in order to maximise their utility. Irigaray takes the part of shattering that illusion: exchange is founded on rape/theft, on the sacrifice of the virgin. She does not contrast that violence with an Enlightenment image of 'peaceful trade', but with an other, more radical, economy, 'that which was always already offered'. She claims that it is the force of the denial of that economy within woman and between women which drives the violence which founds market exchange. In psychic terms, thus, it is not surprising that lips, which are emblematic of openness, are also the site of ritual violation. Market economies rely on systems of distinction: not only the quantification[15] and calculation which motivate economic behaviour, but also fundamental analytic separations of buyer and seller, agent and commodity, worker and means of production.

In the work of Irigaray there is a clearer linking of masculine to men than in the other French poststructuralists here under discussion – I shall go on to discuss the question of sexual difference in the next section. In some of her writing Irigaray appears closer to the Anglo-Saxon radical feminist critique in spirit, although her denser writing, imbued and inter-twined with psychoanalysis and continental philosophy, is very different. Her sometime proximity to Anglo-Saxon feminism may also be seen in her utopian qualities. It is possible to make a distinction between two kinds of

12 Although this term is often treated as one of her coining, it is used by Lacan, for example he remarks 'The soul is conjured out of what is *hommosexual*, as is perfectly legible from history' ('A Love Letter', p. 155). Here the term seems to mean 'outside sex', which would fit with Irigaray's point about the reduction to the same of the masculine economy.

13 See, for example, *Between Men*, New York, Columbia University Press, 1985.

14 See Whitford, *Luce Irigaray*, p. 162 for further comment on this.

15 Irigaray seeks to shift from the quantification of $1 + 1 + 1$ women to a relation with quality – the divine. See *Divine Women*, trans. S. Muecke, Sydney, Local Consumption Occasional Paper, 8, 1986, e.g. pp. 5, 9, 11 for the need for a female 'God'. See also 'Nuptial Quest', *Elemental Passions*, pp. 2, 4. This divine must, however, be a sensible transcendental (*An Ethics of Sexual Difference*, p. 129); it must not be cut off from the flesh.

utopian writing, theoretical and fictional. And yet these necessarily intersect and overlap, in that a utopian narrative inevitably implies certain theoretical points, and theoretical utopian writing tends by definition to slip into description of an imagined state. The pedigree of feminist utopias includes a strong Anglo-American tradition – for instance, the writings of Charlotte Perkins Gilman. Contemporary feminist fictions (such as those of Margaret Attwood, Angela Carter, Suzette Haden Elgin or Joanna Russ) often inhabit, or at least borrow from, the genre of science fiction or fantasy to create either utopias or dystopias. While science fiction initially appeared as a Boys' Own genre – reinscribing tales of Frontier heroics and Imperial expansion into strange new territories inhabited by even stranger populations – the politically rather different subgenre of feminist sci-fi has become a significant one. Sci-fi allows a focus on the desirous and sensuous detailing of the everyday as well as the excitement of remodelled amorous or warlike adventures, with none of the reality chains which bind fiction set in the present or past. I shall take one Franco–American example of a contemporary feminist fiction which deploys utopian tropes (at the same time as rewriting Dante) to illustrate the recurrence of the gift economy motif. And I want to argue that this kind of writing, and this text in particular, has all kinds of intertextual links with Irigaray – in spite of critical writing which sets them apart.

In *Across the Acheron*[16] Monique Wittig describes three markets (*foires*) and then a pair of public meals;[17] these episodes punctuate the text at regular intervals (every nine or ten chapters). Those episodes, which involve men *and* women, are dominated by forms of the masculine economy in which women either act as commodities or help to give value to goods by being excluded from consumption (in other words, by effectively creating scarcity where there is abundance). 'La Foire aux enchères' ('The Auction', chapter 9) is a kind of silent slave-auction, where men bid for women displayed in a ring. 'La Foire d'empoigne' ('The Free-for-All', chapter 30) is more dramatically violent in its allocation of commodities: we see a series of women, who each in turn becomes the object of a struggle between sportsmen who wish to acquire her, and who often tear her limb from limb in the process. 'La Grande Bouffe' ('The Great Gorge', chapter 39) is a banquet where men gorge themselves and starving women watch. Episodes involving women only, or women, lesbians and angels (designated as *elles*) are dominated by a utopian gift economy. 'La Foire aux richesses' ('The Treasure Fair', chapter 19) is a women's market in which the most valuable possessions imaginable are displayed so that those in need can help themselves

16 *Across the Acheron*, trans. D. Le Vay with M. Crosland, London, The Women's Press, 1989.
17 The public meal is an important feature of utopian writing; see, for example, More's *Utopia*.

freely to as much as they require (a reminder of *Utopia*). The final chapter, 'La Cuisine des anges' ('The Angels' Kitchen'), forms a kind of diptych with 'La Grande Bouffe' – it describes the preparation for a sumptuous meal. The very text enacts abundance here in its characteristic lists, which reach a climax in the last chapter, where we have lists of kitchen utensils and implements, colours, birds and birdsong, herbs, fruit and so on.

Wittig's novel is part of a subgenre of science fiction or fantasy written by women, which posits two future societies: a dystopian one, governed by men and characterised by the worst features of patriarchy, and a utopian one, dominated by women, which is a gift economy. Another example would be Slonczewski's *A Door into Ocean*, mentioned in chapter seven. Typically, in this novel, the difference between the two communities is reflected in their speech, as shown in this dialogue between a well-meaning young Valan and a Sharer:

> 'What the devil is "word-sharing"? Does the word for "speak" mean "listen" just as well? If I said, "Listen to me!" you might talk, instead.'
>
> 'What use is the one without the other? It took me a long time to see this distinction in Valan speech.'
>
> Spinel thought over the list of 'share-forms': learnsharing, worksharing, lovesharing. 'Do you say "hitsharing", too? If I hit a rock with a chisel, does the rock hit me?'
>
> 'I would think so. Don't you feel it in your arm?'
>
> He frowned and sought a better example; it was so obvious, it was impossible to explain. 'I've got it: if Beryl bears a child, does the child bear Beryl? That's ridiculous.'
>
> 'A mother is born when her child comes.'
>
> 'Or if I swim in the sea, does the sea swim in me?'
>
> 'Does it not?'
>
> Helplessly he thought, She can't be that crazy. 'Please, you do know the difference, don't you?'
>
> 'Of course. What does it matter.' (pp. 36–7)

Irigaray does not write fictions in this sense, but her theoretical works are flooded with the fictive, the poetic and the utopian. Her descriptions of the gift as a mode of exchange are some of the best examples of her poetic and utopian style: 'A place where everything is still possible. Prior to any difference or distinction. Giving only a world of half-openings. Nothing determinable. The foundation of all giving. A reserve of the dative' (*Elemental Passions*, p. 89).

Irigaray and sexual difference

Discussions of Irigaray's position on sexual difference can thus easily make it seem as if she assumes two opposite and separate sex-worlds, one bad and one good. And yet ultimately, on the one hand, a feminine economy need not be intrasexual; it could be intersexual. On the other hand, the masculine anal economy of rational calculation might be productively brought into relation with a feminine gift economy – another kind of intersexuality. 'Intersexual' is glossed by the Oxford English Dictionary as 'existing between the sexes'. Intersexuality is intended to be a dynamic term – not to refer to some fixed median point between the sexes, but to refer to mutual or reciprocal sexual relations. Irigaray writes: 'Sex is always intersexuality.'[18] The term appears to be calqued on 'intertextuality', which refers to dynamic, passionate and conflictual relations between texts. Theories of intertextuality are sometimes accused of reductionism, of reducing everything to text, and thereby homogenising and neutralising different orders of being (for instance, the material and the superstructural).[19] The converse case would argue for sophisticated readings of different texts in their difference, but still maintain that, at least synecdochically, there is a textual relation to everything, since everything is available as a signifying structure as well. The crucial differences encourage the violent and amorous intercourse between texts. One key question is that of the nature of the differences: are these binary oppositions? hierarchies? *différance*? fixed? mobile?

Sex and sexuality can and should be read as texts, *and* the reading and writing of texts is permeated with the sexual.[20] It is French poststructuralism and so-called 'French feminism' which provide the context and material base with which to examine sexuality textually. As suggested in chapter one, these have a shared concern with language, arguing that radical revolutionary change cannot be brought about by economic, political or technical means alone, that there is a need for a change in the symbolic order. For example, Irigaray writes: 'As women, we have thus been enclosed in an order of forms inappropriate to us. In order to exist, we must break out of these forms.'[21]

While Irigaray shares much of Cixous's diagnosis of the masculine economy, they do have different strategies for escaping it. Cixous, like Derrida, asserts the feminine as something other and radical – however, neither ties the feminine to the biological female. Derrida in addition makes

---

18 'Le Sexe fait comme signe', *Parler n'est jamais neutre*, p. 177.
19 See John Frow, 'Intertextuality and Ontology', in *Intertextuality: Theories and Practices*, ed. M. Worton and J. Still, pp. 45–55.
20 See the introduction to *Textuality and Sexuality: Reading Theories and Practices*, ed. J. Still and M. Worton, Manchester, Manchester University Press, 1993, pp. 1–68.
21 *Je, tu, nous*, p. 109; see also p. 22. She claims that the misunderstanding of her work on the part of 'Anglo-Saxon' feminists 'shows a lack of comprehension of the relations between individual bodies, social bodies, and the linguistic economy' (p. 72; I would translate 'corps social' as 'the social body'), and suggests that this difference between feminists is in part an effect of different languages which mark sexual difference in different parts of speech.

clear that the counter-privileging of the feminine as undecidability is a provisional strategy which is a useful point of insertion when confronted with
a textual privileging of rational decidability.[22] Irigaray's work, however,
notoriously insists on the need for reading sexuality as sexual difference (as
masculine/male versus feminine/female); the biological distinction urgently
needs an imaginary and symbolic dimension, according to her account.[23]
Some feminists would argue that we should rather focus on material questions, while some philosophers who are fascinated by le féminin or l'opération
féminine are quite unsure of any link between these terms and women.
Irigaray brings together political feminism – demands for material, legislative and social changes in women's lot (for example, the construction
of sexuate rights)[24] with a philosophical interest in the feminine. She claims
both that the feminine is barely perceptible under present social and ideological conditions, and that this future feminine is/will be different from the
masculine which is so familiar to us. For example, in *Elemental Passions*
Irigaray is concerned with the question of modes of intercourse, asking the
question: what relationship is possible between two different beings? What
different modes of relationship are possible? She writes:

> this difference creates an abyss. And is there anyone who does not fear the
> abyss? How can there be attraction between different beings in spite of the
> abyss? What risk is there in attraction through difference?
>
> Not in me but in our difference lies the abyss. We can never be sure of
> bridging the gap between us. But that is our adventure. Without this peril
> there is no us. (*Elemental Passions*, p. 28)

For some of her readers this insistence on difference amounts to no more
than (and no less than, we might add) a reprivileging of an old hierarchical
sexual opposition – taking a familiar binary, attempting to swap over the
valorising signs (so that what was negatively marked becomes positively
marked, and vice versa) and taking the attendant risk that with the opposition intact (masculine versus feminine remains, even if we feverishly assert
that feminine equals good), the powerful ideological force which is based
on real material advantages will find the revaluation all the more grist to its

---

22 See, for example, 'Women in the Beehive: A Seminar with Jacques Derrida', in *Men
in Feminism*, ed. A. Jardine and P. Smith, New York and London, Routledge, 1989,
pp. 189–203.

23 This insistence relates to a question of vocabulary. Usually in anglophone feminist
analyses it has been considered important to distinguish between adjectives referring
to biological sex (male and female) and adjectives referring to socio-historical constructions of gender (masculine and feminine). In French one set of terms (*masculin*
and *féminin*) covers both kinds of adjective. Translations of Irigaray move between
male/female and masculine/feminine, because it is often not clear that she would
wish to disentangle the two sets of meanings.

24 See *Je, tu, nous*, chapter 10: 'Why Define Sexed Rights?'

mill (maternity equals good *ergo* yes: all women should be maternal if not actually mothers). Irigaray's gesture would thus be unfavourably compared either with egalitarian sexual indifferentiation (there's no real difference between men and women) or with deconstructionist sexual *différance* (there should be – and note the ethical imperative – lots of sexes, lots of difference).[25] First of all, even if there are dangers associated with Irigaray's strategies, it may nevertheless be worth taking the risk at least of investigating her argument – which has proved seductive to many women – rather than dismissing it out of hand. In the second place, the argument against her is possibly an over-simplification of Irigaray's case which is insufficiently attentive to her attempts at restructuring language; for instance, her valorisation of virginity may sound puritanically disturbing until we recognise that, for her, a virgin is something which you can *become* (*Je, tu, nous*, pp. 141–2). Becoming a virgin in feminine terms is something to do with refusing to be either a use or an exchange value for men.[26] Equally this concerns a refusal to be 'made a woman' by a man: 'Your/my body doesn't acquire its sex through an operation. Through the action of some power, function, or organ. Without any intervention or special manipulation, you are a woman already' (*This Sex Which Is Not One*, p. 211).

Diana Fuss reads this passage as follows: 'Unlike Wittig, who severs the classification "woman" from any anatomical determinants, there can be little doubt that, for Irigaray, a woman is classified as such on the basis of anatomy.'[27] I would read it rather differently – as arguing that it does not take the penis to turn a girl into a woman. I shall quote the three sentences

25 Irigaray comments that when women's movements 'aim simply for a change in the distribution of power, leaving intact the power structure itself, then they are resubjecting themselves, deliberately or not, to a phallocratic order [. . .] But these questions are complex, all the more so in that women are obviously not to be expected to renounce equality in the sphere of civil rights. How can the double demand – for both equality and difference – be articulated?' ('The Power of Discourse' in *The Irigaray Reader*, ed. M. Whitford, Oxford, Blackwell, 1991, p. 128). Another important statement of her position on demands for equality as equality with men is to be found in 'Equal or Different', *The Irigaray Reader*, pp. 30–3. See also the foreword to *Elemental Passions*, 'Nuptial Quest', pp. 2–3.

26 See 'Women on the Market', *This Sex Which Is Not One*, pp. 186–7.

27 *Essentially Speaking*, London, Routledge, 1989, p. 61. The setting up of the opposition between Irigaray and Wittig (as a representative of constructivism or materialism alongside thinkers such as Delphy) requires a skewed presentation of both thinkers. For instance, Wittig is solely the Wittig of *The Straight Mind and Other Essays*, London, Harvester Wheatsheaf, 1992, and no reference is made to her fictional writings. Fuss does this, admittedly, in order to deconstruct the binary from both sides – so that she shows that 'anti-essentialism is made both possible and impossible, at once tenable and tentative, by the essentialist moments upon which it elaborates its own system' (p. 55), and that with respect to Irigaray 'essentialism represents not a trap she falls into but rather a key strategy she puts into play, not a dangerous oversight but rather a lever of displacement' (p. 72).

preceding the three which Fuss quotes: 'Between us, there's no rupture between virginal and nonvirginal. No event that makes us women. Long before your birth, you touched yourself innocently.' In context I believe the passage to be attacking the view that a woman is a virgin (and so not really 'a woman') until (and only until) she has had penetrative (even reproductive) sex with a man. This tradition has entailed the position that lesbian sex does not interfere with virginity, and hence the topos of the sexually experienced virgin – a paradox or puzzle which is relished in a number of erotic fictions such as Balzac's 'The Girl with the Golden Eyes', A. S. Byatt's *Possession* or Donne's 'Sappho to Philaenis':

> Thy body is a natural paradise,
> In whose self, unmanured, all pleasure lies,
> Nor needs perfection; why shouldst thou then
> Admit the tillage of a harsh rough man?
> Men leave behind them that which their sin shows,
> And are as thieves traced, which rob when it snows.
> But of our dalliance no more signs there are,
> Than fishes leave in streams, or birds in air.

Irigaray continues in the passage cited above: 'There is no need for an outside; the other already affects. It is inseparable from you. You are altered for ever, through and through. That is your crime, which you didn't commit: you disturb their love of property.' And later she adds: 'A virgin is the future of their exchanges, transactions, transports. A kind of reserve for their explorations, consummations, exploitations' (pp. 211–12). If a woman can both 'always already' not be a virgin, not be pure, not reserved, a reserve, store or stock of value, but rather 'altered', always already touched by otherness – and simultaneously always a virgin – then a masculine economy is disturbed. And so I read this passage not as making a point about *being*, about identity through essence, as Fuss would have it, but as making a point about *having*, about the disturbance of property rights.[28] I quoted the passage from Donne's poem partly because it raises in a complicated kind of way some of these issues – part of the complication is that a notorious male author (although this authorship has been questioned!) here acts as a ventriloquist for the most notorious lesbian warning another woman about sex with a man, because she wants her herself (as any man would). In the poem Sappho dismisses the claim that a woman requires a man to complete her, to make her perfect (in fact, the reference to fish made me think of the feminist graffito – 'a woman needs a man like a fish needs a bicycle'). She presents man in his two economic guises: as he

---

28 In *Spurs*, Derrida suggests that sexual difference raises the question of propriation as more fundamental, *qua* more undecidable, than the question of being (p. 111).

who makes woman his property, like husbanding virgin territory (the old colonial metaphor which works in both directions to justify taking women and taking land in order to make them fruitful),[29] and as he who steals what is or could potentially be the property of other men, he against whom women must be guarded (by men).

Irigaray's work is a quest for a new feminine Imaginary, which is sometimes critiqued on the grounds that it is a denial of the Symbolic (necessary for differentiation and, therefore, to escape psychosis, according to Lacanians). She argues that the apparent sexual opposition (male vs. female) with which we live is in fact a monosexuality – that the female body, not to mention any other part of the female, has been interred fantasmatically within the male.[30] This burial prevents any exchange between women, or between men and women – any intercourse, interflow, intermingling, interaction or interplay. There is thus a non-relationship in which one party is as if dead. As I have already suggested, a tension exists in much of this language of sexual difference, indeed in that term itself, depending whether we understand, for example, 'women', 'sex' and so on, as referring to Irigaray's hypothesis (or wager) of the *potential* (some would say utopian) meaning, or whether we understand these words as they function in the present phallic linguistic economy. Does 'women' refer to what women could be, or to what they are in contemporary society – and sex likewise? A useful tension, I would argue (similar to that in Cixous's *féminin*), but admittedly one which paves the way to misunderstandings.

Irigaray brings into focus not only the body, but also the sensible in a wider sense – the material. This is part of her return to a pre-Platonic moment, a return which is not a simple, would-be unmediated, celebration, but which often emerges through her dialogue with other philosophers, such as Heidegger.[31] Irigaray's sometimes theological tone has Heideggerian overtones. Heidegger seeks inspiration from the pre-Socratic thinkers (particularly Empedocles) who are clearly a major influence on Irigaray's 'elemental' concerns, and uses them to distinguish between the permanence

---

29 I am grateful to Sabina Sharkey for pointing out to me the powerfulness of the term 'husbandry', and the way it was deployed in English colonialist texts on Ireland.

30 In *Le Corps-à-corps avec la mère*, pp. 16 ff Irigaray argues that – at an earlier stage than that described by Freud in *Totem and Taboo* – western culture is founded on matricide. She analyses the mythological example of Clytemnestra, murdered by her son Orestes. Whitford discusses the woman buried alive (like Antigone), for example in *Luce Irigaray*, pp. 118–20, 157.

31 The influence of Heidegger on contemporary gift thinking is pervasive (for instance, there have been a number of analyses of his *es gibt*, not least by Derrida, for instance in *Given Time*). One of Irigaray's major philosophical reference points is Heidegger's *Introduction to Metaphysics*: in *Divine Women* she cites from it Heidegger's triple etymology for being, i.e. living, emerging and enduring – *vivre, épanouir* and *demeurer* – as it is rendered in French (p. 14). These are all key terms, for instance in Irigaray's *Elemental Passions*.

of being and the flux of becoming.[32] Irigaray directly addresses Heidegger in *L'Oubli de l'air*, another work in what was intended to be an elemental quartet with *Elemental Passions* and *Marine Lover* (interrogating Nietzsche) – she has not written the fourth work, which was to bring out the repression of fire in the writings of Marx. At the same time, 'One of Irigaray's central ideas is the reworking of the Heideggerian theme of the "house of language". The "house" which women need should be a symbolic one – language, representation, imagery, etc.' (*The Irigaray Reader*, p. 75). The loss of home is sometimes termed *déréliction* by Irigaray.

One of the reasons for women's dereliction is their relation to speculation. This is not only significant in the economic sense. The mirror is a recurrent theme in Irigaray's work – particularly in *Speculum*, from the title onwards. Irigaray contrasts the flat (Freudo–Lacanian) mirror, which reflects the female genitals as a hole, with a concave mirror. She plays on the various connotations of speculation and specularisation, imagining, as she does in *Elemental Passions*, other modes of speculation as well as the familiar oppressive ones. She writes in *Speculum*, for instance, of man's demand that woman:

> Must be no more than the path, the method, the theory, the *mirror* for the 'subject' that leads back, via a process of repetition, to re-cognition of the unity of (his) origin.
> But the mother and the woman do not speculate one another in the same way. A double specularization already intervenes in her/them, between her/them. And more. For the sex [*sexe*] of woman is not one. And as *jouissance* explodes in all these/her 'parts', so they can reflect it differently in their bedazzlement. (Translated in *The Irigaray Reader*, pp. 65–6)

In *Divine Women*, Irigaray returns again to the point that women lack a mirror for becoming women, instead they look in the mirror in order to please someone else – feminine beauty is thus no more than a duty imposed by men, rather than a tool for self-love (p. 6). That is an example of a negative reflection, othering or doubling. However, alterity and doubleness or duplicity can enable more fruitful speculation.

In *Spurs*, Derrida critiques Heidegger's reading of Nietzsche for subordinating the question of sexual difference to the apparently more general

---

32 Pure becoming, pure force, cannot exist as such: Heidegger much admired Nietzsche's formulation that it is necessary to '*stamp* the character of Being upon Becoming' (Heidegger, *Early Greek Thinking*, trans D. F. Krell and F. A. Capuzzi, London, 1975, p. 22. Johnson uses this quotation – making this point with respect to Derrida's essay 'Force and Signification', in *System and Writing*, pp. 19, 204. Indeed, this kind of recognition both of the impossibility of pure forms, pure polar opposites, and of the political force underpinning and sustaining their continued ideological hierarchical weight, is common to much of Derrida's and Irigaray's work. The critique of pure Being is implicitly (and sometimes explicitly) a critique of Plato and the Platonic Idea which would exist outside the world of (mortal) becoming; see Whitford, *Luce Irigaray*, p. 105.

question of the truth of being ('Le Coup de don', p. 109).[33] Derrida points out that Nietzsche's analyses of sexual difference are always marked by various forms of *propriation*. Sometimes woman is defined as the one who gives, who *gives herself* ('*se donnant*') while man, by definition, takes and possesses. Sometimes, on the other hand, woman in giving herself '*se donne pour*', simulates and thus assures herself of possessive mastery, or introduces some goal or return to her gesture which erodes her gift as gift. This switches the signs which mark sexual opposition, and so the process of propriation escapes any ontological decidability. Propriation *qua* sexual is thus more potent than the question of being, and 'the process of propriation organises the whole of the process of language or of symbolic exchange in general, including, therefore, all ontological statements' (*Spurs*, p. 111, translation modified).

This argument of Derrida's has been controversial because of the way it may seem to confine women to conventional stereotypes of the historical feminine, not only as self-sacrificing, but also as false, as mimes.[34] However, what Derrida suggests in *Spurs* ('Positions', pp. 95–101), is that Nietzsche's combination of heterogeneous stereotypical statements about women, which can be formalised into three *positions* (two negations or denials and one affirmation), tend to undo each other. This can still be critiqued as a discourse between men over, and with, the metaphor of woman. Irigaray has been less enthusiastic than Cixous about those who are recognised as men and recognise themselves as men, and yet attempt to write in the feminine. However, Irigaray does, like Cixous, accept that, while waiting for the future feminine, numerous strategies must be deployed. For example, the path of deliberately assuming the historical feminine role is characteristic of 'an initial phase'. Irigaray suggests that

> To play with mimesis is thus, for a woman, to try to recover the place of her exploitation by discourse, without allowing herself to be simply reduced to it. It means to resubmit herself – inasmuch as she is on the side of the 'perceptible', of 'matter' – to 'ideas', in particular to ideas about herself, that are elaborated in/by a masculine logic, but so as to make 'visible', by an effect of playful repetition, what was supposed to remain invisible: the cover-up of a possible operation of the feminine in language. It also means to 'unveil' the fact that, if women are such good mimics, it is because they are not simply resorbed in this function. *They also remain elsewhere*: another case of the persistence of 'matter', but also of 'sexual pleasure'. (*This Sex Which Is Not One*, p. 76)

33 For a related critique by Derrida of Heidegger, see '*Geschlecht*: Sexual Difference, Ontological Difference', trans. R. Berezdivin, *Research in Phenomenology*, 13 (1983), 65–83.
34 See G. Spivak, 'Displacement and the Discourse of Woman', in *Displacement: Derrida and After*, ed. M. Krupnick, Bloomington, Indiana University Press, 1983, pp. 169–95.

I want later to examine Irigaray's argument that maintaining, or even constructing, sexual difference is dangerous, but necessary and valuable,[35] and necessarily dangerous in that any safeguard, any guard-rail, returns us to masculine monosexuality. However, first I shall return to Cixous.

Cixous and the gift

The importance of the gift in Cixous's thinking about sexual difference is quite generally acknowledged by her readers; this is, no doubt, influenced by strong statements in some of her best-known works; in *The Newly Born Woman* she writes: 'All the difference determining history's movement as property's movement is articulated between two economies [the feminine and the masculine] that are defined in relation to the problematic of the gift' (p. 80).[36] I would argue that the gift is equally important in the thinking of her compatriot, Derrida, although it is not so regularly signposted by his commentators.[37] To some critics of Cixous the alignment of Cixous and Derrida may seem strange: she has been charged with a number of suspect tendencies (essentialism, biologism, and so on) which appear quite alien to deconstruction. And yet, even before considering conceptual similarities as well as differences in their writing, we might note that in terms of strategic public practices they have been united in a number of significant ways, for example Derrida as the key speaker alongside Cixous at her first *Etudes féminines* conference in 1990, or Derrida interviewed in a *Boundary 2* special issue on Cixous, the piece entitled 'voice ii . . .', after the interview with Cixous entitled 'voice i . . .'.[38] Cixous and Derrida have much in common: a certain background, a range of cultural and philosophical references, a radical questioning of much of what had gone without saying in intellectual debate prior to the late 1960s, and certain aspirations in the ethical and

35 'Sexual difference would represent the advent of new fertile regions as yet unwitnessed, at all events in the west [. . .] it would also involve the production of a new age of thought, art, poetry and language; the creation of a new *poetics*' ('Sexual Difference', *The Irigaray Reader*, p. 165; translated slightly differently in *An Ethics of Sexual Difference*, p. 5).

36 For two examples of critical studies see Brian Duren, 'Cixous's Exorbitant Texts', *Sub-Stance* 10 (1981), 39–51, on *propre* and *impropre* and on the influence of Bataille on Cixous's use of the gift, and my 'A Feminine Economy: Some Preliminary Thoughts', in *The Body and the Text*, ed. H. Wilcox, K. McWatters, A. Thompson and L. R. Williams, New York, Harvester Wheatsheaf, 1990, pp. 49–60.

37 It has not been completely ignored, and yet if I look in the indexes of three books on Derrida taken from my shelves (by Rodolphe Gasché, Christopher Johnson and Christopher Norris), I find no entry for 'gift'.

38 See also Mireille Calle-Gruber and Hélène Cixous, *Hélène Cixous: Photos de Racine*, Paris, des femmes, 1994, in which Cixous refers insistently to a great debt to Derrida, the person to whom she chose to send her earliest writings. Derrida's paper from the *Etudes féminines* conference is reproduced in the middle of the book.

political domain – all these inflect upon their preoccupation with the gift. However, Cixous's domain is that of the creative writer and the literary critic, while Derrida's is that of the philosopher. Both have worked to make their respective domains permeable to a range of discourses to the point where the reminder of disciplinary boundaries may seem quite inappropriate, and yet, I would argue, the difference in the disciplines with which each struggles is part of the gap between them. This chapter will attempt to bring together some of Cixous's references to a possible feminine gift economy with Derrida's theorisation of the impossibility (and necessity) of the gift, in particular in *Given Time I* and in his writings on sexual difference.[39] Cixous herself brings them together with respect to their interrogations of the gift in an interview with Verena Andermatt Conley:

> The question of the gift is a question on which we have worked a lot, marking it and following it, if one may say, with a step as light and as airy, as 'feminine' as possible. The question is of course the following: Is it possible that there is a gift? It is a question that has been treated at length by Derrida in a seminar on the philosophical mode, etc. Is there such a thing as a gift; can the gift take place? At the limit, one can ask oneself about the possibility of a real gift, a pure gift, a gift that would not be annulled by what one could call a countergift. That is also what Derrida worked on.[40]

There has been some debate over Cixous's characterisation of two (libidinal) economies as 'masculine' and 'feminine' – whether these are applied to writing, social relations or intrapsychic structures. Derrida suggests that these cannot be bound to men and women ('voice ii . . .', p. 89), and much in Cixous's writing would support such a claim, whether it be her celebration of a feminine economy in a number of male writers from Shakespeare to Mandelstam or certain of her own explicit statements. Nevertheless, in *The Newly Born Woman*, for example, Cixous argues that until there is radical political, economic, ideological change, and a change in sexuality, most men and women will be caught in a web of cultural determinations which make men more afraid of loss, such that:

> In the development of desire, of exchange, he [the traditional man] is the en-grossing party: loss and expense are stuck in the commercial deal that always turns the gift into a gift-that-takes. The gift brings in a return. Loss, at the end of a curved line, is turned into its opposite and comes back to him as profit. (p. 87)

39 For example, 'voice ii . . .' with V. A. Conley, *Boundary 2*, 12 (1984), 68–93; 'Choreographies' interview with C. McDonald in *The Ear of the Other*, trans. P. Kamuf, Lincoln, Neb. and London, University of Nebraska Press, [1982] 1988, pp. 163–85; *Spurs*; 'Women in the Beehive'.

40 Conley, *Hélène Cixous*, Lincoln, Neb. and London, University of Nebraska Press, expanded edn, 1991, p. 158.

Woman, on the other hand, 'doesn't try to "recover her expenses". She is able not to return to herself, never settling down, pouring out, going everywhere to the other' (p. 87). The feminine, between Cixous and Derrida, slips from a bond with women to an evocation of something which is before or beyond sexual opposition.

Cixous has an avowedly passionate relationship with her intertexts, and her delight at the discovery of Clarice Lispector is well known. At the same time her work is exceptionally open to male writers (such as Joyce or Genet) and political figures (such as Mandela), in whom she can sense a feminine. In, for example, 'Coming to Writing', she (a writer, and therefore a reader) is alternately mother, child, lover, beloved, giving and receiving sustenance in an abundance of fantasmatic relationships which do seem before or beyond any stable economy of sexual opposition, and which she terms 'feminine'.[41] Cixous exhorts us:

> *Win* your freedom: give everything up, vomit everything up, give everything away. Give absolutely everything away, do you hear, *everything*, give your goods away, is it done? Don't keep anything, give away what you hold dear, are you there? (p. 40, translation modified)

And later, she muses on the gift of milk, of nourishment in writing (giving and taking nourishment); hatred eats you alive, she tells us, and

> Anyone who keeps wealth and nourishment for himself is poisoned. The mystery of the gift: the poison-gift: if you give, you receive. What you don't give, the anti-gift, turns back against you and rots you.
> The more you give, the more pleasure overwhelms you, how can they not know that? (p. 49, translation modified)

These references to the gift focus on the psychic benefit to the subject of superabundant generosity. At another time, Cixous is more troubled by the relational aspect of the gift: what relation must there be to the recipient for a gift to take place (can a gift ever take place?). She asks:

> How does one give? It starts in a very simple way: in order for a gift to be, I must not be the one to give. A gift has to be like grace, it has to fall from the sky. If there are traces of origin of the I give, there is no gift – there is an I-give. Which also signifies: say 'thank you', even if the other does not ask you to say it. As soon as we say thank you, we give back part or the whole gift. We have been brought up in the space of the debt, and so we say thank you. Is it possible to imagine that there can be a gift? (interview with Cixous, in Conley, *Hélène Cixous*, pp. 158–9)

At times Cixous seems to agree about the difficulty of the gift – the fall from grace into graces (in the French) or more grace (in the Portuguese)

---

41 In *'Coming to Writing' and Other Essays*, trans. S. Cornell, D. Jenson, A. Liddle and S. Sellers, Cambridge, Mass., Harvard University Press, [1977] 1991.

– a slide into quantification (*Readings*, p. 35). She tells us that you can never have grace – 'it is always given' (*Readings*, p. 67), and that what must be given is something to be taken; love has a part of hatred:

> According to philosophers such as Jacques Derrida, there is no pure gift. One could say, though, that if a gift is to take place, it would be in these scenes of a very heavily symbolized maternity [in Lispector's 'The Foreign Legion'] that goes much beyond an anatomic maternity and consists in letting oneself be taken by the other. It is the most difficult thing in the world. What needs to be given is a gift to take, not a gift of something that is already there. The possibility, the violent right to take something that has been accorded has to be given. ('Apprenticeship and Alienation', in *Readings*, p. 84)

Cixous seems here to suggest that a gift cannot be given, only the possibility of taking can be given. Both Cixous, and perhaps to an even greater extent, Derrida, are struck by the 'impossibility' of the gift: 'there is no "free" gift' (*The Newly Born Woman*, p. 87). And yet both return to the necessity of (faith in) the gift.

Equally, both are aware of the social constraints which necessitate our recognition of sexual opposition – even if sometimes we claim that we are only doing so as a short-term strategy. Cixous is lyrical about the aggressive and amorous exchange between Kleist's Penthesilea and Achilles, or Tasso's Tancredi and Clorinda, or Rossini's Tancredi and Armenaida; her admiration is partly inspired by the shifting masculine and feminine economies – whether Clorinda is assumed to be a man or Tancredi sung by a mezzo-soprano.[42] Cixous, like Derrida, asserts the feminine as something other and radical – however, neither ties the feminine to the biological female. In *Readings*, Cixous talks about the *coup de grâce* (p. 63) in the act of love between Achilles and Penthesilea: 'There is an ephemeral moment of equilibrium that could be called the moment of grace. It is followed by disequilibrium and loss that do not have one and only one cause. One can say – and that is where the question of the other is vital – that Achilles did take the necessary leap.' I should like to juxtapose this with a quote from Derrida:

> But whereas only a problematic of the trace or dissemination can pose the question of the gift, and forgiveness, this does not imply that writing is *generous* or that the writing subject is a *giving subject*. As an identifiable, bordered, posed subject, the one who writes and his or her writing never gives anything without calculating, consciously or unconsciously, its reappropriation, its exchange, or its circular return – and by definition this means reappropriation

42 See, for example, *Readings*, ed. and trans. V. A. Conley, Minneapolis, University of Minnesota Press, 1991, pp. 29, 63–4, or 'Tancredi continues', trans. A. Liddle and S. Sellers, in *Writing Differences*, ed. S. Sellers, Milton Keynes, Open University Press, 1988, pp. 37–53, or *The Newly Born Woman*, pp. 112–22.

with surplus-value, a certain capitalization. We will even venture to say that this is the very definition of the *subject as such*. One cannot discern the subject except as the subject of this operation of capital. But throughout and despite this circulation and this production of surplus-value, despite this labor of the subject, there where there is trace and dissemination, if only there is any, a gift can take place, along with the excessive forgetting or the forgetful excess that [. . .] is radically implicated in the gift. The death of the donor agency (and here we are calling death the fatality that destines a gift *not to return* to the donor agency) is not a natural accident external to the donor agency; it is only thinkable on the basis of, setting out from the gift. This does not mean simply that only death or the dead can give. No, only a 'life' can give, but a life in which this economy of death presents itself and lets itself be exceeded. Neither death nor immortal life can ever give anything, only a singular *surviving* can give. (*Given Time*, pp. 101–2)

Derrida

Of all Derrida's work, the text which proclaims itself most openly to be concerned with the problematic of the gift is *Given Time*. *Given Time* is highly intertextual with respect to Derrida's own *œuvre*, obsessively auto-erotically footnoted, and the *œuvre* is thus revealed to have been obsessively concerned with the gift. Derrida is given to us, displayed, in his footnotes – as fascinated by this impossible thing (not a thing, of course), the gift. Relations between texts (or between 'authors') can themselves be modelled according to different economies – hence Cixous's characterisation of certain writing as *écriture féminine* because of its generous relation to 'the other'. Harold Bloom's theory of the anxiety of influence might be regarded as an account of writing both as fighting over property and fighting with property (an expression sometimes used to designate potlatch). The intertextual relation between Cixous and Derrida could engender and disseminate: it could produce references (direct or indirect) to a series of other intertexts. I want to suggest that this is also a sexed relation between a male philosopher and a female writer – although each of these designations can be called into question.[43] It may even seem that this evocation of intersexuality as well as intertextuality is gratuitous; however, the very question of gratuitousness is itself interrogated by these texts. While the relation between Derrida and Cixous might be seen as an exchange – between subjects who can call each other on the phone as well as comment on each others' texts, Derrida's work as a whole is strikingly characterised by its particular

43 In 'voice ii . . .', Conley claims that Derrida has chosen philosophical discourse, which is strongly marked as masculine; he replies that he is not so sure that he has made that choice (p. 91), although he agrees that some of his early work appears to prove her right. In 'voice ii . . .' itself (and, say, in 'Choreographies'), he presents himself as a dreamer more than as a philosopher – a choice which brings him close to Cixous.

'parasitical' quality. Rather than writing expositions of his own philosophy or theory (as certain secondary works on him would give you to understand he has), he generally chooses to analyse the writing of others. As he bores into these host texts, feeding on their substance, he lays bear his own digestive processes – a reaction takes place as his 'chemistry' meets that of the host who nourishes him, and a new product emerges – perhaps a waste product and perhaps new flesh. This is at once a modest and respectful enterprise, and yet may also be seen as a penetration which undermines or decays. The textual passion which motivates his work may equally be perceived as amorous or lethal.

Given Time is explicitly highly intertextual in its analysis of the problematic of the gift: Heidegger, Mauss and Baudelaire are his chief points of refererence, but many others are evoked (Sahlins, Lévi-Strauss, Poe, Freud, Lacan, Balzac, Gide . . .) – we might even call this network of male writers a homosocial textual economy. Although I should remember and confess (remembrance and confession being part of the problematic of the gift) that he begins with a letter from one woman to another (Mme de Maintenon to a friend), which bemoans the fact that the Sun-King takes all her time. As Derrida explains, only the death of the King will allow that; the King, we might suggest, is the paternal figure of the Law par excellence, who usurps the 'natural' place of superabundant generosity, establishing its pattern, setting up the kind of solar economy analysed in 'Economimesis'. I do not suggest that Derrida is innocently homosocial in his choice of texts: in Given Time his analysis of Baudelaire's poetry (in particular 'Counterfeit Money') is explicit about the libidinal charge between male friends, as one speculates on the other's gift and feels betrayed by his confession that the apparent gift is a counterfeit coin. Derrida informs us that in writing about the gift there must be gift or at least a sign or pledge to give – thus Mauss's The Gift is gift – even if only in so far as it fails to talk on the gift – thus it is what it says, even as it is counterfeit. And the reader (Derrida cites Lévi-Strauss's hommage to Mauss) will betray it, even as he feels betrayed. Derrida's own desire could thus be related intertextually to that of another 'great man' he cites – Montaigne. Instead of the essay Derrida cites, we could choose a different, but equally relevant one, 'On three kinds of relationships', which ranks commerce, relationship, intercourse with the great dead male writers above other kinds of commerce with the living. Given Time is, indeed, a more analytical and 'philosophical' work than, for instance, some of Derrida's writings on sexual differences. And yet its wilful generosity towards Mauss, its refusal to feel betrayed as Mauss fails to produce the gift, even as he insists that there is gift, cannot be reduced to a 'masculine economy'.

For me Derrida's Given Time helps to elucidate why the problematic of the gift has been so problematic, and why our position with respect to Cixous's (or Irigaray's) text might be an ungrateful one. Frequently the reader-response to texts on the gift has been to conjure the gift away, refusing its magic or madness in the name of reason, of reducing everything to economic exchange. One example which Derrida gives is that of Lévi-Strauss reading Mauss; another we could provide is that of those readers of Irigaray or Cixous who wish to reduce the gift in the feminine to unpaid domestic labour. One major difference between Cixous and Derrida has frequently been taken to be sexual difference – Derrida's alleged unwilling-ness to admit that he is a man, that he cannot write in the feminine,[44] that his evocation of woman may be another patriarchal colonisation taking the place of women who might speak for themselves, that his supposed deconstruction of the subject is a deconstruction of the male/masculine subject while a female/feminine subject is yet to see the light of day.[45] While I am not convinced that these charges are absolutely defendable when laid against the letter of Derrida's texts, it might be helpful to note that if male and female writers do not have the same place of enunciation then a dialogue between them could open up the symbolic possibilities of sexual difference.

In 'Choreographies', Derrida recognises the crucial importance of patient laborious feminist struggle (strategy) even as he pleads for it to be interrupted by 'dance'; in 'voice ii . . .' he reminds us that strategy is an effect of the same contract, the same old system which produces sexual opposition: 'Isn't it terrible that it is still necessary to calculate what we say [referring to "masculine" and "feminine"] by accepting the rules of an endless strategy at the moment when we would love to lay down our weapons, when we only love if we lay down our weapons' (p. 86). Is there a gap in strategic calculation, a space for dreaming and giving?

The linking of Derrida with Cixous, and indeed with Irigaray, inevit-ably brings us to the question of voice. Since the first publication of *Of Grammatology* in 1967, Derrida has often been represented as the champion

44 In 'voice ii . . .' Derrida gently questions Conley's assertion that he cannot assume a feminine position (e.g. 93). Conley argues: 'Without awaking you from your dream of a multiplicity of voices – to which one should add of course that of timbre, rhythm, tone, etc. – one could say that those qualifiers about which I spoke to you, "mascu-line" and "feminine", should at the limit disappear. Then, "man" would no longer repress his libidinal economy said to be "feminine". But we are far from it and in these times of transformation which engage each being in her or his singularity in a daily endeavor of questioning, negotiating, etc., rather than simply bypassing, or discarding "femininity" as a masculine construct, should one not at least give woman a chance to speak herself, to write herself from *her* border before acceding to a beyond?' (73).

45 Cf. debates in which Gayatri Spivak ('Displacement and the Discourse of Woman') and Alice Jardine (*Gynesis*, Ithaca, NY and London, Cornell University Press, 1985) have engaged. Irigaray's position is elucidated in Whitford's *Luce Irigaray*, pp. 82–4, in which Whitford suggests that Derrida's dream of sexual multiplicity is a utopian phantasy which bypasses sexual difference.

of writing against speech. His careful analysis of the privileging of speech (and indeed song) as a less or even unmediated form of self-expression and communication in a certain philosophical tradition has sometimes been over-simplified to an alarming degree. This simplification can be used to set him against Cixous, who has not been afraid to refer in a positive fashion to voice . . .

In 'voice ii . . .' (and 'Choreographies'), Derrida refers to a dream of a multiplicity of sexually marked voices, to the way in which the voice is both attached to and detached from the body (p. 79), and can even give birth to another body.[46] He refers to a *writing of the voice* which 'se donne à entendre' (p. 80) – translated by Conley as 'lets itself be heard'. The question of translation runs through Derrida's thoughts on sexual difference here, and through his thoughts on the gift in *Given Time* – for instance the legitimacy of the translations which allow Mauss to recognise gifts in a variety of very different cultures (p. 25). This example from Conley is a fine and accurate translation which must nevertheless lose *se donner*, which literally means either 'to give oneself' or (in the passive voice) 'to be given'. This vocal writing 'speaks otherwise', outside representation, in opposition to the brutality which assigns difference to opposition (sex as a binary). (Thus we cannot escape opposition as we oppose it, other than in the pleasure of the dream.) How does the voice help sexual opposition become sexual differences or sexual differance? 'Perhaps because where there is voice, sex becomes undecided [*le sexe s'indécide*]' (p. 78) – another (unfamiliar) reflexive passive voice in the French. Derrida tells his female interlocutor and translator: 'Vous voyez, pour moi, la traduction entre des langues ou entre des sexes, c'est presque la même chose: à la fois très facile, impossible en toute rigueur, livrée à l'aléa' (p. 78); 'You see, for me translation between languages or between sexes is just about the same thing: both very simple and impossible in any rigorous way, once given over to chance' (pp. 79, 81). I could retranslate this as 'translation between tongues or between sexes is almost the same thing: at once very easy, impossible in a strict sense, a prey to chance.' This retranslation begins to mark what need not be marked; *langue* and *sexe* both refer to bodily organs as well as metonymically (synecdochically?) to categories. Is the relation between your sexual organ(s) and your sex category at once as certain and as uncertain as the relation between your tongue and the language you (naturally? normally?) speak? And what, if any, is the relation between your sex and your tongue – or

46 A point of reference here for Derrida is opera. Cixous gives us the example of Rossini; we could look earlier in time to operas written when some of the greatest singers were castrati – their roles now sung by counter-tenors. Barthes's *S/Z* reminds us how a voice can give birth to a body and unsettle fixed economies not only in the sexual, but also in the linguistic and financial sense. See *S/Z*, trans. R. Miller, New York, Hill and Wang, 1975.

someone else's . . . Derrida makes clear – for example in 'Women in the Beehive' – that the counter-privileging of the feminine as undecidability is a provisional strategy which is a useful point of insertion when confronted with a textual privileging of rational decidability. Derrida tries to open up thinking on sexual difference which would not be 'sealed by a two' ('*Geschlecht*: Sexual Difference, Ontological Difference', p. 80).[47] Derrida's way of opening up, and I want to suggest that it is Cixous's too, is an act of faith (the 'transcendental illusion of the gift' (*Given Time*, p. 30)), is (sexual) differance, the rhythm of the gift, the move in and out of the economic, the setting going (displacement) of the circle. Mauss stubbornly refuses to get rid of the notion of the gift despite all economistic pressures to replace it with, say, the logic of credit (*Given Time*, p. 42), and this very stubbornness is a kind of textual performance, an act of faith.

Irigaray and the other commerce

How does Irigaray's insistence on the need to construct a new feminine identity relate to the question of gift economies – utopian or otherwise? Probably in at least three ways: the new subject would be built according to a gift structure; there would be a (new) way of relating between subjects; and the political and economic organisation of society would be different. A new feminine identity would both enable and be enabled by changes in social and economic relations.[48] The utopian wager made by both Irigaray and by Cixous that another 'feminine' economy could be dreamed if not thought (and that we should try to forge a link to that dream) often appears to entail the wholesale rejection of any property or properties – indeed of the very notion of the *propre*. This would be an attack not only on private

---

47 See also 'Women in the Beehive', for example: 'When we speak here of sexual difference, we must distinguish between opposition and difference. Opposition is two, opposition is man/woman. Difference, on the other hand, can be an indefinite number of sexes and once there is sexual difference in its classical sense – an opposition of two – the arrangement is such that the gift is impossible. All that you can call "gift" – love, *jouissance* – is absolutely forbidden, is forbidden by the dual opposition' (p. 198).

48 See 'Women, the Sacred and Money', trans. D. Knight and M. Whitford, *Paragraph*, 8 (1986), 6–18, e.g.: 'If women are to accede to a different sort of social organization, they need a religion, a language and either a currency of their own or a non-market economy' (p. 9). Or: 'It appears to be impossible, at least in any profound and lasting way, to modify social relations, language, art in general, without modifying the economic system of exchange. They go hand in hand' (p. 12). And again: 'a reordering of social relationships between women necessitates the setting up of an economic system of their own. And, in the first place, respect for a system of exchange' (p. 12) – in French: 'un aménagement des relations sociales entre femmes nécessite la mise en place d'une économie qui leur convient, le respect d'une économie entre elles'(*Sexes et parentés*, pp. 96–7).

property in the restricted sense, but also on ways of thinking which fix essential attributes or properties to (proper) names or, indeed, nouns.

Interestingly, in *Elemental Passions* Irigaray does not quite say that, and indeed she is not promoting the *fusion* which would result from indifferentiation.[49] She wonders whether we could have 'Exchange without property. The possibility of property without being fixed in it. What is possible in 'proper', without being transfixed in it' (*Elemental Passions*, p. 44). Property of some kind has classically been seen as the *sine qua non* of exchange; how can you give something or transfer something to someone if you didn't have that property in the first place and they cannot possess it in the second place? Irigaray allows a trace of property to flicker in the interval of intercommunion. She says to her interlocutor: 'You give me being. But what I love is the fact that you give it to me. Staying there is of little matter to me. I like your giving me a mirror which is not made of ice. Your flowing into me, and me into you. Receiving you melting, molten, and giving that flow back to you. Without end' (*Elemental Passions*, p. 44). In the context of the rest of the work the gift of *being* (which she frequently contrasts with *becoming*) might cause disquiet because of the essential fixity it suggests; here, Irigaray focuses on the gesture of giving and feels free not to pause on or in being. She enjoys the reflective moment of gazing in the mirror of her lover's eyes, where that glass does not capture her image and freeze or petrify her in a single image. Frequently the mirror is a snare: the Woman must be the support of the man's Imaginary whole self, poor amorous Echo, not only mimicking his words with no voice of her own, but also the watery substance in which vain Narcissus can gaze proudly at his fine reflection, as long as no movement stirs the glassy surface; or the petrifying Medusa's head which enables erection as it reminds of castration. But here just as eyes can melt in tears, so can the lovers flow into each other, fluids intermingling. Rigidity is always already released.

Irigaray's focus on, and valuing of, mucus, just like her auto-affective 'two lips', can be (mis)read as an obsessively genital trope – indeed the 'two lips' have been famously interpreted as literal, biological, essentialising – bad news for women as well as tough on men. She writes in *This Sex Which Is Not One*: 'Woman "touches herself" all the time, and moreover no one can forbid her to do so, for her genitals are formed of two lips in continuous contact. Thus within herself she is already two – but not divisible into one(s) – that caress each other' (p. 24). This kind of lyrical and polemical writing has led to a debate over Irigaray's alleged biological

---

49 In 'On the Maternal Order' in *Je, tu, nous*, she discusses with Hélène Rouch, a biologist, the notion of an intra-uterine or placental economy, suggesting that 'These relations, which the patriarchal imagination often presents (for example, in psychoanalysis) as in a state of fusion, are in fact strangely organized and respectful of the life of both' (p. 38).

essentialism.[50] Instead of dwelling on this I should like to quote quite a long passage from *Elemental Passions* which muses on a kiss – this suggests something less obviously genital than other references to two lips in this text:

> Proximity? Two lips kissing two lips. The edges of the face finding openness once more.
>
> Openness is not reflected, not mimed, not reproduced. Not even produced [...]
>
> And how can an endless circulation be set up – in the thing? Or a scansion of space and time in between the poles and the tides?
>
> Openness permits exchange, ensures movement, prevents saturation in possession or consumption. (*Elemental Passions*, p. 63)

As you may guess, I could have gone on quoting even more – *Elemental Passions* is a text which is hard to break up. It has short sentences, but they pour into each other, questioning, responding, guessing, dreaming, in a mode which is simultaneously intimate and abstract, love poetry, philosophical fragments and biblical declamations. In the passage I have quoted two lips kiss two lips. I guess that one pair of lips belongs to our feminine speaker. Usually in this text, her addressee is masculine, but on one or two occasions adjectives suddenly appear with feminine endings. The reader is left suspended between the possibility that the speaker has a female addressee as well as a male one, that she suddenly has a moment's repose in turning to a commerce 'entre femmes', away from the epic amorous battle of the sexes which she has inaugurated, or the possibility that she is hopefully addressing the feminine within her masculine addressee, not the Woman incarcerated in the tomb of the fantasmatic male body, but the feminine libidinal economy which a poetic text can imagine inside a body labelled male (as Cixous regularly does). And so the second pair of 'two lips' could be those of either a female or a male lover. There is an abstraction from any biology, at the same time as there is a biological reference.

The 'kiss', she tells us, is a kind of openness to the other which is not the opposite of being closed. Closedness is important to the watertight compartments fantasised by the masculine Imaginary and legislated over by the Symbolic: the body is wrapped in an impenetrable envelope of skin, spaces are bounded by horizons or surrounded by fences or walls, markers

---

50 Janet Sayers claims that for Irigaray 'femininity [. . .] is essentially constituted by female biology, by the "two lips" of the female sex' (*Biological Politics*, London, Tavistock, 1982, p. 131). Jan Montefiore has responded: 'This metaphor of "two lips" is not a definition of women's identity in biological terms: the statement that they are "continually interchanging" must make it clear that Irigaray is not talking about literal biology' (*Feminism and Poetry*, London, Pandora, 1987). The best exploration of these positions is in Whitford, *Luce Irigaray*, e.g. pp. 171–3.

of property, buildings are erected (homes in which Woman can be incarcerated). Woman is the material with which these constructions are fabricated, the ground on which the erection is sustained, while women – as Margaret Whitford has so lucidly explicated – are truly homeless (confined in homes in the literal sense, they have no homes in the Symbolic order). That closure demands the projection of its opposite: the hole, the gaping wound, the infernal abyss. Irigaray's 'kiss' is thus not open in the sense of the opposite of closed, but 'entr'ouvert'. A structure which might remind us of Barthes's *Le Plaisir du texte*, the pulsing, flickering now half-open, or is it half-closed, of *jouissance*. The male Imaginary figures Woman as hole, and wants to close her up: Irigaray responds to this with a series of figures such as 'l'incontournable volume' in *Speculum* – an expression which is hard to translate, a volume without contours, a volume which cannot be enclosed.[51] This (half-)openness escapes classical economy: it cannot be produced (or reproduced), thus it is not a commodity. Irigaray is concerned elsewhere (for example in her exchanges with Marx such as 'Women on the Market' ('Le Marché des femmes')), and briefly in *Elemental Passions*, with the commodification of women under patriarchy, and with strategies which are inaccessible to commodification. Here she plays with economic vocabulary: exchange, value, interest, appreciation, price, utility or circulation. She suggests that an infinite exchange is set in motion by (half-)openness; which is to be distinguished from the closed (finite) system of classical economy.

In *Elemental Passions*, Irigaray writes as follows:

> The gift has no goal. No for. And no object. The gift – is given. Before any division into donor and recipient. Before any separate identities of giver and receiver. Even before the gift.
>
> Giving oneself, that giving – a transition which undoes the properties of our enclosures, the frame or envelope of our identities. I love you makes, makes me, an other. Loving you, I am no longer; loved, you are different. Loving, I give myself you. I become you. But I remain, as well, to love you still. And as an effect of that act. Unfinishable. Always in-finite. (*Elemental Passions*, pp. 73–4)

The gift has no object – in both senses. It is disinterested and it is not the gift of a commodity. It is pre-essential, prior to any division into giver and receiver, and yet, while undoing division, it prizes (sexual) difference. There is *je* and *toi* – even as I become you, I must be I, in order to love you. It is becoming (and loving) which are the modes of relation between I and you – not being. I am not you. But I am not fixed as 'not you'. It is interesting to note that, for Irigaray, the gift has no 'for'; this contrasts with Derrida's essay on Nietzsche, *Spurs/Eperons*, in which he highlights woman's ability to 'se donner pour' even as she 'se donne'. This functions to

---

51 See Whitford's remarks on this in *The Irigaray Reader*, pp. 28–9.

prevent a hypostasisation of the absolute gift of self, as in giving herself with superabundant generosity, woman also acts that gift.[52] And yet in under-cutting the gift, it could be argued that the gift is lost. This is the problem-atic of *Given Time*. Perhaps, like woman, the gift has to flirt with essentialism – at least as a strategy – in order to exist at all. The utopian genre is one way in which to flirt with essentialism – even for Derrida, even for Wittig.

As is the case with the other contemporary French thinkers with whom I would link her, not all of Irigaray's writing is utopian. Much of her work is critique of the present and of our inheritance from the past. Implicit and explicit in that critique are strategies for now which must make some com-promise with present conditions. However, some of these strategies are related to the utopian. Being can be inflected by becoming. By dreaming, imagining and working on the utopian, change can be effected in the dream-ing, imagining and working subject here and now.

Work is currently being done – particularly within lesbian feminism – and with due homage to Judith Butler's *Gender Trouble* on the argument that sexual difference is grounded in compulsory heterosexuality[53] (*pace* Adrienne Rich). Heterosexuality is compulsory for a number of economic reasons, in the general and restricted sense of 'economic'; the primary reason is taken to be reproduction. Thus it is reproduction – first biological, but also social (the reproduction of labour power, of the relations of produc-tion, etc.) – which necessitates sexual difference. Wittig, for example, claims that lesbians are not women – and that is something to be celebrated – because they do not define themselves relative to men. Irigaray makes a different claim: that women are not women – and that is something to be mourned – because they are trapped in various social roles allocated to them by the patriarchal economy.[54] Women are virgins (pure exchange

---

52 Spivak reads this as a (somewhat literal) statement about the female ability to fake orgasms. It has become a commonplace in certain corners of deconstructionist mytho-logical biology to assert that men can't fake orgasms – since, when one comes to think about it, they obviously can, this is quite a fascinating *lapsus* into the social. (Or perhaps deliberately or otherwise rests on a potent masturbatory fantasy of visible ejaculation, the money shot.)

53 'The heterosexualisation of desire requires and institutes the production of discrete and asymmetrical oppositions between "feminine" and "masculine", where these are understood as expressive attributes of "male" and "female"' (*Gender Trouble*, p. 17). And, again, 'The internal coherence or unity of either gender, man or woman, thereby requires both a stable and oppositional heterosexuality' (p. 22).

54 Butler draws a useful contrast between Irigaray and both Beauvoir and Wittig, who maintain that woman is marked or sexed, whereas Irigaray maintains that the fem-inine sex is a point of absence – both subject and Other are masculine (*Gender Trouble*, pp. 9–13). Butler goes on to suggest that while Beauvoir and Wittig seem over-optimistically content with the humanist notion of the subject, Irigaray's gesture is still as totalising and colonising as the global masculinist signifying economy which she identifies.

value), mothers (use values) or prostitutes (use value which is exchanged) – in none of these positions do women have a right to pleasure as women.[55] Thus for Irigaray, sexual difference is not that which is imposed by the patriarchal economy, but rather that which is repressed. That which is repressed is both *jouissance* between women (which is not monosexual) and *jouissance* within a woman. This is clearly not an invocation of compulsory heterosexuality in the literal sense which underpins Rich's essay of that name. Indeed, apart from Irigaray's lyrical love poetry addressed to women in *This Sex Which Is Not One*, she makes a number of claims about the necessity of our (female) homosexuality as well as of our auto-eroticism. In *Le Corps-à-corps avec la mère* she asserts that socially normative heterosexuality is pathogenic and pathological (p. 31). But the question may be posed whether the inheritance of psychoanalysis (the necessity of accepting sexual difference for psychic health) does lead to the imposition of a psychic heterosexuality on everyone whatever his or her sexual practices. No doubt the challenge will continue to be made: if sexual difference is psychic heterosexuality, is that a necessity? Whitford's is the most convincing argument on Irigaray's behalf with respect to deconstruction: that we have not yet experienced sexual difference, that women are only just beginning to emerge as women,[56] and that it is too soon to embrace Derridean 'sexual differences' positions where male philosophers speak in the feminine. As for the radical lesbian feminist position, it can certainly be argued – and it would be argued by many lesbians – that lesbians do not escape being positioned as 'women', in Wittig's sense, here and now; that would allow a less problematic application of Irigaray's critique of contemporary social organisation, the contemporary Imaginary and Symbolic, and so on. It is an interesting, but maybe less palatable thesis, that abstractions of feminine and masculine are all that we have (will ever have?) to play with.

And the feminine may be another name for the gift, and the masculine another name for economy. Towards the end of *The Other Heading*, Derrida sketches out a series of double duties, of which I shall quote two:

> The *same duty* dictates respecting differences, idioms, minorities, singularities, but also the universality of formal law, the desire for translation, agreement and univocity, the law of the majority, opposition to racism, nationalism and xenophobia.

55 See 'Women on the Market', in *This Sex Which Is Not One*.
56 'And so woman will not yet have taken (a) place' (*Speculum*, trans. D. Macey in *The Irigaray Reader*, p. 53). And again she claims that woman 'cannot relate herself to any being, subject or whole that can be simply designated. Nor to the category (of) women. One woman + one woman + one woman never will have added up to some generic: woman. (The/A) woman gestures towards what cannot be defined, enumerated, formulated, *formalized*. A common noun indeterminable in terms of an identity' (pp. 55–6).

The *same duty* demands tolerating and respecting all that is not placed under the authority of reason. It may have to do with faith, with different forms of faith. It may also have to do with certain thoughts, whether questioning or not, thoughts that, while attempting to think reason and the history of reason, necessarily exceed its order, without becoming, simply because of this, irrational, and much less, irrationalist. For these thoughts may in fact also try to remain faithful to the ideal of the Enlightenment, the *Aufklärung*, the *Illuminismo*, while yet acknowledging its limits, in order to work on the Enlightenment of this time, this time that is ours – *today*. (pp. 78–9)

Afterword

The decision to name this book *Feminine Economies* had a degree of arbitrariness about it: *Gift Economies* might have been a more straightforward choice. To use the term *feminine* in this way is controversial in many quarters; however, that very riskiness has a certain relationship with the gift. Within this book, borrowing from the French poststructuralists who form the subject of the final chapter, *masculine* or *man* has often been used to refer to a colonising structure of neutrality, universality and objectivity (one within which many women operate for substantial portions of their lives), although these terms also 'happen' to refer to biological males. *Feminine* has been used to evoke a structure (or non-structure) of particularity and marginality, of disturbance or *différance*, of exceeding or falling below the norm (a postion which some men, including some celebrated creative artists, inhabit for much of their lives). And yet the term also 'happens' to refer to biological females. Both Cixous and Irigaray complicate any confident assumption that the link between feminine and female is *purely* aleatory or even socio-historical by intermittent reference to the female body (albeit a poeticised body which escapes any familiar rules of biology). In my view, rather than pinning the term down, this insistent, but to some extent self-undermining reference to the body gives it another range of ambiguity. It brings to the debate another element of the feminine, that of materiality (including fluidity and that disturbing half-way state between the solid and the liquid which sometimes provokes the physical reaction of nausea). It also brings a touch of political polemic, of gesture, of defiant celebration. Equally, it creates a necessary disturbance of what could be a too comfortable new neutrality or indifference arising from a deconstruction which points us towards a plurality of sexes.

Kristeva also writes about this strange and shifting feminine which, she claims, must be asserted and yet must not become a refuge or a stronghold:

> Women. We have the luck to be able to take advantage of a biological peculiarity to give a name to that which, in monotheistic capitalism, remains

on this side of the threshold of repression, voice stilled, body mute, always foreign to the social order. A well-deserved luck, for, in fact, in the entire history of patrilineal or class-stratified societies, it is the lot of the feminine to assume the role of *waste*, or of the hidden work-force in the relationships of production and the language which defines them. But *a limited luck*, because others, men, since at least the end of the nineteenth century and in ever-increasing numbers in our time, realize that they have been the 'women' of the community: a misunderstanding, perhaps, that confuses the demands of the female sex (if you like), but which prevents a feminist 'we' from becoming a homogeneous 'secret society of females' and disseminates among others our own unnameable anxiety before all that escapes social restraint. A *luck* that will prove to have been *co-opted* if, after an initial phase – no doubt necessary – of searching for our identity, we lock ourselves up inside it: militant romantics of the final 'cause' to be thus revived, theologians of an inverted humanism rather than its iconoclasts.[1]

The main focus of this book has been the gift, or the feminine, rather than direct political opposition to dominant economic structures. However, it should not be thought that reflection on the gift has the universalising pretension to take over, or substitute for, other forms of struggle, theoretical and practical. Rather that there should be the kind of oscillation which Derrida proposes (between feminist 'work' and feminine 'dance') in 'Choreographies', or Kristeva again in *About Chinese Women*:

> These two extremes condemn us either to being the most passionate bureaucrats of the temporal order (the new wave: women ministers), or to engaging in subversive activity (the other new wave, always following a bit behind the first: promotion of women in the left) [i.e. what is glossed above as feminist 'work']. Or else we remain in an eternal sulk before history, politics, society: the symptoms of their failure, but symptoms betrothed to marginality or to a new mysticism [i.e feminine 'dance' or 'gift'].
>
> To refuse both these extremes. To know that an ostensibly masculine, paternal (because supportive of time and symbol) is necessary in order to have some voice in the record of politics and history [. . . But also] to refuse all roles, in order, on the contrary, to summon this timeless 'truth' – formless, neither true nor false, echo of our *jouissance*, of our madness, of our pregnancies – into the order of speech and social symbolism [. . . .]
>
> A constant alternation between time and its 'truth', identity and its loss, history and the timeless, signless, extra-phenomenal things that produce it. An impossible dialectic: a permanent alternation: never the one without the other. (pp. 37–8)

This oscillation or alternation could also be phrased as, on the one hand, 'Enlightenment' values of progress, reason, universality, opposition to

---

1 *About Chinese Women*, trans. A. Barrows, New York and London, Marion Boyars, [1974] 1977, p. 14.

exploitation, and, on the other hand, listening to the unspoken in speech, calling attention to 'whatever remains unsatisfied, repressed, new, eccentric, incomprehensible, disturbing to the *status quo*' (*About Chinese Women*, p. 38).

In order to illustrate once again the repressed and incomprehensible which shadows the positive side of the Enlightenment, I should like to turn back briefly to the eighteenth century, a major focus in this book, and to an underside of the repeated reference to pins in discussions of the division of labour (that hallmark of reason and progress in the face of feudal stasis): the evocation of feminine pin crime and its punishment. First let us remind ourselves how important the division of labour is. In chapter three I cited *The Spectator*'s Sir Andrew Freeport's views on charity. Instead of letting them rely on 'free' gifts, potential workers should be put to work – leading to a fall in wages and thus greater profits for their kind employers. But also, he claims optimistically, to an even greater general fall in prices *thanks to the increased possibilities of division of labour* – so that even the workers who have suffered a cut in wages in absolute terms benefit in relative terms. Sir Andrew's very name suggests to us that this progressive view depends on the possibility of expanding the market in commodities as well as in labour. Thus three themes are brought together: the division of labour, the expansion of the market in general and the expansion of the labour force. I contrasted this with the feminine utopia of *Millenium Hall* (and other utopian or semi-utopian texts) in which it is true that the work ethic is strong, and the expansion of the labour force to include 'marginals' (frequently women) is a theme. This sometimes leads twentieth-century commentators to relate them to nascent capitalism, and yet, crucially, profit is not the driving motive of these utopian economies, and consequently key economic tenets such as the refusal of cross-subsidisation or the need to make wages equal the marginal product of labour are rejected.

I shall now turn to a rather extreme imaginary crime in the pages of the *Encyclopédie*. I want to bring together the economic theory of the division of labour with sexual difference, remembering that Rousseau, for example, the most perspicacious of eighteenth-century readers of economic inequality, suggests that the very first division of labour is the sexual division of labour in the family – not for Rousseau an absolutely natural or original form, but a social invention.

Pins

Where the historical shift to a commercial society is represented as welcome, it is nevertheless often seen as a kind of feminisation relative to rude warrior societies of yore. Interestingly the feminine is evoked in the repeated reference[2] to the manufacture of the pin in texts of the period; Smith says of his example: 'an example, therefore, from a very trifling manufacture; but one in which the division of labour has been very often taken notice of' (*The Wealth of Nations*, p. 14); in fact he repeats the term 'trifling' four times on that page, in his 'Early Draft' it was instead 'very frivolous'. While it is a standard example, it still needs a kind of apology (or *apologia*) because it is so slight. The pin is furthermore an ambiguous and mobile object which reminds me of the various psychoanalytically charged images in Derrida's *Spurs*: Nietzsche's umbrella, the sail, the dagger and so on. In the fourth volume of the plates of the *Encyclopédie*, *épingle* is lodged fortuitously between *éperon* (spur), and *escrime* (foil). Pin exists happily in the singular, and yet, surely, we usually think of pins in the plural – like the needlewoman's mouth bristling with pins, almost like the petrifying snakes on Medusa's head, which so fascinate Freud. In the *Encyclopédie* a pin is defined by Deleyre as 'a small instrument [. . .] which is used as a detachable means of fastening linen and fabrics, as a way of fixing the various folds made in them when one is dressing, sewing or making a package'.[3] In the *Encyclopédie* the alphabetical arrangement enables the eye to slip down the page in a metonymic progression which juxtaposes and links words which may or may not be related. After 'Epingle' comes the homophone 'Epingles' (ascribed to A.) which apparently means gifts (usually jewellery) given to women. These are described emphatically as 'presents given of your own free will', but are hardly disinterested, since they are given 'to the wife or daughters of a seller to persuade them to agree to the sale'. Indeed they run the risk of being a further step away from a free gift, as they may be a fraudulent means of escaping tax. Four lines after that entry comes 'Délit d'épingle', which tells the ancient story of an evil woman (definitely not a Parisian and perhaps not even French, we are reassured) who 'put out the two eyes of a two-year-old child and committed *the pin crime*, something which is, they say, extremely cruel'. The story comes from Sauval, who claims not to know what the term in question means; the author of the article (A.) suggests that it means precisely putting out someone's eyes with a pin (no further crime is required). The woman was 'crucified, she was executed with her hair loose, wearing a long robe, and with her two legs bound below with a rope'. This story, whose very inclusion in the *Encyclopédie* does not seem self-evident, is marked by a series of emphasised twos (eyes, years and legs). The binding of the woman's legs suggests a repudiation of

2 Apart from the *Encyclopédie*, the editors of *The Wealth of Nations* (p. 15, notes 3 and 4) cite the entry for 'pin' in *Chambers' Cyclopaedia* (4th edn, 1741) and Smith's own *Lectures on Jurisprudence* (both the report of 1762–3 and the report dated 1766).

3 The article closes with a statement from the Editor which makes the article and author (a specialist on Bacon) emblematic of the *Encyclopédie* as a whole, a bringing together of the most sublime philosophy with the least important mechanical details.

her sexual potential – and potential to reproduce – since she is not fit. The two legs match the two eyes she puts out – a kind of castration. All the women of Paris came to see her die 'on account of the novelty', some saying that her torment was appropriate to her place of origin, others to the need that all women should long remember her fate, others that the enormity of her crime would have made an even more severe punishment appropriate. The feminine association with pins is thus a complex and disturbing one – from clothes (and women's fine clothes are a favourite example of the fruits of trade) to jewels, which slip deceitfully between trading gifts and fraud, to the most horrible violent crime and one which is peculiarly related to women. We associate the Enlightenment with a rejection of the spectacle of torture; the body will henceforth be subjected instead to a regime of surveillance and incarceration. There is a rejection, for instance, of the time-honoured method of detecting a witch by testing the sensitivity of her flesh with a pin. But here no criticism of the medieval horror is voiced – the woman who betrays her maternal character and *blinds* an infant must herself be crucified in front of all other women. The 'remarkable female thief [*insigne larronesse*] whose country is not known' is punished in a biblical way which may also remind us of the exorbitant and unnatural punishments visited on rebellious slaves in front of the assembled slave population.

This is reminiscent of Diderot's introduction of slavery as a punishment for post-menopausal women who engage in sex in his Tahiti (analysed in chapter four). The wilful choice of these crones to put their pleasure before the reproductive needs of their society means that they are either banished from society altogether (exile) or forced into productive labour on behalf, we presume, of society as a whole. The transparency of Tahiti encourages some readers to view Tahitian sex as work – for the erotic needs the veil. And the evocation of excessive punishments may indeed be the totalitarian side of the 'Enlightenment' values also found in Plato's *Republic* and More's *Utopia*: universality, sameness, transparency. However, there is a veil in Diderot's *Supplement* (and in Plato's and More's writing): it is a linguistic one – the use of wit and the subtleties of dialogic structure.

Celebrations of the gift as sovereign symbolic exchange (such as we find in Bataille or Baudrillard) deploy the feminine in its cruel and radically eccentric guise – where feminists may find material for offence. Equally many readers have found something incomprehensible and disturbing in Montaigne's praise of cannibalism. Here I would turn to the question of the reading relation – at least as crucial as (and interdependent with) the dialogic structure of the writing. I would turn also to the question of the relative roles of seriousness, play and the ethical, roles which are intertwined as hosts and parasites or guests.

If language structures, then it also re-structures the subject – and hence the importance of avant-gardist texts (conventionally understood), but also of canonical texts, such as those of Rousseau, which may be read differently, and recuperated texts such as Scott's *Millenium Hall*. The economy of abundance (as opposed to the market economy of scarcity) is not only located *in* certain works, but in the relation between reader and text. Likewise, the lover's dream or the floating of sexed traits. In the last chapter I quoted a passage from *A Door into Ocean* in which a young man (a kind of ephebe) helplessly asks a Sharer, 'Please, you do know the difference, don't you?', and she replies, 'Of course. What does it matter'. This example from popular culture evokes another in my mind: the line from an American TV comedy series quoted by de Man in his introduction to *Allegories of Reading*. When asked by his dutiful wife if he wants his shoes laced over or under, Archie Bunker replies 'What's the difference'. I close the quotes before the punctuation, since the difference between the mark of a question (grammatical) and the full stop which marks an assertion (rhetorical) is what makes it self-undermining – what takes it towards being arche debunking, as de Man puts it. These two examples, with their very different sexual politics, remind us finally of the importance of women's work. In the realist comic text, the wife's apparent dedication to her exploiter still has potential to disrupt and challenge the patriarchal economy (as we see even more clearly in the original British version, *Till Death Us Do Part*). While the husband utters the key phrase, it is the wife's refusal to hear his rhetorical snub, and her laborious explanation of the difference between lacing over and lacing under, which brings out the ungrammaticality of the familiar cliché. Where does stupidity end and defiance begin? In the more serious science-fiction example, it is the young man who is the butt, the one who desires clear distinctions between subjects and objects and fails to understand a fluid logic of reciprocity.

Feminine economies need not be pinned down, and should certainly not attempt to *replace* other forms of critique or opposition, a gesture which would only mimic the totalitarian drive to universality and sameness. Feminine economies can only exist in relation . . .

Bibliography

Aglietta, M., *A Theory of Capitalist Regulation: The US experience*, trans. D. Fernbach, London, Verso, [1976] 1979.

Anderson, W., *Diderot's Dream*, Baltimore, Johns Hopkins University Press, 1990.

Astell, M., *A Serious Proposal to the Ladies for the Advancement of their True and Greatest Interest* [3rd corrected edn, 1696]: excepts in *The First English Feminist: Reflections on Marriage and other Writings by Mary Astell*, ed. and intr. by Bridget Hill, Aldershot, Gower Publishing, 1986.

Baker, F., 'Remarques sur la notion de dépôt', *Annales Jean-Jacques Rousseau*, 37 (1968), 57–93.

—— [Review of] 'James F. Jones, *La Nouvelle Héloïse: Rousseau and Utopia*', *Modern Language Review*, 75 (1980), 195–8.

—— 'La Route contraire', in *Reappraisals of Rousseau: Studies in Honour of R. A. Leigh*, ed. S. Harvey, M. Hobson, D. Kelley and S. B. Taylor, Manchester, Manchester University Press, 1980, pp. 132–62.

—— 'La Scène du lac dans *La Nouvelle Héloïse*', in *Le Préromantisme hypothèque ou hypothèse?*, Colloque de Clermont-Ferrand 29–30 juin 1972, Actes et Colloques, 18, 129–52.

Baker-Smith, D., 'The Escape from the Cave: Thomas More and the Vision of Utopia', *Dutch Quarterly Review of Anglo-American Letters*, 15 (1985), 148–61.

Barker, E., *The Political Thought of Plato and Aristotle*, London, Methuen, 1959.

Barthes, R., *Critical Essays*, trans. R. Howard, Evanston, Northwestern University Press, [1964] 1972.

—— *The Eiffel Tower and Other Mythologies*, trans. R. Howard, New York, Hill and Wang, 1979.

—— *Mythologies*, trans. A. Lavers, London, Paladin, [1957] 1973.

—— *New Critical Essays*, trans. R. Howard, Berkeley and Los Angeles, University of California Press, [1964] 1990.

—— *S/Z*, trans. R. Miller, New York, Hill and Wang, [1970] 1975.

Barthes, R., Baudry, J.-L., Hollier, D., Houdebine, J.-L., Kristeva, J., Pleynet, M., Sollers, P. and Wahl, F., *Bataille*, Paris, U.G.E. 10/18, 1973.

Bataille, G., *Œuvres complètes*, Paris, Gallimard, 1971.

—— *The Accursed Share*, trans. R. Hurley, New York, Zone Books, [1967] 1988.

—— *Eroticism*, trans. M. Dalwood, London, John Calder, [1957] 1962.

Bataille, G., *My Mother; Madame Edwarda; The Dead Man*, trans. A. Wainhouse, London, Marion Boyars, (1989) 1995.

—— *Story of the Eye*, trans. J. Neugroschal, Harmondsworth, Penguin, [1928] 1982.

—— *Visions of Excess. Selected Writings, 1927–1939*, trans. A. Stoekl with C. R. Lovitt and D. M. Leslie, Jun., Minneapolis, The University of Minnesota Press, 1985.

Bataille, G., Leiris, M., Griaule, M., Einstein, C., Desnos, R. and writers associated with the Acéphale and Surrealist groups, *Critical Dictionary* [1929–30] in *Encyclopaedia Acephalica*, trans. I. White *et al.*, London, Atlas Press, 1995.

Baudrillard, J., *Symbolic Exchange and Death*, trans. I. Hamilton Grant, London, Sage, [1976] 1993.

—— 'When Bataille Attacked the Metaphysical Principle of Economy' (first published in 1976), trans. D. J. Miller, *Canadian Journal of Political and Social Theory*, 11 (1987), 57–62.

Beauvoir, S. de, *The Second Sex*, trans. and ed. H. M. Parshley, London, Jonathan Cape, [1949] 1953.

Becker, G., *The Economic Approach to Human Behaviour*, Chicago, University of Chicago Press, 1976.

Bennington, G., 'Introduction to Economics, I: Because the World is Round', in *Bataille: Writing the Sacred*, ed. C. Bailey Gill, London and New York, Routledge, 1995, pp. 46–57.

Benot, Y., *Diderot, de l'athéisme à l'anticolonialisme*, Paris, Maspéro, 1970.

Benrekassa, G., 'Loi naturelle et loi civile: l'idéologie des Lumières et la prohibition de l'inceste', *Studies on Voltaire and the Eighteenth Century*, 87 (1972), 115–44.

Berneri, M. L., *Journey through Utopia*, London, Freedom Press, [1950] 1982.

Bernheimer, C. and C. Kahane, eds, *In Dora's Case*, London, Virago, 1985.

Black, M., 'When Montaigne Conducts You on a Visit to his Cannibals, Take Care not to get Eaten by the Guide', *Dalhousie French Studies*, 16 (1989), 15–36.

Blum, C., *Rousseau and the Republic of Virtue: The Language of Politics in the French Revolution*, Ithaca, NY and London, Cornell University Press, 1986.

Bougainville, L. A. de, *Adventures in the Wilderness. The American Journals of Louis Antoine de Bougainville, 1756–1760*, trans. E. P. Hamilton, Norman, University of Oklahoma Press, [1924] 1964.

—— *Voyage autour du monde*, Paris, Cercle du Bibliophile, 1969.

Bourdieu, P., *Algérie 60* [Algeria 1960], Paris, Minuit, 1977.

Bowie, M., *Lacan*, London, Fontana, 1991.

Brooks, P., *The Novel of Worldliness. Crébillon, Marivaux, Laclos, Stendhal*, Princeton and London, Princeton University Press, 1969.

Buck-Morss, S., 'Envisioning Capital: Political Economy on Display', *Critical Inquiry*, 21 (1995), 434–67.

Burgard, P. J. (ed.), *Nietzsche and the Feminine*, Charlottesville, University Press of Virginia, 1994.

Butler, J., *Gender Trouble*, London, Routledge, 1990.

Cady, A., ed., *Women Teaching French: Five Papers on Language and Theory*, Loughborough, Loughborough University Research Centre, 1991 (Studies in European Culture and Society, 5).

Carretta, V., 'Utopia Limited: Sarah Scott's *Millenium Hall* and the *History of Sir George Ellison*', *The Age of Johnson: A Scholarly Annual*, 5 (1992), 303–25.

Cave, T., *The Cornucopian Text: Problems of Writing in the French Renaissance*, Oxford, Clarendon Press, 1979.

Cavendish, M., *The Description of a New World, Called the Blazing World*, ed. Kate Lilley, London, William Pickering, [1666] 1992.

Certeau, M. de, 'Le Lieu de l'autre. Montaigne: "Des cannibales"', *Œuvres et Critiques*, 8 (1983), 59–72.

Chambers, R. W., *Thomas More*, London, Jonathan Cape, 1935.

Chanter, T., *Ethics of Eros: Irigaray's Rewriting of the Philosophers*, New York and London, Routledge, 1995.

Chinard, G., *L'Amérique et le rêve exotique dans la littérature française au XVIIe et au XVIIIe siècle*, Paris, Droz, 1934.

Cixous, H., *'Coming to Writing' and Other Essays*, trans. S. Cornell, D. Jenson, A. Liddle and S. Sellers, Cambridge, Mass., Harvard University Press, [1977] 1991.

—— *Portrait of Dora*, trans. A. Barrows, London, John Calder, [1976] 1979.

—— *Readings: The Poetics of Blanchot, Joyce, Kafka, Kleist, Lispector and Tsvetayeva*, ed. and trans. V. A. Conley, Minneapolis, University of Minnesota Press, 1991.

—— 'Tancredi Continues', trans. A. Liddle and S. Sellers, in *Writing Differences*, ed. S. Sellers, Milton Keynes, Open University Press, 1988, pp. 37–53.

—— 'voice i . . .', *On Feminine Writing: A Boundary 2 Symposium*, ed. V. A. Conley and W. V. Spanos, *Boundary 2*, 12(2) (1984), 51–67.

Cixous, H. and Calle-Gruber, M., *Hélène Cixous, Photos de Racine*, Paris, des femmes, 1994.

Cixous, H. and Clément, C., *The Newly Born Woman*, trans. B. Wing, Manchester, Manchester University Press, [1975] 1986.

Cixous, H., Gagnon, M. and Leclerc, A., *La Venue à l'écriture*, Paris, 10/18, 1977.

Cleveland, G., Gunderson, M. and Hyatt, D., 'Child Care Costs and the Employment Decision of Women: Canadian Evidence', *Canadian Journal of Economics/Revue canadienne d'Economique*, 29 (1996), 132–51.

Conley, V. A., *Hélène Cixous: Writing the Feminine*, Lincoln, Neb. and London: University of Nebraska Press, expanded edn, 1991.

Connelly, R., DeGraff., D. and Levison, D., 'Women's Employment and Child Care in Brazil', *Economic Development and Cultural Change*, 44 (1996), 619–56.

Crittenden, W. M., *The Life and Writings of Mrs Sarah Scott*, Philadelphia, Thesis Presented to the University of Pennsylvania, 1932.

Crocker, L. G., *Jean-Jacques Rousseau: A New Interpretative Analysis of his Life and Works*, New York, Macmillan, 1968–73.

Davidoff, L. and Hall, C., *Family Fortunes: Men and Women of the English Middle Class, 1780–1850*, London, Hutchinson, 1987.

Deleuze, G. and Guattari, F., *Anti-Oedipus: Capitalism and Schizophrenia*, trans. R. Hurley, M. Seem and H. R. Lane, London, Athlone Press, [1972] 1984.

Delphy, C., *Close to Home: A Materialist Analysis of Women's Oppression*, trans. D. Leonard, London, Hutchinson, 1984.

Delphy, C. and Leonard, D., *Familiar Exploitation*, Cambridge, Polity Press, 1992.

Derrida, J., 'Choreographies', interview with C. McDonald in *The Ear of the Other*, trans. P. Kamuf, Lincoln and London, University of Nebraska, Neb. Press, [1982] 1988, pp. 163–85.

Derrida, J., *Dissemination*, trans. B. Johnson, Chicago, The University of Chicago Press, [1972] 1981.

—— 'Economimesis', trans. R. Klein, *Diacritics*, 11 (1981), pp. 3–25.

—— 'Geschlecht: Sexual Difference, Ontological Difference', trans. R. Berezdivin, *Research in Phenomenology*, 13 (1983), 65–83.

—— *Given Time, I: Counterfeit Money*, trans. P. Kamuf, Chicago and London, The University of Chicago Press, [1991] 1992.

—— *Of Grammatology*, trans. G. Spivak, Baltimore, The Johns Hopkins University Press, [1967] 1976.

—— *The Other Heading*, trans. P.-A. Brault and M. B. Naas, Bloomington and Indianapolis, Indiana University Press, [1991] 1992.

—— *The Post Card. From Socrates to Freud and Beyond*, trans. A. Bass, Chicago and London, The University of Chicago Press, [1979] 1987.

—— *Spurs*, trans. B. Harlow, Chicago and London, The University of Chicago Press, 1979.

—— 'voice ii . . .' with V. A. Conley, *Boundary 2*, 12 (1984), 68–93.

—— 'Women in the Beehive: A Seminar with Jacques Derrida', in *Men in Feminism*, ed. A. Jardine and P. Smith, New York and London, Routledge, 1989, pp. 189–203.

—— *Writing and Difference*, trans. A. Bass, London, Routledge, [1967] 1978.

Dex, S., Joshi, H. and Macran, S., 'A Widening Gulf among Britain's Mothers', *Oxford Review of Economic Policy*, 12 (1996), 65–75.

Dickason, A., 'Anatomy and Destiny in Plato's Views of Women', in *Women and Philosophy: Towards a Theory of Liberation*, ed. C. Gould and M. Wartofsky, New York, Capricorn Books, 1976, pp. 45–53.

Diderot, D., *Œuvres politiques*, ed. P. Vernière, Paris, Garnier, 1963.

—— *Rameau's Nephew and Other Works*, trans. J. Barzun and R. H. Bowen, Indianapolis, Bobbs-Merrill Company, 1964.

Diderot, D. and d'Alembert, J., eds, *Encyclopédie, ou dictionnaire raisonné des sciences, des arts, et métiers*, 17 vols, Paris, 1751–65.

Duchet, M., *Diderot et l'Histoire des Deux Indes, ou l'Ecriture fragmentaire*, Paris, Nizet, 1978.

Dunne, L., 'Mothers and Monsters in Sarah Robinson Scott's *Millenium Hall*', in *Utopian and Science Fiction by Women*, ed. J. L. Donawerth and C. A. Kolmerten, New York, Syracuse University Press, 1994, pp. 54–72.

Duren, B., 'Cixous's Exorbitant Texts', *Sub-Stance* 10 (1981), 39–51.

During, S., 'Rousseau's Patrimony: Primitivism, Romance and Becoming Other' in *Colonial Discourse/Postcolonial Theory*, ed. F. Barker, P. Hulme and M. Iversen, Manchester, Manchester University Press, 1994, pp. 47–71.

Duval, E. M., 'Lessons of the New World: Design and Meaning in Montaigne's "Des Cannibales" (I: 31) and "Des coches" (III: 6)', *Yale French Studies* (*Montaigne: Essays in Reading*), 64 (1983), 95–112.

Eagleton, T., *The Rape of Clarissa: Writing, Sexuality and Class Struggle in Samuel Richardson*, Oxford, Basil Blackwell, 1982.

Earle, P., *The Making of the English Middle Class. Business, Society and Family Life in London 1660–1730*, London, Methuen, 1989.

Eigeldinger, M., *Jean-Jacques Rousseau: Univers mythique et cohérence*, Neuchâtel, Editions de la Baconnière, 1978.

Ellrich, R. J., 'Rousseau's Androgynous Dream', *French Forum*, 13 (1988), 319–38.

Faderman, L., *Surpassing the Love of Men: Romantic Friendship and Love Between Women from the Renaissance to the Present*, New York, Morrow, 1981.

Fallaize, E., *French Women's Writing*, London and Basingstoke, Macmillan, 1993.

Felman, S., *Jacques Lacan and the Adventure of Insight: Psychoanalysis in Contemporary Culture*, Cambridge, Mass. and London, Harvard University Press, 1987.

—— (ed.) *Literature and Psychoanalysis. The Question of Reading: Otherwise*, Baltimore, Johns Hopkins University Press, 1982.

Fontenay, E. de, *Diderot, ou Le Matérialisme enchanté*, Paris, Grasset, 1981.

Foucault, M., *The History of Sexuality*, vols I (*An Introduction*) II (*The Use of Pleasure*) and III (*The Care of the Self*), trans. R. Hurley, Harmondsworth, Penguin, [1976] 1978, [1984] 1985, [1984] 1986.

—— *The Order of Things*, trans. A. Sheridan, London and New York, Routledge, [1966] 1989.

France, P., *Diderot*, Oxford, Oxford University Press, 1983.

Frayling, C., 'The Composition of *La Nouvelle Héloïse*', in *Reappraisals of Rousseau: Studies in Honour of R. A. Leigh*, ed. S. Harvey, M. Hobson, D. Kelley and S. B. Taylor, Manchester, Manchester University Press, 1980, pp. 181–214.

Freud, S., *Jokes and their Relation to the Unconscious*, Harmondsworth, Penguin, 1976.

—— *On Psychopathology*, Harmondsworth, Penguin, 1979.

—— *The Psychopathology of Everyday Life*, Harmondsworth, Penguin, 1975.

Fuss, D., *Essentially Speaking*, London, Routledge, 1989.

Godbout, J. with Caillé, A., *L'Esprit du don*, Beauceville, Boréal, 1992.

Goodman, D., 'The Structure of Political Argument in Diderot's *Supplément au Voyage de Bougainville*', *Diderot Studies*, 21 (1983), 123–37.

Goux, J.-J., *Les Monnayeurs du langage*, Paris, Galilée, 1984.

Graffigny, F. de, *Letters from a Peruvian Woman*, trans. D. Kornacker, New York, The Modern Language Association of America, [1747] 1993.

Greenhalgh, C., 'Male–Female Wage Differentials in Great Britain: Is Marriage an Equal Opportunity?', *The Economic Journal*, 90 (1980), 751–75.

Grosz, E., *Sexual Subversions. Three French Feminists*, Sydney, Allen and Unwin, 1989.

Haggerty, G. F., ' "Romantic Friendship" and Patriarchal Narrative in Sarah Scott's *Millenium Hall*', *Genders*, 13 (1992), 108–22.

Hanrahan, M., 'Cixous's *Portrait de Dora*: The Play of Whose Voice?', forthcoming.

Harvey, D., *The Condition of Postmodernity*, Oxford, Basil Blackwell, 1989.

Homans, M., 'The Woman in the Cave: Recent Feminist Fictions and the Classical Underworld', *Contemporary Literature*, 29 (1988), 369–402.

Horowitz, M. C., 'Montaigne's "Des Cannibales" and Natural Sources of Virtue', *History of European Ideas*, 11 (1989), 427–34.

The Irigaray Reader, ed. M. Whitford, Oxford, Blackwell, 1991.

Irigaray, L., *Le Corps-à-corps avec la mère* (*The Bodily Encounter With the Mother*), Montreal, les éditions de la pleine lune, 1981.

—— *Divine Women*, trans. S. Muecke, Sydney, Local Consumption Occasional Paper, 8, 1986.

Irigaray, L., *Elemental Passions*, trans. J. Collie and J. Still, London, Athlone Press, [1982] 1992.

—— *An Ethics of Sexual Difference*, trans. C. Burke and G. C. Gill, London, Athlone Press, [1984] 1993.

—— *Je, tu, nous: Toward a Culture of Difference*, trans. A. Martin, London, Routledge, [1990] 1993.

—— *Marine Lover of Friedrich Nietzsche*, trans. G. C. Gill, New York, Columbia University Press, [1980] 1991.

—— *Parler n'est jamais neutre* [Speaking is never neutral/neuter], Paris, Minuit, 1985.

—— *Sexes and Genealogies*, trans. G. C. Gill, New York, Columbia University Press, [1987] 1993.

—— 'Sorcerer Love: A Reading of Plato's Symposium, Diotima's Speech', trans. E. H. Kuykendall, *Hypatia* 3 (1989), 32–44.

—— *Speculum of the Other Woman*, trans. G. C. Gill, Ithaca, NY, Cornell University Press, [1974] 1985.

—— *Thinking the Difference*, trans. K. Montin, London, Athlone Press, [1989] 1994.

—— *This Sex Which Is Not One*, trans. C. Porter with C. Burke, Ithaca, NY, Cornell University Press, [1977] 1985.

—— 'Women, the Sacred and Money', trans. D. Knight and M. Whitford, *Paragraph*, 8 (1986), 6–18.

Jardine, A., *Gynesis: Configurations of Woman and Modernity*, Ithaca, NY and London, Cornell University Press, 1985.

Jauss, H. R., *Toward an Aesthetic of Reception*, trans. T. Bahti, Minneapolis, University of Minnesota Press, 1982.

Johnson, C., *System and Writing in the Philosophy of Jacques Derrida*, Cambridge, Cambridge University Press, 1993.

Jones, J. F., *La Nouvelle Héloïse: Rousseau and Utopia*, Geneva and Paris, Librairie Droz, 1978.

Jones, V., *Women in the Eighteenth Century. Constructions of Femininity*, London and New York, Routledge, 1990.

Joshi, H. and Owen H., 'How Long is a Piece of Elastic? The Measurement of Female Activity Rates in British Censuses, 1951–1981', *Cambridge Journal of Economics*, 11 (1987), 55–74.

Kamuf, P., *Fictions of Feminine Desire: Disclosures of Héloïse*, Lincoln, Neb., University of Nebraska Press, 1982.

—— *Signature Pieces. On the Institution of Authorship*, Ithaca, NY and London, Cornell University Press, 1988.

Kautsky, K., *Thomas More and his Utopia*, trans. H. J. Stenning, London, Lawrence and Wishart, 1979.

Kavanagh, T. M., *Enlightenment and the Shadows of Chance: The Novel and the Culture of Gambling in Eighteenth-Century France*, Baltimore and London, Johns Hopkins University Press, 1993.

Klossowski, P., *Roberte ce soir and The Revocation of the Edict of Nantes*, trans. Austryn Wainhouse, London, Calder and Boyars, [1953] 1971.

—— *La Monnaie vivante*, Paris, Losfeld, 1970.

Knight, D., 'Roland Barthes in Harmony: The Writing of Utopia', *Paragraph*, 11 (1988), 127–42.

Kofman, S., *Le Respect des femmes*, Paris, Galilée, 1982.

Kristeva, J., *About Chinese Women*, trans. A. Barrows, New York and London, Marion Boyars, [1974] 1977.

—— *Pouvoirs de l'horreur: Essai sur l'abjection*, Paris, Seuil, 1980.

—— *Powers of Horror: An Essay on Abjection*, trans. L. S. Roudiez, New York, Columbia University Press, 1982.

—— *Tales of Love*, trans. L. S. Roudiez, New York, Columbia University Press, [1983] 1987.

Lacan, J., *The Four Fundamental Concepts of Psychoanalysis*, trans. A. Sheridan, Harmondsworth, Penguin, [1973] 1977.

—— 'God and the *Jouissance* of The Woman' and 'A Love Letter', in *Feminine Sexuality*, ed. J. Mitchell and J. Rose, trans. J. Rose, London and Basingstoke, Macmillan, 1982, pp. 137–61.

Laplanche, J. and Pontalis, J.-B., *The Language of Psycho-analysis*, trans. D. Nicholson-Smith, London, Hogarth Press, [1967] 1973.

Lasowski, P. W., *Libertines*, Paris, Gallimard, 1980.

Leclerc, A., *Parole de femme* [Woman's Word], Paris, Grasset, 1974.

Leigh, R. A., *Rousseau and the Problem of Tolerance in the Eighteenth Century*, Oxford, Oxford University Press, 1979.

—— 'Liberté et autorité dans le *Contrat social*', in *Jean-Jacques Rousseau et son œuvre*, Paris, Klincksieck, 1963, pp. 249–64.

Lestringant, F., 'Le Cannibalisme des "Cannibales" I: Montaigne et la tradition', *Bulletin de la Société des Amis de Montaigne*, 9–10 (1982), 27–40.

—— 'Le Cannibalisme des "Cannibales" II: De Montaigne à Malthus', *Bulletin de la Société des Amis de Montaigne*, 11–12 (1982), 19–38.

—— 'Le Nom des "Cannibales" de Christophe Colomb à Michel de Montaigne', *Bulletin de la Société des Amis de Montaigne*, 17–18 (1984), 51–74.

Lévi-Strauss, C., *The Elementary Structures of Kinship*, trans. J. Harle Bell and J. R. von Sturmer, ed. R. Needham, London, Eyre & Spottiswood, [1949] 1969.

Lipsey, R., *An Introduction to Positive Economics*, London, Weidenfeld and Nicolson, [1963] 1983.

Longxi, Z., 'The Cannibals, the Ancients and Cultural Critique: Reading Montaigne in Postmodern Perspective', *Human Studies*, 16 (1993), 51–68.

Lyotard, J.-F., *Libidinal Economy*, trans. I. Hamilton Grant, London, Athlone Press, [1974] 1993.

—— *The Postmodern Condition: A Report on Knowledge*, trans. G. Bennington and B. Massumi, foreword by F. Jameson, Manchester, Manchester University Press, [1979] 1984.

Mably, Abbé de, *Doutes proposés aux philosophes économistes sur l'ordre naturel et essentiel des sociétés politiques*, Paris, La Haye, 1768.

Macey, D., *Lacan in Contexts*, London, Verso, 1988.

McKendrick, N., Brewer, J. and Plumb, J. H., *The Birth of a Consumer Society. The Commercialisation of Eighteenth-Century England*, London, Europa Publications Ltd, 1982.

Man, P. de, *Allegories of Reading*, New Haven, Yale University Press, 1979.
—— *The Rhetoric of Romanticism*, New York, Columbia University Press, 1984.
Mandeville, B., *The Fable of the Bees: Private Vices, Public Benefits*, ed. P. Harth, Harmondsworth, Penguin, [1724] 1970.
Marc 'Hadour, G., 'Thomas More in Emulation and Defense of Erasmus', in *Erasmus of Rotterdam, the Man and the Scholar*, ed. J. Sperna Weiland and W. Th. M. Frijhoff, Leiden, Brill, 1988, pp. 203–14.
Marchak, C., 'The Joy of Transgression: Bataille and Kristeva', *Philosophy Today*, (Winter 1990), 354–63.
Marin, L., *Utopics: Spatial Play*, trans. R. A. Vollrath, London and Basingstoke, Macmillan, 1984.
Marks, E. and de Courtivron, I. (eds), *New French Feminisms*, Brighton, Harvester Press, 1981.
Martin, J. and Roberts, C., *Women and Employment, a Lifetime Perspective*, London, HMSO, 1984.
Masters, R., *The Political Philosophy of Rousseau*, Princeton, Princeton University Press, 1968.
Mauss, M., *The Gift. Forms and Functions of Exchange in Archaic Societies*, trans. I. Cunnison, London, Routledge and Kegan Paul, [1925] 1966.
—— *Sociologie et anthropologie*, Paris, Presses Universitaires de France, 1950.
Ménard, C., 'L'autre et son double', in L. Giard (ed.), *Michel Foucault. Lire l'œuvre*, Grenoble, Jérôme Millon, 1992, pp. 129–40.
Miller, J., *Rousseau, Dreamer of Democracy*, New Haven, Yale University Press, 1984.
Mirabeau, V. R., Marquis de, *L'Ami des hommes, ou Traité de la population*, Avignon, 1756.
Moi, T. (ed.), *French Feminist Thought*, Oxford, Basil Blackwell, 1987.
Montaigne, M. de, *Essays*, trans. J. M. Cohen, Harmondsworth, Penguin, [1580–92] 1958.
—— *The Essays of Michel de Montaigne*, trans. and ed. M. A. Screech, Harmondsworth, Penguin, 1991.
Montefiore, J., *Feminism and Poetry*, London, Pandora, 1987.
Montesquieu, C., *The Spirit of the Laws*, trans. T. Nugent, New York, Hafner Publishing Company, [1748] 1949.
More, T., *Utopia*, trans. R. Robinson, introduction by R. Marius, London, Dent, [1516] 1985.
Morelly, J., *Code de la nature ou le véritable esprit de ses lois de tout temps négligé ou méconnu*, introduction by V. P. Volguine, Paris, Editions Sociales, [1755] 1953.
Mühl, E. von der, *Denis Veiras et son Histoire des Sévarambes 1677–79*, Paris, Droz, 1938.
Mui, H.-C. and Mui, L. H., *Shops and Shopkeeping in Eighteenth-Century England*, London, Routledge, 1989.
Nicholson, C., *Writing and the Rise of Finance: Capital Satires of the Early Eighteenth Century*, Cambridge, Cambridge University Press, 1994.
O'Brien, C. C., *The Independent Magazine*, 12 December 1992, p. 62.
Papin, B., 'L'Utopie tahitienne du *Supplément au Voyage de Bougainville* ou le "modèle idéal" en politique', *L'Information littéraire* 36 (1984), 102–5.

Plato, *The Republic of Plato*, ed. F. M. Cornford, Oxford, Oxford University Press, 1941.

Pocock, J. G. A., *The Machiavellian Moment: Florentine Political Thought and the Atlantic Republican Tradition*, Princeton and London, Princeton University Press, 1975.

Raymond, M., 'Montaigne devant les sauvages d'Amérique', *Etre et dire* (1970), 13–37.

Raynal, G. T. F. Abbé de, *Histoire philosophique et politique des Deux Indes*, ed. Y. Benot, Paris, Maspero, 1981 (extracts from *Histoire philosophique et politique des établissements et du commerce des Européens dans les deux Indes* [1770, expanded edn, 1781])

Reeve, C., *Plans of Education; with Remarks on the Systems of other Writers*, London, T. Hookham and J. Carpenter, 1792.

—— *The Progress of Romance*, introduced by Suzi Halimi, Paris, Editions d'Aujourd'hui, [1785] 1980.

Reid, T., *Practical Ethics; Being Lectures and Papers on Natural Religion, Self-Government, Natural Jurisprudence, and the Law of Nations*, ed. K. Haakonssen, Princeton and London, Princeton University Press, 1990.

Rohrlich, R. and Baruch, E. H. (eds), *Women in Search of Utopia: Mavericks and Mythmakers*, New York, Schocken Books, 1984.

Rousseau, J.-J., *Œuvres complètes*, ed. B. Gagnebin and M. Raymond, Paris, Bibliothèque de la Pléiade, 1959–95.

—— *The Confessions*, trans. J. M. Cohen, Harmondsworth, Penguin, [1781] 1953.

—— *Discourse on Political Economy and The Social Contract*, trans. C. Betts, Oxford and New York, Oxford University Press, 1994.

—— *Emile*, trans. B. Foxley, London, Dent, [1762] 1974.

—— *Julie*, trans. J. H. McDowell, University Park and London, The Pennsylvania State University Press, [1761] 1968.

—— *Politics and the Arts: Rousseau's Letter to d'Alembert*, trans. A. Bloom, New York, Cornell University Press, [1758] 1960.

—— *The Social Contract*, trans. M. Cranston, Harmondsworth, Penguin, [1762] 1968.

Rubin Suleiman, S., 'Bataille in the Street. The Search for Virility in the 1930s', in *Bataille: Writing the Sacred*, ed. C. Bailey Gill, London and New York, Routledge, 1995, pp. 26–45.

—— 'Mothers and the Avant-Garde: A Case of Mistaken Identity?' *Avant Garde*, 4 (1990), 135–46.

—— 'Pornography, Transgression and the Avant-Garde: Bataille's *Story of the Eye*', in *The Poetics of Gender*, ed. Nancy K. Miller, New York, Columbia University Press, 1986, pp. 117–36.

Sahlins, M., *Stone Age Economics*, Chicago and New York, Aldine Atherton Inc., 1972.

Sayers, J., *Biological Politics*, London, Tavistock, 1982.

Schnorrenberg, B. B., 'A Paradise like Eve's. Three Eighteenth-Century English Female Utopias', *Women's Studies: An Interdisciplinary Journal*, 9 (1982), 263–73.

Schor, N., 'This Essentialism Which Is Not One: Coming to Grips with Irigaray', in *Engaging with Irigaray*, ed. C. Burke, N. Schor and M. Whitford, New York, Columbia University Press, 1994, pp. 57–78.

Schumpeter, J., *History of Economic Analysis*, Oxford, Oxford University Press, 1954.

Schwartz, J., *The Sexual Politics of Jean-Jacques Rousseau*, Chicago, The University of Chicago Press, 1984.

Scott, S., *The History of Sir George Ellison*, London, A. Millar, 1766.

—— *Millenium Hall*, introduction by W. M. Crittenden, New York, Bookman Associates, [1762] 1955.

—— *Millenium Hall*, introduction by J. Spencer, London, Virago, 1986.

Sedgwick, E. K., *Between Men: English Literature and Male Homosocial Desire*, New York, Columbia University Press, 1985.

Shell, M., *The Economy of Literature*, Baltimore, Johns Hopkins University Press, 1978.

Shiach, M., *Hélène Cixous: A Politics of Writing*, London and New York, Routledge, 1991.

Shklar, J. N., *Men and Citizens. A Study of Rousseau's Social Theory*, Cambridge, Cambridge University Press, 2nd edn, 1985.

Showstack Sassoon, A., ed., *Women and the State: The Shifting Boundaries of Public and Private*, London, Hutchinson, 1987.

Slonczewski, J., *A Door into Ocean*, London, The Women's Press, 1987.

Sly, F., 'Women in the Labour Market, Results from the Spring 1995 Labour Force Survey', *Labour Market Trends*, 104 (1996), 91–113.

Smith, A., *The Wealth of Nations*, Oxford, Clarendon Press, 1976.

Sollers, P., 'Le Toit', in *L'Écriture et l'expérience des limites*, Paris, Seuil, 1968, pp. 105–38.

The Spectator, ed. D. F. Bond, 5 vols, Oxford, Oxford University Press, [1711–14] 1965.

Spender, D., *Man-Made Language*, London, Routledge and Kegan Paul, 1980.

Spivak, G., 'Displacement and the Discourse of Woman', in *Displacement: Derrida and After*, ed. M. Krupnick, Bloomington, Indiana University Press, 1983, pp. 169–95.

—— *In Other Worlds: Essays in Cultural Politics*, New York and London, Routledge, 1988.

Spurr, D., *The Rhetoric of Empire: Colonial Discourse in Journalism, Travel Writing and Imperial Administration*, Durham, NC and London, Duke University Press, 1993.

Starobinski, J., *Jean-Jacques Rousseau: Transparency and Obstruction*, trans. A. Goldhammer, Chicago, The University of Chicago Press, [rev. edn 1971] 1988.

—— 'Rousseau and Modern Tyranny', trans. P. France, *The New York Review*, 29 November 1973, 20–5.

Still, J., 'Dreams of the End of Markets: The Model of Women's Work in Plato, More and Rousseau', *Paragraph*, 15 (1992), 248–60.

—— 'From Eliot's "raw bone" to Gyges' Ring: Two Studies in Intertextuality', *Paragraph*, 1 (1983), 44–59.

—— 'From the Philosophy of Man to the Fiction of Woman: Rousseau's *Emile*', *Romance Studies*, 18 (1991), 75–87.

—— *Justice and Difference in the Works of Rousseau*, Cambridge, Cambridge University Press, 1993.

—— 'Lucretia's Silent Rhetoric', *The Oxford Literary Review*, 6 (1984), 70–86.

Still, J. and Worton, M. (eds) *Textuality and Sexuality: Reading Theories and Practices*, Manchester, Manchester University Press, 1993.

Stowe, W. W., 'Diderot's Supplement: A Model for Reading', *Philological Quarterly*, 62 (1983), 353–65.

Strauss, L., *The City and the Man*, Chicago, Rand McNally, 1964.

Talmon, J. L., *The Origins of Totalitarian Democracy*, London, Secker & Warburg, 1952.

Taylor, B., *Eve and the New Jerusalem: Socialism and Feminism in the Nineteenth Century*, London, Virago, 1983.

Todorov, T., 'L'Etre et l'Autre: Montaigne', *Yale French Studies* (*Montaigne: Essays in Reading*), 64 (1983), 113–44.

Trousson, R., *Jean-Jacques Rousseau*, Paris, Tallandier, 1988–89.

Van Den Abbeele, G., 'Utopian Sexuality and its Discontents: Exoticism and Colonialism in the *Supplément au Voyage de Bougainville*', *l'esprit créateur*, 24 (1984), 43–52.

Veblen, T., *The Theory of the Leisure Class*, New York, Penguin Books USA, [1899] 1953.

Veiras d'Alais, D., *Histoire des Sévarambes*, Paris, 5 vols, 1677–79.

Voltaire, F. M., *Candide and Other Stories*, trans. R. Pearson, London, Dent, 1992.

—— *Letters on England*, trans. L. Tancock, Harmondsworth, Penguin, [1734] 1980.

—— *The Manners and Spirit of Nations*, Harmondsworth, Penguin, [1749] 1977.

—— *Mélanges*, ed. J. van den Heuvel, Paris, Bibliothèque de la Pléiade, 1961.

—— *Zaïre*, ed. E. Jacobs, London, Hodder and Stoughton, 1975.

Wegemer, W., 'The Rhetoric of Opposition in Thomas More's *Utopia*: Giving Form to Competing Philosophies', *Philosophy and Rhetoric*, 23 (1990), 288–307.

Whatley, J. S., '*Un Retour secret vers la forêt*: The Problem of Privacy and Order in Diderot's Tahiti', *Kentucky Romance Quarterly*, 24 (1977), 199–208.

Whitford, M., *Luce Irigaray: Philosophy in the Feminine*, London and New York, Routledge, 1991.

—— 'Luce Irigaray: The Problem of Feminist Theory', *Paragraph*, 8 (1986), 102–5.

Wilcox, H., McWatters, K., Thompson, A. and Williams, L. R. eds, *The Body and the Text: Hélène Cixous, Reading and Teaching*, New York, Harvester Wheatsheaf, 1990.

Wilson, A. M., *Diderot*, New York, Oxford University Press, 1972.

Wittig, M., *Across the Acheron*, trans. D. Le Vay with M. Crosland, London, The Women's Press, 1989.

—— *The Straight Mind and Other Essays*, London, Harvester Wheatsheaf, 1992.

Wooden, W. J., 'A Reconsideration of the Parerga of Thomas More's *Utopia*', in *Quincentennial Essays on Saint Thomas More*, ed. M. J. Moore, Boone, NC, Albion, 1978, pp. 151–60.

Worton, M. and Still, J. (eds) *Intertextuality: Theories and Practices*, Manchester, Manchester University Press, 1990.

Young, R., *White Mythologies: Writing History and the West*, London and New York, Routledge, 1990.

Index

Note: 'n.' after a page number indicates the number of a note on that page.